THE RECONSTRUCTION OF BELIEF

THE HOLY SPIRIT AND THE CHURCH

THE RECONSTRUCTION OF BELIEF

THE HOLY SPIRIT AND THE CHURCH

BY CHARLES GORE, D.D.

HON. D.D. EDIN. AND DURHAM, HON. D.C.L. OXFORD, HON. LL.D. CAMBRIDGE AND BIRMINGHAM, HON. FELLOW OF BALLIOL AND TRINITY COLLEGES, OXFORD, FELLOW OF KING'S COLLEGE, LONDON, FORMERLY BISHOP OF OXFORD

WIPF & STOCK • Eugene, Oregon

Wipf and Stock Publishers
199 W 8th Ave, Suite 3
Eugene, OR 97401

The Holy Spirit and the Church
By Gore, Charles
ISBN 13: 978-1-60608-119-8
Publication date 2/5/2009
Previously published by John Murray, 1924

PREFACE

Dr. John Donne, the famous Dean of St. Paul's, published, about 1630, certain *Paradoxes and Problems*, of which one was the problem, "Why doe young lay-men so much study divinity?" I do not suppose that anyone would consider himself called upon to investigate this problem to-day. But there is still a large number of men and women, young or old, for whom the questions of 'divinity' are the most interesting and important of all questions, and it is in their interest that these volumes on "The Reconstruction of Belief" have been written.

In the earlier volumes—*Belief in God* and *Belief in Christ*—no reference was made to the authority of the Church or the Bible. I endeavoured to pursue a purely critical method. I sought to construct the fabric of belief which seemed to me the most probable on the evidence. In result it appeared that the intellectual construction which best satisfied the requirements of reason and criticism was substantially the traditional faith of Christendom.

I

This method has been misunderstood from different quarters. On one side it has been accused of rationalism and individualism. But I think unjustly. I never concealed from my readers that the method pursued in these books was not in my case, any more than with the vast majority of mankind, the method by which my intellectual convictions had been actually obtained. Almost all men in some sense come to believe whatever they believe, whether about nature or about God, on authority of some sort and by various kinds of emotional and moral attractions. But, however we come to believe, the test of the rationality of our faith lies in its submission to the light of reason and history. It is, as I contend at length in this volume, quite a false view of authority which represents it as precluding free enquiry. It is our intellectual duty and responsibility to think freely. In recent times a vast deal of language has been used which presents the position of tradition as opposed to the position of reason and criticism—as if we had to choose between authority and reason. The best way to show that this is not the case is to abstain from all appeal to authority and to show that the construction which best responds to all the evidence is a construction which is, in its general effect and all its main lines, conservative of tradition. For this free appeal to reason and criticism there is precedent of the most weighty kind in some of the greatest names among the theologians of the Church.

There is, of course, a risk in thinking freely. Free thinking, free criticism, may lead us away from the faith. And I cannot deny that at the last resort it is a man's duty to follow his conscience and reason even if they lead him (as I think) widely astray. And I believe that, as God is good, for such a man the way of reason and conscience sincerely and faithfully followed will be ultimately the way to the light. Of course a minister of the Christian religion who, by thinking freely, is led by irresistible conviction outside the central tradition of the faith he was ordained to maintain, must cease to hold office as a minister of the Church. None the less he is morally bound to follow his personal convictions. I cannot deny this. But I believe that the main reason, intellectually speaking, why so many men have been led (as I think) astray in their personal convictions on religious subjects, is because the Church has appeared to them not to be encouraging free thinking or criticism. It has been asking for an irrational submission. And I think the best service that a student can do for the faith is to show that the conclusions which are the most probable, on the evidence freely examined, are the conclusions which are embodied in the Creed of the Church. That is what I have been trying to do. I repudiate the charge that, as an orthodox professor of religion, I am 'reasoning in chains.' However I got my faith, I am convinced with an ever-growing conviction that, far better than any other hypothesis, it satisfies the evidence; though in order to do this it has in each age to purge itself of inherited mistakes and misunderstandings.

Of course the majority of men have not the vocation or the opportunities of a student. They also must 'test all things'; but the testing will be mainly the testing of moral experience. But students are part of the equipment of the Church; and the intellectual reassurance of the average Christian lies largely in the consciousness that the students of the Church are facing the facts, and are open to the light, whencesoever it comes, and however novel or even revolutionary it seems; and are showing themselves constantly able to express what is substantially the old Creed in terms of the new knowledge. If men do not feel this—as has too often been the case—the average Christian becomes ashamed of his faith and intellectually disheartened. Thus in these volumes it has been my aim to consult the interests of the ordinary educated man by presenting properly intellectual and critical reasonings and conclusions in language which the unacademic mind can understand.

II

From the side of 'Modernism' I have been charged with not going far enough. 'If you accept such and such critical conclusions, e.g. that this or that reported saying of our Lord in the First Gospel cannot be relied on, you ought to go much further and accept such and such a representation of Christ which is seriously opposed to the tradition.' This sort of argument is not at all impressive in the abstract. In almost every intellectual movement which deeply stirs mankind there is an element of solid advance in perception of the truth and also a great deal of exaggeration. It seems to me (as to St. Chrysostom of old) quite impossible to maintain the literal infallibility of the Gospel records. On the other hand, it seems to me certain that these records, if they are approached on genuinely critical lines, yield historical results which are as certain as historical results can be; and that the purely humanitarian or non-miraculous estimates of Christ, or even such an estimate of Him as the late Dr. Emmet and Miss Dougall recently presented in *The Lord of Thought*, does violence to the evidence on the largest scale.[1] I do not think the verbal accuracy of the Gospels can always be defended. But I think their substantial truth is what alone can account for the earliest history of the Christian Church and for its deepest spiritual experience.

III

What I have done so far is to vindicate to my own satisfaction the rationality of the traditional faith in God and in Jesus Christ as the incarnation of God.

[1] In the above I have had in mind a review of *Belief in Christ* in *The Church Quarterly*, April 1923, p. 24, by the late Dr. Emmet. As one who knew him not only as a friend and as a Biblical critic, but also as an excellent parish priest, I desire to pay him the tribute of a deep regret.

But as He passes from the scene there takes His place in history "the Church which is His body," inspired by His Spirit, claiming to be His appointed representative and the organ of His continual life among men. Thus, to complete my plan, I must set myself to study the faith in the Holy Spirit and in the Church. And this enquiry must be in the first instance again purely critical. It is widely denied that the Church represented the deliberate intention of Jesus Christ. He founded no Church, we are told, and instituted no sacraments. The idea of the sacramental church, which already in the New Testament occupies the ground, does not belong to the Jewish root of Christianity and is not to be ascribed to Jesus. Its real origin is to be found in the 'mystery religions,' which had a vast influence on the primitive Gentile communities. These critical questions have to be considered, and the idea of the religion of the Spirit in the Church, as it is presented in the New Testament, has to be set in as clear a light as possible (chaps. i–iv).

When this is done, we shall find ourselves face to face with the question of church authority, which has hitherto been deliberately ignored, and on which, to judge from the reviews of my books, the curiosity of 'the religious world' is mainly centred. I strive to present what I think is the true and original idea of authority in religion (v), and to distinguish it from its perversion (vi), and to distinguish the true from the false idea of the development of Christian doctrine (vii), and to maintain the authority of Holy Scripture in a sense which seems to me compatible with historical science (viii). This leads on to an attempt to summarize the results of accepting the authority of the Church and of the Scriptures, and to answer the question 'What then is of faith?' or 'What is essential orthodoxy?' (ix).

Then, to reassure those who are alarmed at a long

string of 'articles of faith,' I seek to show that there is a strong solidarity amongst them; and that they follow with a certain inevitable sequence from the fundamental acceptance of the Biblical conception of God and man and human sin, or, from another point of view, are coherent with the principle of the Incarnation. There is only one principle at stake, not a variety of independent principles (chap. x).

Then finally (xi) I attempt to show the bearing of all this body of conclusions on the problem of the present day and on the vocation of that district of the Catholic Church to which I belong. But this can, of course, only be done in outline. I am, as every good Christian must be, deeply moved by the revived interest in the reunion of Christendom; and I have been always quite ready—perhaps too ready—to take my part in the controversies which the question of reunion raises about Romanism, Orthodoxy, Anglicanism, and Protestantism. But of one thing I feel sure. There will be no real progress towards fellowship except so far as men are prepared to view the questions about the Creed and the Church and the sacraments and the ministry afresh, laying aside their traditional assumptions as far as possible in order to ask again the question—What is the mind of Christ concerning the propagation of His religion? Does it not after all appear to be in a high degree probable that the New Testament documents interpret it aright, and that we cannot get behind them or away from them?

And this volume, no less than those which preceded it, is a challenge to men to think freely. We are apt to 'reason in fetters.' And to-day the fetters are quite as likely to be the fetters of what professes to be 'criticism' but is really a false philosophy which denies the transcendence of God and (very probably) the real freedom of man, as the fetters of an unreasoning orthodoxy. And when we come down to the region of current ecclesiastical controversies, the fetters are likely to be those of the spirit of our party, which is apt to be singularly enslaving. But whatever the source of possible enslavement, the challenge of these books to men is to dare to think freely.

I cannot help expressing my regret that a book about the Holy Spirit, which one would wish to make devotional, should by the necessities of the case be so dominantly argumentative. Nevertheless I dare to invoke His blessing in sending it out into the world.

C. G.

6 Margaret Street,
London, W.1.
Epiphany, 1924.

CONTENTS

CHAPTER VI

CHAPTER VII

CHAPTER VIII

CHAPTER IX

CHAPTER X

CHAPTER XI

THE HOLY SPIRIT AND THE CHURCH

CHAPTER I

THE RELIGION OF THE SPIRIT IN THE NEW TESTAMENT

WE are to-day constantly being told, and quite truly, that what we need to make our religion more real, more full of power, and more attractive, is a deeper apprehension of the presence and activity of the Holy Spirit of God. This call for "the religion of the Spirit" comes from many quarters. Thus Pope Leo XIII, in his Encyclical *Divinum illud munus* of 1897,[1] expressed his bitter regret that Christians have but a very meagre knowledge of the Holy Spirit. "They often use His name in their exercises of piety, but their faith is surrounded with dense darkness"; and he charges all preachers and those who have charge of souls to regard it as a duty to teach their people "more diligently and more richly" on what concerns the Holy Spirit, so that the lamentable "ignorance of these great and fruitful mysteries may be completely banished." Similar lamentations

[1] The teaching of the encyclical is summarized in Cavallera's *Thesaurus Doctrinae Cath.*, pp. 288 ff. (Paris: Beauchesne, 1920). The references in the text above are taken from Marmion (the Abbot of Maredsous), *Le Christ Vie de l'Ame*, p. 125 (Paris: Desclée, de Brouwer et Cie, 1923). The Abbot Marmion himself uses what, judging from our experience in England, I should have ventured to hope was exaggerated language about the prevailing ignorance of the Holy Spirit: "Combien pourtant de chrétiens d'aujourd'hui qui ne le connaissent que de nom et ne savent presque rien de ses opérations dans les âmes."

and exhortations come to us from quite opposite quarters; and to feel how much they are needed we have only to realize that the gift of the Holy Spirit, and the meaning and consequences of the gift, constitute one at least of the dominant themes of the New Testament. If you had asked an original disciple in Jerusalem, or one of the members of the Churches founded by St. Paul, what it was to be a Christian, you would probably have got one of two answers: either that 'it is to confess that Jesus is Lord' or that 'it is to have received the Spirit.'

And up to a certain point there is a more or less general agreement among seriously religious people as to the meaning of life in the Spirit. It is to be possessed, and feel ourselves to be possessed, by an inward power and presence greater than ourselves, a power and presence which we acknowledge to be God working in us, to give us spiritual enlightenment as to the purpose of life, and the knowledge of Himself, and personal guidance, and power to control our passions, and the pre-eminent gift of love.

So far there is not much difference among us. But when you pass from the practical consideration of "the fruit of the Spirit" as seen in the individual, to the consideration of the methods by which this Divine Spirit works, and the conditions under which His presence is to be looked for and relied upon, the differences between what I may call the 'modern' and the Scriptural point of view become somewhat startling.

I

Since the day when Hegel wrote about the philosophy of spirit, and gave a great impulse to the comparative study of religions, what has been meant commonly in intellectual circles by a Religion of the Spirit is fairly evident, and I will seek to describe it.

1. The comparative study of religions has led us

to entertain the idea of religion as in all its phases and varieties essentially one. Everywhere we find the human spirit becoming conscious of its relation to something vaster than itself—to something divine—which at last is conceived of as one and universal. By the human 'spirit' which has become awakened to fellowship with the universal spirit is meant something more than understanding or intellect. Spirit involves intelligence, but it is in feeling and conation, even more than in intelligence, that this "sense sublime" is awakened and sustained. And it is this awakening and growth of spirit which, broadly, is what is meant by religion. The fascination of such a book as *The Golden Bough* is that, surveying the rude and savage origins of religions all the world over, it makes us feel that mankind is one, and his religion one in essence, all the way up from its crudest to its most exalted forms. Throughout the whole process there is an awakening and realizing within the man of his fellowship with divine spirit. This is the religion of spirit as we moderns like to conceive it.[1]

This general idea of the religion of spirit may take a more pantheistic form, as when the conception suggested is that of an impersonal spirit of the universe coming to the consciousness of itself in man; or a more theistic form, as when the conception is that of a personal God, who is spirit, disclosing Himself and imparting Himself to man, more or less in all countries and through all phases of his civilization[2]; but whether the religion of spirit is more

[1] I had a variety of books in view in writing the above. Perhaps I may refer to essays i, viii, ix, in the volume entitled *Spirit: God and His Relation to Man considered from the Standpoint of Philosophy, Psychology, and Art*, edited by Canon B. H. Streeter, with the motto "In him we live, and move, and have our being."

[2] In very modern days, as in the theology of Mr. H. G. Wells, it takes the form of asserting a fellowship of the human spirit with a spirit in the world which is striving for good, which is greater than man or the individual man, but is very far indeed from being universal or cosmic. On this, see *Belief in God*, pp. 47–8.

pantheistically or more theistically conceived of, in either case it is of a universal process that we like to think, by which mankind everywhere, under all sorts of religious beliefs and institutions, becomes conscious of something which is already within him and only needs to be awakened, or something which is available for him individually, as a gift, without regard to any 'institution.'

The process, it is acknowledged, may have moments of culmination. It may be acknowledged that it has so far found its climax in Jesus and the Christian religion. But essentially all religions represent one movement, and the truth or value of all alike is a question of more or less. There is no one absolutely true religion in contrast to a number of false ones. That ancient claim made alike by Judaism, Islam, and Christianity is a pretension which must be abandoned.[1] The religion which actually won Europe and is called Christianity owed almost as much to the Greek as to the Jew; and if India is to call itself Christian, its Christianity will, again, owe as much to India as to the Europe which evangelized it.

2. Thus the religion of spirit, as it is commonly conceived of in modern intellectual circles, though, as has been said, it can tolerate the idea of a relative culmination attained in the past, does not readily tolerate the idea of a final culmination once for all attained. It wants a continuous process of religious discovery by the absorption of new elements and the correction of the old. If it is prepared to express this as being "not the supersession but the interpretation of the Christ," yet it resents the idea of a standard of truth, whether about God or about man, expressed in written scriptures or credal forms of the past, which claim to lay their restraining hand upon modern developments of belief or modern reconstruc-

[1] This feeling was much promoted by Lessing's famous drama *Nathan der Weise*.

tions of formulas and ideals.[1] "The letter killeth," we hear it said, but "the Spirit giveth life." The Spirit must be free to "lead us into all the truth,"[2] and we must expect to see the standards and formulas of the past, however venerable, superseded in the light of increasing knowledge, and the sacred books of the past read in a light their authors would not have recognized.

This idea of the fluidity of all the religions of history and the transitoriness of their specific forms is expressed in an uncompromising form by Dr. Kirsopp Lake in the opening paragraph of his *Landmarks in the History of Early Christianity*[3]:

"At first sight the historian of religions appears to be faced by a number of clearly distinguished entities, to each of which he feels justified in giving the name of a separate religion; but on further consideration it becomes obvious that each one of these entities has been in a condition of flux throughout its history. Each began in a combination or synthesis of older forms of thought with comparatively little new in its composition; each ended by disintegrating into many elements, while the best were taken up into new life in some new religion. The movement was more marked at some times than at

[1] See Auguste Sabatier's *The Religions of Authority and the Religion of the Spirit* (Engl. trans., Williams & Norgate, 1909).

[2] These two texts, it should be remembered, are very frequently quoted in a sense alien to their original meaning. By the "letter that killeth" (2 Cor. iii. 6) St. Paul meant the law "written and engraven in stones," with its authoritative prohibitions, "thou shalt not." This was divinely given *to kill*, i.e. to make men conscious of their state of alienation from God, because of their inability to keep the law. Then only, when man had been duly "killed," i.e. made conscious of his inability and his need, the offer of redemption could be made and accepted, and the Spirit entering into the man could empower him and strengthen him to become actually righteous; cf. Rom. ii. 27–9, vii. 6. The phrase is not concerned at all with the relation of a religion of authority, "the letter," to a religion of individual inspiration, "the spirit." Again, "all the truth" into which the Spirit is to lead the disciples in St. John xvi. 13 is defined and explained in the context, xvi. 14; cf. xiv. 26. It is the truth as it is in Jesus.

[3] Macmillan, 1920.

others, and the differentiation of the various religions depends chiefly on the recognition of these moments of more rapid change. But the process never really stopped; from beginning to end new elements were constantly absorbed and old elements dropped. For religion lives through the death of religions. Nothing illustrates this so well as the history of Christianity, for no religion is so well known."

This is an extreme statement, to which perhaps few would completely assent. But the ideas of universality of process and continuous progress towards an unattained ideal are certainly the ideas which in modern literature are commonly associated with "the religion of the Spirit."

3. But there is also a more old-fashioned conception of the religion of the Spirit or of spiritual religion, associated with Protestantism throughout its history, which has still a very wide hold upon our English mind. It is that which puts what is spiritual into antithesis with what is external or material. Spiritual religion is still spoken of as if it were concerned only with the inward relation of the single soul with God, and as if anything which represented it as (so to speak) embodied, or in some way *annexed* to external rites or social institutions, were a derogation from its spirituality.

I have thought it well to call attention at starting to the ideas which seem to be preoccupying our minds when we use the phrase "the religion of spirit" or "a spiritual religion," because we need to be on our guard against entertaining prejudices which may turn out to be misleading, and deceiving ourselves by using Scriptural phrases in a sense quite different from what they were intended to bear. And what I am claiming of my readers is that they should make a determined effort, first of all, to consider the religion which in history has made the chief claim to be the religion of the Spirit—I mean, of course, the Christian religion—objectively and as it appears at its origin. It is a difficult thing to divest ourselves of prejudices and read the history of the past simply according to the intentions of those who were the actors in it. Let it be granted that it cannot be done perfectly. But the claim of historical criticism is that it can be done, if not perfectly yet with some measure of real effectiveness. Let us make a serious effort, then, first to examine the idea of the Spirit and of the religion of the Spirit, as it is suggested in the Old Testament and as it presents itself in full flood in the New, before we make any attempt to estimate its value and truth.

The first point that will strike us when we seek frankly to appreciate the Bible teaching about the Holy Spirit is that it speaks of it or Him not as something which men naturally possess and only need to realize, but as a gift given, so to speak, from outside and (especially in the New Testament) under definite and objective conditions.

II

The idea of spirit (breath, or wind) as the invisible principle of life, and the idea of spirits, that is, invisible but living beings good or bad, is, I suppose, approximately universal among men. But what specially distinguishes the Old Testament among ancient literatures is the development of the idea of the one Spirit of the living God—the Spirit of Jehovah or His Holy Spirit.[1]

As the Israelites came to believe in one only God, the living God, the Creator of all things, they spoke of His spirit or active energy as going forth

[1] The teaching of Zoroaster about the good Spirit, which is very closely identified with God, if not identical, is very striking. But Zoroaster, if he is not clearly dualistic, never clears himself from dualism.

2

into the whole creation. "The spirit of God was brooding upon the face of the waters." "Thou sendest forth thy spirit, they [the creatures] are created; and thou renewest the face of the ground." "Whither shall I go from thy spirit?" "By his spirit the heavens are garnished." So particularly of man: "The spirit of God hath made me, and the breath of the Almighty giveth me life." "The spirit of the Almighty giveth men understanding."[1] Also any remarkable gifts of individuals, the strength of Samson, the skill of Bezalel, are ascribed specially to the spirit of God.[2]

So far, then, the spirit of God is universal in its action and, though a communicated influence, is in some sense necessary to the very being of a living creature. But the most characteristic idea of 'the holy spirit,' even in the Old Testament, is that which specially identifies it with the divine process of redemption, which, if it is ultimately to become universal, runs as yet exclusively through the channel of the chosen people, Israel. It is the prophets who are the special organs of the spirit, and, as the features of true prophetic inspiration become more and more distinct, the prophets appear as the instruments of a continuous self-revelation of God which is to reach its culmination in the days to come. To be the scene of this self-revelation is the special vocation of Israel. The gift of the spirit is moral, and as such is sometimes spoken of as the normal agent of moral recovery. Thus "Take not thy holy spirit from me" is the cry of the penitent heart. But on the whole it is thought of as at present the endowment of the prophets, but to be expected in the future in its fullest richness in the person of the Messiah or the Servant of Jehovah, and then to be

[1] Gen. i. 2; Ps. civ. 30, cxxxix. 7; Job xxvi. 13, xxxiii. 4, xxxii. 8.
[2] Exod. xxxi. 3; Judg. xiii. 25, xiv. 6.

poured out on the whole of the redeemed Israel in the day of culmination, the day of the Lord.[1]

In the Book of Wisdom, which was written under Hellenistic influences, the spirit of God is practically identified with His (personified) wisdom, the operation of which is universal. Thus it is said, "The spirit of the Lord hath filled the world," and "Thine incorruptible spirit is in all things"; and when we read "From generation to generation passing into holy souls, she maketh men friends of God, and prophets,"[2] we wonder whether the author is not contemplating an inspiration beyond the limits of Israel. But nothing of this kind is suggested in the canonical books; and in the New Testament, to which we pass, it is very noticeable that while the idea is conveyed to us of a universal activity of God in nature and in the minds of men, the idea is associated with His Son or Word,[3] and not with the Spirit. The gift or activity of the Spirit is exclusively associated with Christ and the Church. Let us consider the facts, even though it involves a little repetition of what was said in the previous volume.

The Jews of the latter days had come to believe that for many centuries there had been no inspired prophets among them; but a revival of prophecy was expected.[4] And the New Testament at once

[1] For the Holy Spirit as guiding the people as a whole, see Isa. lxiii. 10 f., Hag. ii. 5, Zech. iv. 6, Nehem. ix. 20; for the Holy Spirit in the heart of the individual Israelite, Ps. li. 10 f., cxliii. 10; for the Spirit in the Messiah, Isa. xi. 1, 2; in the servant of Jehovah, Isa. xlii. 1, lxi. 1; in the whole people in Messianic days, Ezek. xi. 19, xxxvi. 24 ff., xxxvii. 14, xxxix. 29, Isa. xxxii. 15, xliv. 3, lix. 21, Zech. xii. 10, Joel ii. 28 ("all flesh" = all Israel of all ages and both sexes).

[2] Wisd. i. 7, xii. 1, vii. 27, ix. 17.

[3] See below, p. 17. The only possible exception is in Rev. i. 4, where "the seven Spirits which are before the throne of God" and "the seven Spirits sent forth into all the earth" (iv. 5, v. 6) represent the universal activities of God. See Zech. iv. 10 and Swete, *in loc.*

[4] 1 Macc. iv. 46, ix. 27, 54, xiv. 41.

proclaims the revival in John, the son of Zacharias, who was "filled with holy spirit [1] even from his mother's womb." And his father Zacharias "was filled with holy spirit, and prophesied," and Simeon was "in the Spirit" when he recognized the Lord's Christ. Thus prophecy revives to herald the Christ. And Jesus is the perfect work of the Holy Spirit. He it is who quickens the germ of life in the womb of the virgin mother so that she conceived her son of the Holy Spirit. He it is who consecrates Him for His mission in the world at His baptism; Jesus leaves the place of His baptism "full of Holy Spirit" and was "led by the Spirit" to the wilderness of temptation. "In the power of the Spirit" He returns to Galilee, and in the synagogue at Nazareth applies to Himself the prophecy uttered concerning the servant of Jehovah, "the Spirit of the Lord is upon me." "In the Spirit of God" He is said to cast out devils. So evident ought it to be to all men that there is in Him a victorious action of God over the spirits of evil, that to ascribe His powers to Satan is to "blaspheme against the Holy Spirit." His own inner life was lived in the Spirit: "He rejoiced in the Holy Spirit." St. Peter in the Acts summarizes the story of Jesus in the words "God anointed him with Holy Spirit and power: who went through the land doing good, and healing all who were being overpowered by the devil." After His resurrection His last injunctions were given to the apostles "through the Spirit." [2]

[1] It cannot be maintained that, where there is no article used in the Greek, there the reference always is to the gift and not the person. For "Holy Spirit" without the article may be used as a proper name. But "the Holy Spirit" with the article always does refer to the person, and "holy spirit" without the article often = inspiration: see Robertson, *Grammar of the Gr. N.T.*, p. 756.

[2] In Heb. ix. 14 Christ is said to have offered Himself to God upon the cross in "eternal spirit." But this seems to refer not to the Holy Spirit specifically, but to the divine quality of His self-oblation.

This is the witness of the Synoptic Gospels and specially of St. Luke. In all of them John the Baptist is represented as bearing witness that His greater successor is to have power to do what he could not do, "to baptize with holy spirit."[1] There is very little said in any of the first three Gospels about the preparing of the disciples for this supreme gift.[2] But at the beginning of the Acts St. Luke represents the risen Lord as reminding the disciples about "the promise of the Father, which (said he) ye heard from me," and these particular words, as well as the atmosphere of expectation in the minds of the disciples, imply some such preparation of the disciples' minds as the Fourth Gospel records at length. There we have a plain statement that whereas in the future the believers were to receive the Spirit, yet during the ministry of Jesus on earth "Holy Spirit was not yet," because Jesus was not yet glorified.[3] And in the later discourses the disciples are assured that even the loss of Christ's visible companionship would be more than compensated by the greater gift of the Spirit, the "other helper," whom, after Jesus was gone out of their sight, He would send upon them, or the Father would send in His name, both to supply His absence and to accomplish His presence within them.

[1] "And with fire" St. Luke adds (Luke iii. 16). But "and with fire" is omitted in Acts i. 5.

[2] See, however, Mark xiii. 11 and parallel passages, and Luke xi. 13.

[3] Recent writers in *The Journal of Theological Studies*, vol. xxiv, Professor C. H. Turner (No. 93, pp. 66 ff.) and Mr. F. J. Badcock (No. 94, pp. 169 ff.), have been urging us to follow some ancient and modern authorities and to punctuate these verses (John vii. 37–9) so as to read thus: "If any one thirst let him come unto me, and let him drink that believeth on me; as the scripture has said, Out of his belly shall flow rivers of living water. This spake he of the Spirit, which they that believed on him were to receive; for the Spirit was not yet (given), because Jesus was not yet glorified." So also Burney, *Aramaic Origin of the Fourth Gospel*, p. 110. This must surely be right. Whatever the exact meaning of the reference to Scripture, it is plain that in the writer's mind the vessel of the Spirit, out of which it is to flow, is not the believer, but Christ.

The actual bestowal of the gift of the Spirit is described with great particularity, and with a profound sense of its importance, in the Acts. The bestowal is made upon the whole body of disciples [1] at a particular moment, with external signs accompanying its coming and proving its arrival within their souls and bodies. It takes possession of them and shakes the very foundation of their being. Henceforth as the Church expands it becomes the normal possession of each member of the new Israel, according to the prophecy. But it is bestowed on each as an objective gift following baptism, and the normal instrument of its bestowal appears to be the laying on of apostolic hands. The effect of the Holy Spirit within them is represented as a life of fellowship in which they are knit into one, joyfully inspired with courage and faith, guided and sanctified in their personal lives, corporately enlightened to make right decisions touching the development of the Church, and endowed with special gifts—"tongues" and prophecy and the working of signs and wonders.[2]

And the Church in which the Spirit is given appears as a body organized under officers. Renan spoke of "the divine institution of the hierarchy" as a "favourite thesis" of St. Luke and P. Sabatier speaks of "hierarchical pretensions" as character-

[1] That, I think, is implied especially at ii. 17 f.

[2] Some critics are inclined to speak as if St. Luke was so much interested in the wonderful manifestations of the Spirit, such as tongues, prophesyings, and miraculous healings, as to have little or no perception of His permanent indwelling and its normal moral fruits. I do not doubt that St. Paul gives us a fuller theology of the Spirit (and of Christ) than St. Luke, who was not a theologian. But Luke certainly gives us a very vivid picture of the life of fellowship and love into which the Spirit bound the Church (ii. 42, 44–46, iv. 32), and of the joy and goodness of their common life. We should remember the phrase "He was a good man, and full of the Holy Ghost" (xi. 24). Certainly "love, joy, peace, long-suffering, kindness, goodness, faithfulness," are in the Acts "the fruit of the Spirit."

izing the conciliar decree in the Acts.[1] I do not like either expression. But at least they have the advantage of recognizing a fact which many of our contemporaries are fond of ignoring—viz. the existence and recognition from the first (according to our records as they stand) of the authority of the apostles—not as witnesses only but as rulers—which was inherent in them from the first by Christ's appointment of them. St. Peter in his speech immediately after the Ascension speaks of a "ministry and apostleship" and (by a quotation from the Psalms) "overseership."[2] The special position of the apostles within the community is vividly represented in the text[3] "And by the hands of the apostles were many signs and wonders wrought among the people; and they [the apostles] were all with one accord in Solomon's porch. But of the rest [of the disciples] durst no man join himself to them: howbeit the [Jewish] people magnified them; and believers were the more added to the Lord."

There were, it appears, from the beginning three bonds of unity for the Church: the common teaching —"the apostles' teaching" accepted as "the word of God"—and the sacramental rites which were the instruments of divine gifts—baptism and the laying on of hands and the breaking of the bread—and the ministry of the apostles, the later development of which under their authority we can more or less clearly discern. Upon these matters I shall have to return, and upon the contention of those who suggest that the picture in the Acts reads back upon the first beginnings of the Church what was in fact

[1] Renan, *Les Apôtres*, p. xxxix; P. Sabatier, *La Didaché*, p. 155.

[2] Acts i. 17, 20, 25; see more in detail in chap. iv.

[3] Acts v. 12. See Rackham's note. For the meaning of "the rest" see Luke xxiv. 9, "The eleven and all the rest." κολλᾶσθαι, as in Acts ix. 26 (cf. 1 Macc. iii. 2, vi. 21), means to join oneself to others, as one of their number. The note on this passage in the new Clarendon Bible, *Acts*, p. 153, seems to me unsatisfactory.

a somewhat later cycle of ideas. Here I am only insisting that, as the records stand, the gift of the Holy Ghost is in the Acts represented as a gift given, so to speak, objectively to a definite and visible society, claiming to be the true Israel, and to it, as far as appears, exclusively, and to individuals only as members of the society. To the reception of the Spirit there is no gate but baptism in the name of the Lord Jesus.[1] Even when the acceptableness of the Gentile Cornelius has been demonstrated by a manifest effusion of the Spirit upon him and his pious associates, still they are baptized in the name of Jesus Christ.[2] Those at Ephesus who had been baptized by John's baptism, but had not heard that the Holy Ghost had been given, were baptized afresh in "the name of the Lord Jesus," and received the Holy Spirit with the laying on of St. Paul's hands. What is presented to us is the picture of a community of which the Holy Spirit is the animating presence. To lie to the apostles is to "lie to the Holy Spirit." The Holy Spirit guides all their movements and their development. They associate the Holy Spirit with themselves in their collective decision: "It seemed good to the Holy Spirit and to us." It is the apostle who appoints the presbyters in a local Church, but he declares that it is "the Holy Spirit who has made them bishops." The total effect is that we recognize the gift of the Holy Spirit as a gift embodied in the Church.

When we turn from the Acts to St. Paul's Epistles, the picture is just the same. St. Paul loves individuality. He loves to recognize the variety of the Spirit's gifts. But there is no trace of any such individualism as would admit of his recognizing the Spirit as a gift belonging to or given to an individual

[1] Acts ii. 38, "Repent ye and be baptized every one of you in the name of Jesus Christ unto the remission of your sins; and ye shall receive the gift of the Holy Ghost."

[2] Acts x. 47.

apart from the body. There is no conception of any membership of Christ except by baptism, which is incorporation into "the body"—the Church. "By one Spirit were ye all baptized into one body." When he talks about the reception of the Spirit, he talks about it as a gift received at an assignable moment. "Received ye the Spirit," he asks, "by the works of the law or by the hearing of faith?"[1] He is recalling to their minds a particular incident of their lives. Those, again, who have become Christians and received the Spirit are exhorted not to "grieve" the Spirit, or to "stir up the gift" they have received, or to yield themselves to "be filled with the Spirit," but never to *ask for* the Spirit. He has already become a permanent endowment of their life; and it is an endowment which they have received as "members" of the Body. Their union with Christ in the Spirit is indistinguishable from their union with the Church. Even more manifestly than in the Acts the Spirit in the Epistles of St. Paul is a spirit which has taken to himself a body, and thereby provided for Christ, whose Spirit He is, a visible organ and instrument in the world. The principle of unity in the body is the Spirit, which might be described as its soul: but there are necessary external conditions of union also, and they appear to be, as in the Acts, the acceptance of the common "teaching" or "tradition" or "faith"; and the sacraments of fellowship, baptism, and the eucharist; and the authority of the apostles, upon which, at the last resort, St. Paul, as will appear, is prepared to insist very strenuously.[2]

And there is nothing in the Epistles other than St. Paul's to suggest that any other teacher of the Church would have hesitated to identify the gift of the Spirit with the fellowship of the Church.

[1] Cf. Swete's *Holy Spirit in the New Testament*, pp. 202, 204, 215 (Macmillan).

[2] 2 Cor. xiii. 10.

III

We have now contrasted broadly two different views of the religion of the Spirit—that with which we are familiar in a great deal of the modern literature on the subject, which would represent it as universal in humanity, with that which is presented in the New Testament, where it appears that the gift of the Spirit is given only in the Church. At the same time we must not exaggerate the contrast. The modern view also is in part countenanced in the Old Testament and in the New. Thus it is the fundamental doctrine of the Bible that man was made in the image of God and after His likeness, and that there is a spirit in mankind everywhere, breathed into him by God, which responds, or may respond, to the offer of God. This is why the preachers of the Gospel can make their appeal to the universal conscience—"commending ourselves," as St. Paul says, "to every man's conscience in the sight of God."[1] It is everywhere in the Bible taken for granted that the good which men see in the disciples of Christ will appeal to them as responding to their best instincts—"that they may by your good works, which they behold, glorify God in the day that he shall visit them."[2] Thus Christians are not to despise human nature as it stands, but to "honour all men." Our Lord in the Gospels appreciates tenderly what we should call 'natural goodness,' even in trivial examples—"a cup of cold water only." There are men of faith outside the Kingdom who are already prepared to enter it.[3] So we hear of the Lord "having much people"[4] even in a singularly corrupt city like Corinth. And St. Paul appeals to natural virtue in the world at large as a fit subject for the contemplation of the disciples of Christ—"if there

[1] 2 Cor. iv. 2.
[2] 1 Pet. ii. 12.
[3] Matt. viii. 11.
[4] Acts xviii. 10.

be any virtue, and if there be any praise." [1] He also, in spite of his strong conviction of human corruption, believes in the natural conscience, individual and social, and speaks of some men who know not the law, that is are Gentiles, as "doing by nature the things of the law." [2] He thinks, that is, of the law of Sinai, like the Schoolmen, as being the republication of the original law of nature, never quite obliterated in men's consciences.

Moreover, it is the function of the natural reason and conscience in all men everywhere to "seek God, if haply they might feel after him, and find him, though he is not far from each one of us; for in him we live, and move, and have our being; for as certain Stoic poets said, We are also his offspring." [3] All this is a recognition of spirit in man in the modern sense, and of a movement of God towards man everywhere, and of a universal presence of God in nature; only in the New Testament, in which the Son or Word of God is distinguished from the Spirit, this movement of God towards all men and in all men, and in nature as a whole, is ascribed not to the Holy Spirit, but to the Son, or Word. "The life," i.e. the life of the Word, "was the light of man." He (the true light), who was coming into the world (in His incarnation), was all along "the light which lighteth every man." And "All things were made by him; and without him" (the Word) "was not anything made which hath been made." [4] "Through him" (the Son) "are all things." "All things have been created through him, and unto him . . . and in him all things consist" or have their coherence.[5] "He upholds all things by the word of his power." [6] Thus in the vision of the City of God in the Apocalypse we are made to see that the

[1] Phil. iv. 8.
[2] Rom. ii. 14-15.
[3] Acts xvii. 27–8.
[4] John i. 4, 9, 3.
[5] 1 Cor. viii. 6; Col. i. 16, 17.
[6] Heb. i. 3.

perfecting of its beauty requires that the glory and honour of all nations should be contributed to it.[1] They have all something to give which it needs.

So St. Paul and the writer of the Epistle to the Hebrews and St. John must have been conscious that the current Hellenic philosophy of the *Logos* or divine reason in all things contained a considerable element of truth which they needed; and in fact, as the religion of Israel had assimilated elements from Persia and Greece before Christian days, so Christianity assimilated more or less largely from Hellenism. As "the Law" had been for the Jews a guardian to bring them to Christ, so their philosophy had been to some at least of the Greeks. This the Alexandrian fathers recognized, and St. Paul and St. John would, perhaps, not have protested against this view. Justin Martyr, who had been "a philosopher" before he became a Christian, and remained so afterwards, recognized in all who were true to their best light, before Christ came in the flesh—in Socrates and Heracleitus no less than Abraham and Elijah, "friends of Christ" and "Christians" before their time. Like Justin, so also Augustine, two centuries later, knew that in his own case the Platonic philosophy had brought him to Christ. And not only so, but also Augustine, like Origen before him, deliberately approved of Christianity "borrowing" from Hellenism.[2]

As I have said, however, all this divine influence outside the limits of the Church was attributed by the New Testament writers to "the Word," not to "the Spirit." But when Origen, in a strange passage,[3] drew from the New Testament the positive

[1] Rev. xxi. 24–6.

[2] See Appended Note A on *Borrowing from Hellenism*, p. 31.

[3] The most distinct passage of Origen is quoted in Greek by Dr. Westcott (*Dict. of Chr. Biog.*, iv, p. 136, col. 2). No reference is given and I cannot at present find the passage. (I call it "strange" because it represents the activity of the Word or Son

conclusion that the Holy Spirit did not in fact act universally in the world, like the Father, nor even like the Son in all rational creatures, but only in "the saints," the later Church refused to follow him in this positive restriction of the Holy Spirit's action; and in developing the theology of the Holy Trinity they constantly insisted that the Holy Spirit, "the Lord, and Giver of life," must be recognized as in some sense operative wherever life is.[1] Thus there is much in the New Testament and in Christian fathers to encourage, and nothing to forbid, the modern missionary in China or Japan or India seeking diligently for the elements of truth in non-Christian religions, and making the most of them as preparations for Christ. They can rightly present the religion of Christ to Indians and Chinese and Japanese as the consummation and satisfaction of the highest thought and aspiration of their own sages.

1. Nevertheless, when all this is said and acknowledged, there remains a difference, so great as to be startling, between the popular modern view and that of the New Testament. The root of the difference lies in the New Testament emphasis on sin. It had not wholly obliterated the image of God in man. But it had thoroughly defaced it. It had turned what was meant to be a world of light into dreadful darkness. It had brought it about that the whole movement of God towards man must become a movement to redeem or buy back, under extreme difficulty, a world which had come to lie in the evil one—it must be a movement to seek and to save that which was lost. How dominant this view of mankind is both in our Lord's attitude towards men

as extending only to rational beings, whereas in the New Testament His activity is extended very distinctly to all creation.) But a similar passage is to be found in Latin in *de Princip.*, lib. i, cap. iii, 5.

[1] See *Lux Mundi: The Holy Spirit and Inspiration* (ed. 15), p. 232.

and in that of the New Testament writers I have tried to make plain already.[1] It cannot be denied. It pervades all the books. St. James and St. Peter are as 'pessimistic' in their view of the world, as it is, as St. Paul or St. John. Thus, if the New Testament does not *exclude* the idea of the universal operation of the Holy Spirit of which we get glimpses in the Old Testament, it says nothing about it. It represents mankind as needing a new effusion of the Holy Spirit. It deliberately concentrates our whole attention upon the divine purpose and enterprise of redemption, and views this purpose and enterprise as taking concrete shape first in Israel, then in the Christ, in whom the purpose of Israel was fulfilled, and then in the Church, the New Israel, the society which is commissioned to make effectual among men the offer of salvation, and which is the shrine of the Spirit and the body of Christ. There alone were men entitled to expect and receive the Spirit, and to find that sonship to God for which they were divinely created, and that brotherhood which is essential to the life of humanity, actually realized.[2]

Thus all the efforts of Christian missionaries, from the apostles downward, was to present the offer of God, of which all men ought to feel their need, in a concrete shape, a thing of "here" and now. "Behold, now is the day of salvation." "Neither is there any other name under heaven, that is given among men, wherein we must be saved." And the shelter of that name belongs to those only who have had it invoked upon them in baptism and have received

[1] *Belief in Christ*, chap. ix.

[2] It must not be forgotten that the N.T. consistently proclaims not that all men are sons of God and brothers, but that they are meant to be so and in Christ have really become so. See John i. 12, 1 Pet. ii. 17, "Honour all men: love the brotherhood"; cf. 2 Pet. i. 7, where "love of the brethren" is to be the school of universal "love." See also Dr. Pollock (Bishop of Norwich), *The Brotherhood of Man* (S.P.C.K.).

the Spirit of Jesus within them, "Repent and be baptized every one of you in the name of Jesus Christ unto the remission of your sins; and ye shall receive the gift of the Holy Ghost." So it is that, without denying that there is some truth in all religions, they unhesitatingly identify the "word of truth" with "the Gospel,"[1] the definite Christian message, and "the spirit of error" with all that withholds men from accepting it,[2] and they talk of the past of those who have come from contemporary heathenism as a shameful past, as darkness compared to light and foulness to cleanliness—speaking certainly as if those they are addressing would agree with them—"your vain manner of life handed down from your fathers"—"your former lusts in the times of your ignorance"—gross vices and "abominable idolatries"—"God hath called you out of darkness into his marvellous light."[3] "We all once lived in the lusts of our flesh, and were by nature children of wrath," "having no hope and without God in the world," "led away unto those dumb idols," "sacrificing to devils."[4] Relatively at any rate and in practical fact, they do declare that the Christian faith is the one true religion, and all others are by comparison false. For Jews indeed all that was necessary was that their eyes should be opened to the true tendency of their own religion. But for the Gentiles what was needed was the acceptance of a new religion. As Remigius told Clovis centuries later, they must "burn what they have adored." We must have the courage to face this fact.

2. St. Paul and St. John in different ways recognize, as we have seen,[5] that development will be necessary in the understanding and appropriation of the treasures of wisdom and knowledge which lie hid

[1] Eph. i. 13. [2] 1 John iv. 6.
[3] 1 Pet. i. 14, 18, ii. 9, iv. 3.
[4] Eph. ii. 3, 12; 1 Cor. x. 20, xii. 2.
[5] See *Belief in Christ*, pp. 318 f. See also below, chap. vii, on the development of Christian life and doctrine.

in Christ; and they sanction by their example the appropriation of contemporary ideas and terms from non-Christian philosophies and religions, which proved to be part of the method by which the Christian faith developed. Nevertheless their emphasis is on the finality of the Christ and of the message concerning Him of which the apostles were the stewards. This message constitutes the tradition which the Church is to hand down unimpaired and unaltered. A good deal more will have to be said about the finality of the Church's Creed. At present all we need do is to recognize that the emphasis on finality is far more marked in the New Testament than the recognition of development.

3. Finally, to recur to the third feature in the contemporary estimate of the meaning of a spiritual religion which we referred to above, we cannot discover in the New Testament any trace of that unwillingness to associate the Spirit's action or presence with material forms which traditionally has characterized Protestantism. There is hardly to be found in the Bible, Old Testament or New, any echo of the Oriental or Hellenistic horror of matter, or the material body, as evil and the source of defilement. According to the Bible, everything which exists was made by the one good God and is in its original nature very good. "Every act of giving [on God's part] is good, and every [divine] gift perfect, coming down as it does from above from the Father of lights."[1] Sin has its source, not in the body or material forces, but in the perverted or rebellious will. "Sin is lawlessness," not materiality. God had no hatred of flesh as such. On the contrary, the climax of His manifestation is incarnation. "The Word was made flesh." The human "flesh" became the organ of very God. So when the Spirit came down to fulfil the presence of Christ among men, He too

[1] Jas. i. 17.

took body in a visible institution,[1] the old Israel reformed, with visible sacraments, the baptism of water and the laying on of hands and the bread and wine of the eucharist. There is no sign in the New Testament of horror at this sort of "materialism." So in the glorious prospect of the final consummation there is no idea of a world of pure unclothed spirits. The prospect is of a resurrection of the body, after the pattern of Christ's, and of a "restitution of all things"—a glorified nature.

No doubt God is pure spirit, and there are spirits, good and evil, who are not material, at least in our sense; and in our present bodies there is a grossness and corruptibility which will not belong to the "spiritual body" of our future perfection. In this sense "flesh and blood" cannot inherit the Kingdom of God. But what the future holds in store for us is still a real embodiment, like the "glorious body" of Jesus. For us men the material is the sphere and organ of the spiritual, and is to be so to all eternity. We shall have to recur to this great principle later on, and to examine certain specific charges made against St. Paul of attributing sin to the flesh or the body. But I hope the general estimate which I have given of Bible teaching about the body and the material world will be accepted as true and unexaggerated.

The result is that "spiritual" in the New Testament is put in opposition to "carnal," or to the body only as polluted and distorted by sin and habituated to sinful ways. It is not put in opposition to the bodily-as-it-ought-to-be and may be. Isaac's birth, according to St. Paul, was "after the Spirit," not because it was less material than Esau's, which was "after the flesh,"[2] but because it was in accordance with a spiritual purpose and a promise

[1] On the idea of an "invisible Church," see Appended Note B, p. 32.
[2] Gal. iv. 29.

of God. And life " in the Spirit " is not life alienated from material things and common interests, but life dominated by spiritual purpose, just as life " in the flesh " is life controlled from below by the selfish lusts and passions—and it is contrary to man's true liberty to be controlled from below.

Thus if, as we shall see more in detail, the New Testament uses very simply the language of sacramentalism, there is nothing in this to surprise us. The horror of the material as the vehicle of the spiritual is simply not there—nor the conception of the spiritual as the disembodied. This is particularly apparent in respect of marriage and man's sexual nature. Our Lord indeed tells us that all the conditions of marriage will have passed away from our perfected humanity; and St. Paul in the First Epistle to the Corinthians, still under the dominance of the expectation of an immediate end of the world, thinks marriage a less wise course than celibacy for Christians—though in later Epistles he talks about marriage in a way which suggests some change of mind; but the sexual nature of man in itself is never in the New Testament disparaged or treated as evil, but always as good. It is " honourable in all respects, and the bed undefiled."

And surely there is no restraint upon anti-sacramental language so effective as is to be found in this region. Is not the production of a new personality —a soul or spirit destined for an immortal life in God, but liable also to the most awful spiritual disaster— is not this the greatest of spiritual events in the world and the most wonderful of the activities of the creative spirit? And is not this entrusted by God to a material process the most liable, as experience shows, to carnal misuse? In view of this momentous fact, can any of the arguments have any value at all which would treat the sacramental system of the Church as wholly unacceptable, and something we cannot attribute to God, because it puts spiritual realities under the control of men who may be bad men, and material things which may be unspiritually used? We may wonder at the divine adventure, but we cannot deny that that is the way of God.

But in thus declining a false argument, we must not be blind to the exceedingly important element of truth which Protestantism has sought to guard even while it has distorted it. Outward forms are notoriously liable to become formal, and religious ceremonies very easily become unspiritual; because the spirit is slumbering or occupied in other regions while the sacred actions are being performed, or because it is relying on the mere performance of a sacred routine, or on the satisfaction of the imagination by splendour of ceremonial. Nothing, in fact, is more conspicuous in the history of the Church than this sort of degradation of sacraments and sacred rites. They very easily become charms. It was the sense of this peril, intensified by their horror of the magic and the imposing ritual of the pagan mysteries, which made some of the Fathers use such puritan language about Church ceremonies [1]; and it was their experience of the misuse of externals in Christian worship which made some of the leaders of later monasticism use similar language. But a religious rite is not less material or less necessary because it is simply performed. And the safeguard of the

[1] Cf. Tertullian, *de Baptismo*, 2: "There is really nothing which so blinds men's minds as the simplicity of divine operations contrasted with the magnificence of their promised effect. So in the case of baptism, since all that happens is that with the greatest simplicity, without pomp or any novel apparatus, and without any expenditure, a man is brought down into the water and washed to the accompaniment of a few words, and comes up again little or no cleaner, therefore it is regarded as incredible that he should thereby obtain eternal life. I am a liar if, on the contrary, the solemnities and sacred rites of the idols do not produce their impressiveness and authority from their elaborate apparatus. Yet what a miserable incredulity is this which leads you to deny to God His special properties—simplicity with power!"

sacramental method lies only in an insistence, like St. Paul's, on the spiritual valuelessness for the individual of everything external except in proportion to the faith which uses it and the good living which results from it.

I hope enough has now been said, by way of preliminary, to call attention to the New Testament idea of the method of the Spirit—the embodiment of the Spirit in the visible Church—and to put it in contrast to certain dominant modern views of the religion of the Spirit which would detach it from visible institutions, and sometimes also from particular historical events and from any unique or authoritative Gospel. And we are now to proceed to ask whether the set of views about the Spirit and the Church which so plainly characterize the New Testament as a whole can really be ascribed to Christ Himself—whether He did really found, or refound and equip, the Church as a visible society—or whether all the sacramental ideas of the Church, already apparent in St. Paul, come, as so many moderns would have us believe, from the Hellenistic atmosphere in which the early Christian disciples found themselves, and have little or nothing to do with Christ. But I am conscious in this matter of being up against a vast wall of prejudice. The Catholic Church of history has by its superstitions, its moral and intellectual weaknesses, and its narrownesses—specially at certain periods—alienated such a vast body of the world's best feeling, that the very idea of the Church as the one home of the Spirit ("*Extra ecclesiam nulla salus*") excites the sort of resentment which seems to deprive many men of the very capacity for fresh enquiry. Now I want to ask for fresh enquiry, such as leaves out of sight for the moment all present-day questions, and seeks simply to examine the origin of Christianity, and to ask what seem to have been the intentions of Christ Himself and of His first interpreters; and to facilitate that, I want, before I proceed to argue as to the facts, to urge some considerations which may serve in some measure to disarm prejudice and make the idea and principle of the Church at least more intelligible.

1. There is nothing, I think, more central to the mind of Christ than the principle that you can only love God in fellowship—that you can only love God by and in loving your neighbour. And then, when you ask "Who is my neighbour?" it appears that your neighbour is every man; and that the function of the Church is to give a home to all men indiscriminately, if only they want to live the good life; and to let men see in the Church what brotherhood means, there where the motives of men are sufficiently purged to make real brotherhood possible. Unfaithful to this principle as Catholic Christianity has sometimes shown itself to be, this is its root principle. It was comparatively easy for the first disciples to love one another, for they were all Jews, united by a common tradition of patriotism. But when they found out that they were required to live on equal terms with Gentiles, it was another matter. Yet St. Paul, in the spirit of Christ, insists on catholicism—that is, on the brotherhood of all men in Christ. "Receive ye one another, even as Christ also received you." Now human nature in its races and sects and competing individualities is appallingly disruptive. Nothing in Christianity could have kept believers in Christ together except the positive obligation of the one body—the obligation of membership by baptism, grace by sacraments, adherence to the apostolic ministry. The sacraments are social ceremonies as well as visible ceremonies. The "tying" of grace to sacraments in the Church embodies for each person the principle that he can only have fellowship with God by abiding in "the brotherhood."

It is because the mass of men are, as they stand, beyond the appeal of brotherhood, that the method of God is to gather those who respond to the appeal of the Gospel into an organized society which shall show, embodied in fact, what human brotherhood really means. I do not believe that till we have fully appreciated this law or fact we shall ever have a chance of understanding what Catholicism at its root means; and Church History really deserves the name only by exhibiting the principle of brotherhood in actual practice. "Ecclesiastical" ought to mean "brotherly." It did really mean this in the days when it cost men much to call themselves Christians. It may come to be so again in no distant future, and the Church may regain its ancient meaning. Meanwhile no one ought to be able to study afresh the origins of Christianity without perceiving that the principle of Church and sacraments lies neither in materialism nor in narrowness of spirit, but in the recognition that mankind cannot realize divine sonship except in brotherhood, and that mankind as it is can realize neither except by being redeemed. If the first Christians had not been bound together by the necessity of adherence to the one Church and its sacraments and ministry—if they had not identified salvation with membership in the one divine society represented by the local Church—the disruptive tendencies of class and race and tradition would have rendered the divine attempt to establish a catholic fellowship nugatory from the beginning. Here we get the fundamental reason why "credo in sanctam, catholicam ecclesiam" follows at once on "credo in Spiritum Sanctum." How to make the principle of this sequence effective again in modern society is, I think, actually the most important matter for consideration by Christians at the present day.

2. I do not think it can be denied that St. Paul

and St. Luke and St. John teach implicitly that "extra ecclesiam nulla salus," but I think we easily fail to understand what is or should be meant by "salvation." Salvation or redemption describes a great and continuous and consummated action of God in history for the realizing of His original purpose for man, which sin had baffled and almost obliterated. It is, as represented in the Bible, an action of God, public and covenanted. God, as it were, comes out into the open with His great offer. "There is the salvation." The offer was made in stages. There was an old covenant and a new. But in both stages alike the offer is made publicly, visibly, under covenant. By their relation to this great offer men are to be tested. To accept it is to be approved. To reject it or to ignore it is to be judged and (in proportion to the moral clearness with which it has been presented to man) to be condemned. This is the constant language of the New Testament. The preaching of the Gospel is by St. Paul compared to a triumphal procession through the world, the incense of which fills the air, but which (so to speak) smells differently in different nostrils, according to the different moral dispositions of men. It smells of life to those who are being saved, who welcome it as the satisfaction of their deepest need. It smells of death to those who are perishing—that is, who love the world too well to listen to it. This is the judgement.[1] And St. Paul and the other preachers of the Gospel triumphantly proclaimed the going forth of this self-acting judgement into the world. They appear to have no doubt that the good will hear and obey, and the evil or the proud only will refuse. Their experience seemed to justify that. They are not perplexed by the problem of "the good man without faith." And in fact we feel that the moral splendour of the Christian Church, as it showed itself

[1] 2 Cor. iii. 14-15.

in the comparative purity of its first history, made this triumphant proclamation legitimate. But the history of the Church has been a strange one. If its appeal varies in force with its general moral character—as St. John and St. Paul and St. Peter lead us to believe—it has often and in many different places made a sadly weakened appeal. It has had to depend on something different from the visible evidence of sanctity and especially of brotherhood. Some will argue, no doubt, from this that the nature of the appeal must be fundamentally altered. Those, on the other hand, who believe this conclusion to be mistaken, will still feel that the responsibility of men for not yielding to the appeal of the Church has been a very variable responsibility, because the Church has itself given them so many excuses for gainsaying. Those who feel this—though their sense of the undying purpose of God through the Church will not be weakened, though they would have the Church reformed and not rejected—nevertheless will rejoice to reflect that the Covenant of Salvation does not represent the whole action of God.

Apparently now all parts of the Church agree on this. In old days the Church does seem to have believed itself entitled to pronounce the final sentence upon anyone who in fact rejected its message or refused its authority. But by emphasizing "invincible ignorance," or by considering more broadly the conditions of human responsibility, we have quite passed out of this frame of mind. "We know in part, and we prophesy in part." We are to "judge nothing before the time." It is the Church's duty to declare the message of God, and (while at the same time it makes sure that what it is delivering is "the message" and nothing else) to refuse to reduce it. It may be its duty to judge and to excommunicate this or that individual or group. But this is to leave them to God—not to profess to pass the final sentence on them. The Church was surely going quite beyond its commission and authority when it sought to formulate an answer as to what would be the destiny of unbaptized infants, or unconverted heathen, or of anyone however rebellious and sinful. It has got authority to bear a certain witness. It is set to administer a covenant of redemption or salvation. It must let men know the warrant by which it speaks and acts. But it can pronounce no final sentence. It has no authority to draw up any list of the lost or any infallible catalogue of saints. The day of judgement, we are assured, will be a day of surprises, and we are to " judge nothing before the time."

Nevertheless, here in the New Testament we find this covenant of salvation offered to us in the Church on the authority of Christ. Is it rightly so offered? Did Christ really found such a Church as appears in the New Testament, or was the conception due to other influences and had Christ nothing to do with Church and sacraments? That is the question which next claims our attention.

APPENDED NOTE A (to p. 18)

ON BORROWING FROM HELLENISM

St. Augustine *de Doctrina Christiana,* cap. xl, xli, gives a suggested allegorical explanation of the Israelites " borrowing of the Egyptians jewels of silver, and jewels of gold, and raiment," and so " spoiling the Egyptians." They were commanded to take these things, he says, to convert them to a good purpose. In the same way in more recent times the heathen have not only false superstitions and heavy burdens, which Christians, when they go out from their fellowship, ought to hate and avoid, but also (he is speaking, he says, specially of the Platonists) liberal instruction and moral principles and some true things about the worship of the only true God, which they did not invent, but dug, as it were gold and silver, out of the mines of God's providence which is universal; and all this Christians shall "convey" to good uses. So also their useful social institutions, which may be represented by the "raiment" of the Egyptians. Such "borrowing" St. Augustine attributes to innumerable Greek Christian authors and among the Westerns to Cyprian, Lactantius, Victorinus, Optatus, and Hilary. The suggested interpretation, which Augustine does not wish to press, is based probably upon Origen's letter to Gregory of Neo-Caesarea, though Origen appears to restrict what may be "borrowed" with more caution than Augustine. Cf. Dr. McNeile's *Exodus* (Westminster Commentaries), p. 74.

So also Origen and Augustine call attention to Moses receiving enlightenment from Jethro (see Origen, *Hom. in Ex.* and Aug. *de Doctr. Christ.*, prolog. § 7). "For Moses," says Augustine, "knew that a wise counsel, in whatever mind it might originate, was to be ascribed not to the man who devised it, but to Him who is the truth, the unchangeable God." For Justin Martyr, see *Apol.*, i, 46.

APPENDED NOTE B (to p. 23)

ON THE IDEA OF THE INVISIBLE CHURCH

From the sixteenth century, beginning with the teaching of Luther, down to modern times, an idea has been associated with Protestantism that while *the* (local) *churches* of which we read in the New Testament were indisputably visible and mixed bodies—with good members and bad—*the Church*, the one home of salvation, the Church of which such glorious things are spoken in the Epistle to the Ephesians and elsewhere, was an invisible company of the elect known only to God in His predestinating love and independent of all local and visible attachments. I do not think it is necessary to argue against this at any length. Since Rothe wrote his *Anfänge der Christlichen Kirche* (1837) it has passed into disrepute in Germany, its first home. Its present status may be seen in Harnack's *Constitution and Law of the Church,* especially in his controversy with Sohm, pp. 176 ff. I may refer also to the discussion in *The Church and the Ministry,* chap. i, and to Dr. Mason's essay on "Early Conceptions of the Church" in *The Early History of the Church and Ministry* (Macmillan).

In the Acts and in the Epistles of St. Paul we hear constantly of "the churches," i.e. the local churches established at each place. In the New Testament these local churches do not seem to be regarded (at least not generally) as federated into one Church or as component elements of the one Church. Rather they are regarded as each of them representative of the one Church. Each church is *the* Church; and the members of each local church are thereby members of the one Church, baptized by one Spirit into one body. To put it conversely, the one Church of God—the Church refounded in Jesus Christ—is not composed of all the different churches of Judæa, Asia, Achaia, etc., but it is composed of all the individual members of all the local churches. But this one Church of God is, just as much as the local churches, a visible body, save that the Head (Christ) and the members departed this life are of course out of sight. This may now be taken for granted, and I will content myself with quoting Dr. Hort, as he writes in his posthumous book *The Christian Ecclesia,* p. 169, in which he assuredly does not exhibit any ecclesiastical bias.

"I said just now that the one ecclesia of [the Epistle to the] Ephesians includes all members of all partial ecclesiae. In other words, there is no indication that St. Paul regarded the conditions of membership in the universal ecclesia as differing from the condition of membership in the partial local ecclesiae. Membership in a local ecclesia was obviously visible and external, and we have no evidence that St. Paul regarded membership in the universal ecclesia as invisible and exclusively spiritual, and as shared by only a limited number of the members of the external ecclesiae, those, namely, whom God had chosen out of the great mass and ordained to life, or those whose faith in Christ was a genuine and true faith. What very plausible grounds could be urged for this distinction was to be seen in later generations; but it seems to me incompatible with any reasonable interpretation of St. Paul's words."

We notice that St. Paul writes in his earlier epistles to "the churches of Galatia," "the church of the Thessalonians," "the church of God at Corinth," but in his later Epistles to "the saints" at Philippi and Ephesus and Colossae. But still we get the local "church" in Phil. iv. 15 and Col. iv. 16, and the use of "church" for the congregation assembling in a particular house.

CHAPTER II

DID JESUS CHRIST FOUND THE CHURCH?

THE Bible record divides itself naturally into three stages. First, in the Old Testament, we have the story of the long process by which Israel's God, Jehovah, becomes defined in character as the one and only God, the Creator of all that is, perfect in goodness and power, who has chosen Israel for His organ or instrument of self-disclosure, and is one day to manifest Himself through Israel to all the world in the perfection of His kingdom. Part of the first volume of this series was devoted to vindicating this claim of Israel to be the prophet of the real God.[1] Next, in the Gospels, there comes into the forefront the figure of Jesus of Nazareth, and He comes to be defined in the minds of His disciples as the Christ, the fulfilment of the purposes of God, His true and only Son incarnate, "the Word made flesh." The validity of this definition was the subject of our second volume. Finally, as Jesus passes out of sight into the heavens, whence He is to come again to wind up the history of this world, the stage which He has left is occupied (in the Acts and the Epistles) by the coming and activity of the Holy Spirit—the Spirit of the Father and the Son—and He too receives embodiment—that is, the Spirit appears as inspiring and fashioning the Church, and the Church appears as the only organ of the Divine Spirit and instrument of the great salvation.

[1] *Belief in God*, chaps. iv, v, vi, and see also *Belief in Christ*, chap. i.

Here again, however, at this last stage of divine self-disclosure, we advance upon the ground of controversy old and new. For (1) various traditions of Protestantism have refused to assign so high a function to the visible Church; and indeed the history of the Church has made it sadly evident that it cannot be regarded as the manifestation of the Spirit in that complete and perfect sense in which Jesus Christ is the manifestation of God. There is plainly here a good deal that requires discussion, and we know too well what strong prejudices of different kinds make frank enquiry in this field singularly difficult to many of us.

2. Upon the old controversy between Catholic and Protestant something has been said in the last chapter—that is, it was argued that the high conception of the function of the Church is unmistakably present in the New Testament as it stands. And this, we note, is now commonly conceded by modern critics. But also they commonly attribute this conception, with much besides in traditional Christianity, to St. Paul and other influences which helped to form the mind of the early disciples, and would have us believe that it was read back upon Jesus without historical justification. Here, then, we get upon one of the chief grounds of modern controversy which will occupy us in this and the following chapter—the question whether really Jesus of Nazareth is responsible for the Church at all.

I

In the volume which preceded this we had to give consideration to an idea of Christ which has been specially associated with the names of Schweitzer and Loisy, and which has had in England both eager partisans and strenuous opponents.[1] According to

[1] *Belief in Christ*, pp. 37–8, 151 ff.

these adherents of what is called the "apocalyptic" idea of Jesus Christ, it is impossible to attribute to Him the foundation or equipment of the Church, because that involves His making more or less elaborate provision for an indefinite future; whereas in fact He anticipated no future for the world at all. His death was to be the signal for the divine intervention. He would be at once raised to the glory of God, and as the Messiah from heaven would be sent to end the world and judge the world and inaugurate the Kingdom of God, in which His elect would share with Him eternal felicity. It was only the complete breakdown of the expectation of the immediate coming of Christ (which He Himself proclaimed) which made room for and also made necessary the institution of the organized Church, and the idea of the Church as in some sense already the Kingdom of God on earth. But all this was an afterthought due to the experience which proved that the apocalyptic proclamation of Christ was a delusion.

We have already seen cause to reject this whole view of the position and teaching of Christ as singularly one-sided. In particular we saw reason to believe that our Lord when on earth had explicitly declared that He had no map of the future spread before His eyes, and later had warned His disciples that the "times or seasons" were not to be disclosed to them; and that, though He certainly prefigured His final coming and the end of the world, He also paid much attention to the intervening period—the length of which He wholly refused to define—which was to be occupied with the growth of the Kingdom on earth and the preaching of the Gospel in all the world, and warned His disciples of the severe testing of their faith which "the divine delay" would involve.[1] The rejection of the extreme position of Schweitzer has become general. Nevertheless the

[1] See on all this, *Belief in Christ*, chap. v.

apocalyptic idea is still frequently made the ground for the assertion that Jesus can have founded no permanent Church, and instituted no sacraments or ministry, and given it no rules or directions [1]; and, on other grounds, it is so commonly denied that He founded any such rite of perpetual memorial [2] as the Lord's Supper, and the connexion of Church institutions, such as appear plainly in the Acts and the Epistles, with the historical Jesus is so frequently repudiated, that the whole question must be carefully examined—the question, I mean, whether our Lord really made any such provision for the future of the movement inaugurated during His lifetime, and if so, what it was.

We must, of course, proceed as before purely on the historical and critical basis—asking simply what is the most probable conclusion on the evidence.

It has been already remarked that if you had asked one of the early converts what it was to be a "Christian," he would have replied either that it was to believe that "Jesus is the Lord" or that it was to have "received the Spirit." The original Creed, which summarized the first experience of the Christians prior to any reflection or theory, may be said to have consisted of these two articles—the one being concerned with a past experience, the experience of the crucifixion and glorification of their Master; the other with a present experience of the activity of the ascended Christ, in both of which experiences they saw the fulfilment of prophecy.[3] If you had had the opportunity further to question this primitive Christian, you would have found that he and his fellows anticipated no long continuance for the Church. The death of any one of their fellow-Christians was

[1] As by Dr. Inge, see *Outspoken Essays*, series i (1919), pp. 227 f. and 249; also see below, p. 39.

[2] As by Dr. Rashdall, *Idea of Atonement*, p. 59.

[3] See App. Note A, p. 64, on N.T. interpretation of prophecy.

a shock to them. For their eager hopes led them to expect a very speedy "coming" of Christ in glory to end the present order and establish His kingdom in the world. But you would have taken note that this expectation of the speedy dissolution of the world, and absorption of the Church in the Kingdom, did not hinder their sense of present duties. Alike at Jerusalem, at Antioch, at Corinth, and elsewhere, you would have seen the Church behaving like a permanent society which has to take counsel for the future, and organize itself and use its resources. It has certain sacred meetings and sacred rites, and it is under a certain rule or order which was delivered to it ("the tradition") by its apostolic founders.

Dr. Inge, writing about the vexed question of divorce, has recently used a very unfortunate argument. He has said that—

> "the real difficulty in appealing to the Gospels [on this subject] is a different one. Our Lord was not in a position to repeal either the law of Moses or the laws of the Roman Empire, nor did He ever think of doing so. He was not legislating even for the Church, for there was no Church to legislate for; none of His disciples had any suspicion that 'the Church' was anything more than a brief stop-gap till the Messianic Kingdom of God should come." [1]

Now, to me it appears quite certain that our Lord did, not indeed repeal, but revise by His own authority the law of Moses in general ("It was said to them of old time . . . but I say unto you") as one who was establishing Israel and its law on a new basis; and if words have any meaning and if the combined authority of our earliest documents really gives us trustworthy witness about Christ, He did revise the law of Moses in respect of divorce particularly, quite definitely and trenchantly, though there

[1] The words are quoted from an article called "A Defence of our Divorce Laws" in the *Evening Standard* of December 21, 1922.

is a discrepancy in the reports touching one single point. But I am not being drawn away from the course of my argument by the particular question of divorce. My point is this. Dr. Inge would have us believe that the expectation of a speedy end of the world renders absurd the idea of Christ having legislated for the Church. This argument I call "unfortunate," because we do precisely know that in the minds of the first disciples there was no such incompatibility between the expectation of the speedy end and the belief that they were, as a Church, in this particular respect under a law. St. Paul when he wrote the first Epistle to the Corinthians certainly expected the speedy coming of the end before his own death. But none the less he shows himself throughout the epistle an organizer of the Church, zealous to confront and meet its present difficulties, as one who builds for the future. And in the task of organizing the Church he is conscious of a certain "tradition" which is common to him and the rest of the apostles [1]; and at the centre of this tradition there are certain "words" or commands "of the Lord" to which he appeals from time to time as of final authority,[2] amongst them being a word of Christ prohibiting divorce, which St. Paul carefully distinguishes from his own judgement on matters touching marriage [3]—judgements which at one point at least are affected by his expectation of an immediate end of the world.

Quite certainly then in St. Paul's mind the expectation of the speedy end of the world was not inconsistent with the belief that Christ had in the matter of divorce and in other matters legislated for the Church while He was on earth. St. Paul regarded himself certainly as an officer in the Church, which was indeed to have a very short existence in this

[1] 1 Cor. xv. 1–3, 11. [2] See *Belief in Christ*, p. 89.
[3] 1 Cor. vii. 10, 12, 25.

world, but was meanwhile "under the law to Christ." And this confirms the conclusion which we draw from all the Gospels, that Christ did both announce His future coming—though in fact He definitely refused to say anything about the time or season of the coming—and also in certain particulars made careful provision for the intermediate period, whether it should prove to be long or short.

No doubt "the Lord," whose words St. Paul occasionally refers to, was by him predominantly thought of as the glorified Christ in the heavens, who, as he believed, had called and commissioned him as one of His apostles. But the conditions of his call he knew to have been exceptional. "Those who were apostles before him" had been already so when Christ appeared to them after His resurrection on the third day.[1] He knew therefore that they were appointed during Christ's lifetime on earth; and from the beginning of his converted life he had received the "tradition" of the institution by Christ of the eucharist for the continual memorial of Himself.[2] Certainly, then, St. Paul held that it was during His life on earth that our Lord had, in part, equipped His Church with officers and a solemn rite, as well as certain specific commands. And if this is sufficiently evident in St. Paul's epistles, it is at least as evident in the Acts. There at starting the necessary condition for apostolate is described as being a long companionship with Christ on earth—from the preaching of John the Baptist to the Ascension. This is one of the links which binds the Acts to the Third Gospel as two volumes of one work. What you see occurring in the Acts was prepared for and provided for during the earthly life of Jesus.

But if it be acknowledged that the apostles themselves were more or less mistaken about the im-

[1] Gal. i. 17; 1 Cor. xv. 4–11.
[2] This is argued in *Belief in Christ*, pp. 99 ff.

mediate Coming, is it not possible that St. Paul and St. Luke were mistaken about the origin of the Church, and threw back upon Christ while on earth what was in fact only or mainly the growth of necessity after He had disappeared ? I think there is a very great difference between the possibilities of mistake in the two cases. But we will ignore this. Whatever might have been possible in the way of a mistake, I think the whole historical situation, as the Gospels represent it, no less than particular sayings ascribed to Christ, which show the surest evidences of authenticity, compels us to believe that Christ did in fact make precise provision for His Church.

II

It is, however, a mistake to ask whether Christ while on earth *founded* the Church, for it was already in existence. We understand nothing if we do not understand this. 'The Church' is in the first instance the holy people of God—Israel. St. Stephen in his speech before the Jews gives us the clue. He is represented as saying of Moses that "he was with the church in the wilderness."[1] The Church, that is, was at least as old as the redemption of Israel from Egypt and its foundation as a nation. The word *ecclesia* was the common Greek word to describe the official assembly of any people. In the Greek Bible it is used in this sense with another word 'synagogue' to translate two Hebrew words for the assembly of the holy people—the "congregation of the children of Israel." But in New Testament times the second word ('synagogue') is used to describe the place of religious assembly for the Jews other than the temple, and the first word ('ecclesia') had in the Greek Bible tended to mean the holy people itself, whether assembled or not. It was in this sense

[1] Acts vii. 38.

especially, though not exclusively, that it passed into the language of the New Israel[1]; and this is the sense in which Stephen uses it. It means the same as Israel or the people of God. Into this people our Lord was born. In it He was educated in the Scriptures, and there are the most evident signs in His frequent references to the Scriptures that, while He in no way anticipated the scientific investigation of later ages, He not only had meditated deeply upon them but interpreted them, by contrast to Pharisees and Scribes and apocalyptic fanatics, with a profound spirituality of insight. In the Scriptures he found the Messianic hope, the expectation of the Kingdom of God, and, as we have seen, reconstructed that hope, partly by the elimination of certain gross elements of unreal expectation, partly by recalling to vivid expression forgotten elements, and proclaimed a doctrine of Messiah, which was both old and new—in which sense He Himself was the Christ who was to come. But the coming of the Christ meant the consummation of Israel's hope, not its extinction. In the days of the Christ, according to the prophets, the holy people were to be consecrated under a New Covenant: it was to receive a new outpouring of the Spirit; it was to witness the Resurrection of the dead; it was to become the centre of religion for the world.[2] The Christ is not an isolated figure. He is the central figure in a renewed people. His coming is or implies the coming of the Kingdom, and it is in the Kingdom or universal reign of God that the hope of Israel is to be consummated. All

[1] Harnack, *Constitution and Law of the Church* (Engl. trans., Williams & Norgate), p. 15, says: "Qāhāl—in the LXX translated as a rule by ἐκκλησία—is the community in its relation to God." *The Vocabulary of the Greek Testament*, by Moulton and Milligan (Hodder & Stoughton), says: "It is the LXX term for the community of Israel, whether assembled or no." These statements are much too absolute, as a concordance to the LXX will show us. However, there is tendency towards this meaning.

[2] See *Belief in Christ*, pp. 14–19.

this we see clearly to have been in the mind of Jesus of Nazareth. It was the atmosphere which He breathed.

But the record of Israel, generation after generation, had shown it to be a body obstinately refusing to walk after the counsel of God. "Israel doth not know, my people doth not consider" is the complaint of God through the prophets. "Ye stiff-necked and uncircumcised in ears," exclaimed Stephen, "ye do always resist the Holy Ghost: as your fathers did, so do ye." But the failure in the people and their leaders is not to defeat the purpose of God through Israel—it only narrows its channel temporarily. There is always a faithful remnant, "the meek of the earth," who, though politically insignificant, become the channel of the divine purpose. This is the interpretation of history offered by Isaiah, Micah, Zephaniah, the second Isaiah—indeed we may say all the true prophets. So it was in our Lord's day. The people and their rulers reject the counsel of God. They refuse the Christ. But there was again a faithful remnant, "the meek and lowly in heart," who accepted Him. This then again is the true Israel, in our Lord's eyes. "Fear not, little flock," He is recorded to have said to them; "it is your Father's good pleasure to give you the Kingdom." [1]

[1] Luke xii. 32. The particular phrase is peculiar to Luke. But the sense of it is common to all the Evangelists. Thus (1) the preaching of John the Baptist has for its object to provide a new Israel, true children of Abraham, "a people prepared for the Lord." (2) The revision of the Law, including the divorce law, by our Lord means that the vocation of Israel is being fulfilled and not annulled. (3) The exclusive mission of Christ: "I am not sent but unto the lost sheep of the house of Israel" means that He is come to reconstitute Israel, so far at least as it will consent to listen. (4) The claim that "Jesus is the Christ" or "the Christ is Jesus" is of itself sufficient proof that the believers in Him are the true Israel.

After the statements of the case made from very different points of view by Harnack (in his *Constitution and Law of the Church*,

There was a crisis in the Galilean ministry which may be identified with the murder of John the Baptist, and the mission of the Apostles, and the feeding of the five thousand (St. Mark vi.), when Jesus appears to have taken for granted His rejection by the Jews as a whole and by their leaders. They would not have Him at all, or they would only have Him on terms with which He would make no compromise. Yet His time was not yet come to go up to Jerusalem and die. He has a preliminary task to fulfil. This appears to be the training of the Twelve, and on this accordingly He concentrates Himself. There ensues a period of journeyings outside the dominions of Herod, who had murdered John and was suspected of a like design upon Jesus,[1] and for a time outside the Jewish territory altogether, which brought Jesus and His Apostles at last round to Caesarea Philippi, the scene of Peter's confession; which again is followed by the last slow progress to Jerusalem.[2] The training of the Twelve is all through this period the central occupation of the Lord; and He appears to be

pp. 221, 224, and in *Expansion of Christianity*, i, 300 f.), and by Dr. H. F. Hamilton (*People of God*, vol. ii, pp. 29 ff.), it is hardly necessary to repeat the proofs that the Christian Church from the first believed itself to be the old Israel reconstituted. The sense of this is constantly in St. Paul's mind, as in his whole appeal to the Old Testament, or when, writing to Gentiles, he speaks of the old Jews as "our fathers," 1 Cor. x. 1, or in his argument in Gal. iii. 16 and Rom. ix. 6 ff. and xi. 5, 16 ff. It is the assumption of St. James in the Acts (Acts xv. 14–18) and of the Epistles of St. Peter (1 Pet. i. 1) and St. James (i. 1), and of the Apocalypse (see Swete's note on vii. 4–8, pp. 96 f.), and of the Epistle to the Hebrews. The sense that only the believers in Christ constitute the true Israel is equally apparent after it has become obvious that the old Israel has in the mass rejected Christ (Apoc. ii. 9, iii. 9), and also, as in the beginning of the Acts, while the hope is entertained that they still may welcome Him. Even in St. James's Epistle you still feel the unwillingness of the writer sharply to distinguish the Old Israel and the New. Nevertheless it is the Christians whom he addresses as "the twelve tribes."

[1] Luke xiii. 32.

[2] See Headlam's *Life and Teaching of Jesus Christ*, chap. vii (Murray).

training them not only as disciples, but as apostles, as rulers and pastors of the Israel to be.

Thus in the parable of the husbandmen the vineyard is Israel, and the point of it is that the vine dressers, the actual rulers of Israel, who are in charge of its destinies, are to be utterly rejected, and the vineyard entrusted to "others" (Mark and Luke) or "other husbandmen." I think this most naturally means the apostles. It is only they who can be said to take the place of Scribes and Pharisees and Chief Priests in order to "render" to God "the fruits of the vineyard [Israel] in their season."[1]

Again, in the parable of the household, during the prolonged absence of the Master,[2] we have "servants" left in "authority." And when Peter asks the question, "Lord, speakest thou this parable unto us [the Twelve], or even unto all?" our Lord, as usual giving no direct answer, suggests by another question that he (Peter) or they (the Twelve)[3] are in the position of the "faithful and wise steward, whom his lord will set over his household, to give them their portion of meat in due season." Here we have another figure of the house of Israel under new government or management. The Twelve are being prepared to be its "stewards." Once more in the day of the Kingdom, the day of Christ's sovereignty, the Twelve are to be found seated upon twelve thrones, judges of the twelve tribes of Israel, as well as participants in the heavenly feast.[4] In a sense, as we have seen,[5] the glorification of Christ and the mission of the Spirit *was* the coming of Jesus in His

[1] In Matt. xxi. 43, after the change of metaphor from vineyard to building, we have the words, "The Kingdom of God shall be taken from you, and given to *a nation bringing forth the fruits thereof.*" This, I suppose, would be the Church of the believers in Jesus.

[2] Mark xiii. 34–7; cf. Luke xii. 36–48.

[3] On the relation of Peter to the other apostles, see Appended Note B, p. 65.

[4] Matt. xix. 28; Luke xxii. 30.

[5] *Belief in Christ*, pp. 144–5.

Kingdom; and nothing is more certain than that in the beginning of the Acts the Apostles appear as the judges and pastors or rulers of the New Israel. Nothing seems to me to be more idle than the attempt to deny either that St. Luke in the Acts represents the apostles as divinely appointed officers of the body of the disciples, or that St. Paul conceives the apostolate which he shared with the Twelve as instituted in the first instance by Christ on earth and as possessed of official authority by divine appointment.[1] Their position after Pentecost confirms what the parables and sayings of St. Mark and St. Luke suggest, that our Lord constituted and trained the Twelve as the future officers of Israel. Critical scholars are not willing to rely on the record of the First Gospel when it is unsupported by the others without scrupulous examination, and that for substantial reasons. But I think the famous passage [2] which, in the First Gospel alone, follows the Confession of Peter falls in so precisely with the story of the Gospel and the Acts as a whole that we may or must accept it as true. Every word of it tells and reflects the historical situation.

The confession of the Messiahship of Jesus by His disciples was confessedly a crucial event. It was most natural that Jesus should have met it with His solemn benediction, as something wrought in the soul of Simon by God Himself. "Blessed art thou, Simon Bar-Jonah: for flesh and blood hath not revealed it unto thee, but my Father which is in heaven." [3] But also the sense of relief to the soul of the Master which the confession brought, and which is suggested by the rich benediction pronounced upon

[1] On the Acts, see above, pp. 12 ff. On the authority of the apostles in St. Paul, see Appended Note C, p. 68.

[2] St. Matt. xvi. 17–19.

[3] See Bruce as quoted in Dr. Box's excellent commentary in *The Century Bible*, p. 263.

Simon, is unmistakably genuine.[1] Jesus elsewhere shows the value He set on a solid foundation for a spiritual fabric. Such a foundation He could not find in the shifting and untrustworthy faith of the multitude. He "did not"—indeed He could not—"trust himself unto them." But, by a process of selection and training, now at last there had been engendered in the Twelve, or in Simon their spokesman, a faith at least capable of being solidified into such a rock as could be safely built upon. So He blesses Simon, under a name which the Fourth Gospel tells us He had found for him on first meeting him. "I also say unto thee, that thou art Peter—Rock-man—and on this rock[2] I will build my Church," or, as Dr. Hort would render it, "My Israel," the true Israel acknowledging the Christ. And as the old prophets had always proclaimed the nucleus of Israel indestructible, so Jesus proclaims the Israel of His new foundation—"the gates of death [hades] shall not prevail against it."[3] And just as Isaiah, under divine commission, had appointed Eliakim, son of Hilkiah, steward of the house of David, with the power of the keys to open and shut, in place of the worthless Shebna, so Jesus promises to appoint Peter steward of the new house of David (Isa. xxii. 22),[4]

[1] H. S. Holland's memorable sermon in *Creed and Character*, p. 49.

[2] The rock is surely the *person*: cf. a remarkable Rabbinic saying concerning Abraham, "When God saw Abraham who was going to arise, he said, Lo, I have discovered a *petra* to build and to found the world upon. Therefore he calls Abraham 'rock,' as it is said (Isa. li. 1)." See Taylor, *Sayings of the Jewish Fathers*, p. 160.

[3] Two points should be noticed. (1) The foundation was no doubt a *re*foundation; cf. St. James's quotation of the "prophets," "I will build again the tabernacle of David" (Acts xv. 16). (2) What is promised to the new Israel is neither more nor less than that it shall not, any more than the Christ Himself, be swallowed up by death.

[4] "The keys of the Kingdom of heaven" I think it cannot be doubted that here "the Kingdom" is identified with the Church, though doubtless in general it is a wider and a vaguer term.

and He assigns to him the authority to " bind " and " loose "—which was well recognized among the Jews, and meant official authority to prohibit or allow—a legislative power in the Church, that is, but no absolute power, for, to the Jews, these words implied a divine law to be interpreted. It was this interpretative authority which the Jewish rabbis had so grievously misused. " They had made the word of God of none effect by their tradition." This authority, then, is to pass from the present Jewish authorities to Peter.[1] The authority, we note, is by Christ reconstituted, although it has been so grievously abused, but with the warning subsequently given that it may be so again.[2]

In a later passage of St. Matthew's Gospel our Lord is again reported to have referred to the power of binding and loosing, now apparently as inhering in the smallest church, or community of believers, who shall meet in His name, and here the power is so described as to be plainly not only legislative but also disciplinary over the individual—" to bind " carries with it exclusion from the community.[3]

At this point we must pass from the First Gospel to the Fourth. There our Lord is represented on the evening of His resurrection as commissioning " the disciples," which here in all probability, as throughout the later part of the Gospel, means the Twelve,[4] to perpetuate His own apostolate: " As the Father hath

[1] On the relation of Peter to the other apostles, implied here and elsewhere in the N.T, see Appended Note B, p. 65.

[2] Luke xii. 45–8.

[3] This passage, Matt. xviii. 15–20—which follows very closely on Jewish precedents, see Dr. Box's notes—must be noted here because of the importance of the *disciplinary* power which is attached to binding and loosing. Taken in general, it suggests a situation where there are a number of small Christian communities. That is a later situation, and accordingly critical scholars doubt its authenticity. I wish to use it only as showing the meaning assigned to " binding " and " loosing." It may be, however, that vers. 18–20 should be detached from vers. 15–17.

[4] See Appended Note D on the meaning of John xx. 21, 22, p. 68.

sent me, even so send I you. And when he had said this, he breathed on them, and saith unto them, Receive ye Holy Spirit: whose soever sins ye forgive, they are forgiven unto them; whose soever sins ye retain, they are retained." If we interpret the authority to bind and loose promised to St. Peter in St. Matthew, chap. xvi., as it is interpreted in chap. xviii., viz. as including the authority of discipline over individuals, it will be seen that it is substantially the same authority which was then promised to Peter which is here bestowed upon all "the disciples." It is the authority to admit individuals to the Church or to exclude them as unfit, to excommunicate and to absolve, and it implies as its background the kind of legislative power which was ordinarily carried by the phrase "binding and loosing." And again in the appendix to the Gospel (chap. xxi.) Peter is given the commission of a shepherd—which in Jewish language means a ruler—to govern and feed the flock of Christ, the circumstances of this commission strongly suggesting that what we are witnessing is the restoration of Peter after his fall, and that we are not meant to draw the conclusion that the pastoral office was peculiar to St. Peter.[1]

These passages of St. Matthew and St. John will be estimated differently by scholars, no doubt, according to their differing estimates of the trustworthiness of these Gospels. They appear to me to indicate as belonging to the apostolate just the kind of authority which in fact we see belonging to it, and unquestioned, in the Acts and in St. Paul's Epistles.[2] This unquestioned authority attributed to the apostles seems to me to require some specific acts of Christ to explain it. Thus I see no reason to doubt that the texts we have been considering are really historical.

[1] See below, p. 65.

[2] See below, p. 68.

But whatever be the historical estimate formed of these passages, the evidence of the Acts and St. Paul's Epistles must not be underrated, nor the indications in St. Mark and St. Luke explained away. If it be asked why the same explicit stress is not laid by these two evangelists on the apostolic commissions as appears in St. Matthew and St. John, I suppose the right answer probably is, that when these Gospels were written there was no dispute about the apostolic authority, as being derived from Christ Himself, such as would have suggested any particular enquiry into what exactly Christ had done; that St. Mark's selection of incidents was probably determined in the main by a previous selection made by St. Peter for the instruction and edification of converts; and that St. Luke appears to have been under pressure of space and he may naturally have felt that enough about apostolic authority appeared in the Acts. On the other hand, I think it is very likely that the emphasis on St. Peter's position which is apparent in the First Gospel was due to the need the author felt to correct the tendency in Jewish-Christian circles to make St. James the chief of the apostles. And the Epistles of St. John show us plainly why he should have wished to emphasize the apostolic commission by recalling what were to him well-remembered incidents. But the reason why this or that incident does not appear in a historical record is, we know, a matter of very uncertain speculation.

Jesus then, let us conclude, did not found a new Church, but He did refound the old Church on the new basis of faith in His Messiahship, and did equip it with teaching, new as well as old, and also, in the persons of the Twelve, with authoritative officers.

III

Further, we have no critical justification for calling in question the institution by Christ, as sacraments or sacred rites of His New Israel, the ordinances of baptism and the eucharist. Baptism, it would seem, was already in the time of our Lord (with circumcision and sacrifice) the rite for the incorporation of Gentile proselytes into the community of Israel.[1] The whole ceremony was their " new birth " as Israelites [2] ; and as circumcision of course applied only to males and sacrifices were confined to Jerusalem, baptism assumed the chief importance. As used by John the Baptist, baptism was based upon the need to constitute " a people prepared for the Lord," that is, an Israel based, as in the teaching of the ancient prophets, not merely upon physical descent, but also upon moral fitness ; and, according to the Fourth Gospel, John's baptism was carried on in the circle of the disciples of Jesus.[3]

But in John's teaching, as represented in the foundation records (Mark and Q), it was announced that He who was to come, whose precursor John was, would baptize with a new sort of baptism, to administer which John could make no claim. " He shall baptize you with the Holy Ghost," or " wit the Holy Ghost and with fire." If these words stood alone, it might be doubted whether the baptism here spoken of was to be literal or symbolical ; but the

[1] See a note with references in Headlam's *Life and Teaching of Jesus Christ*, pp. 137–8, and Edersheim's *Life and Times of Jesus the Messiah*, App. xii.

[2] See references to the Rabbis in Edersheim, *l.c.*: " As he stepped out of these waters he was considered as 'born anew' —in the language of the Rabbis, as if he were a 'little child just born' or 'a child for one day.' One who makes a proselyte was as if he created a soul." These quotations of course are later than the New Testament and it cannot be proved that the idea of the proselyte as 'new born' dates from our Lord's time.

[3] John iv. 2.

abundant pouring out of the gifts of the Spirit was from of old associated with the coming of the Messiah and the Kingdom. Very little is said about it in the Synoptic Gospels; but at the beginning of the Acts it is unmistakably implied that Jesus before His departure had assured the disciples that the "promise of the Father" would e fulfilled to them within a few days. And on the day of Pentecost they were accordingly "baptized" with the gift of the Spirit and its accompanying power. As the matter is described in the Acts, the gift of the Spirit was given in the first instance to the original nucleus of believers by a sudden effusion, accompanied by outward signs, which was unique; but for subsequent adherents of the new fellowship it was given (without any apparent question or deliberation) through baptism, which was regarded as the instrument of the forgiveness of sins and incorporation into the community, and was accompanied or followed by the gift of the Spirit, normally attached to the laying on of hands. We should thus be led to suppose that baptism in the literal sense was an institution of Christ's which the apostles administered from the first on His instructions. And in the First Gospel at its conclusion we have the express direction of Christ given to the Eleven, "Go ye and make disciples of all the nations, baptizing them into [or 'in'] the Name of the Father, and of the Son, and of the Holy Ghost." Now, there is no good reason to doubt that all these words formed part of the original text of St. Matthew; yet critics may not unreasonably doubt whether our Lord on this occasion can have so solemnly and emphatically pronounced the threefold name of God. If it had been so, we cannot but suspect, the early teaching in Jerusalem would have been somewhat different. But it is probable enough that, so far at least as the command to go out and baptize is concerned, the First Gospel was following the lost ending of St. Mark.[1] This no doubt is only conjecture, but the unquestioned position of baptism in the Church from its very beginning would certainly seem to indicate that it was an appointment of Christ. St. Paul's language also (in Eph. v. 25–6) seems to attach it to Christ. Further, in the Fourth Gospel we have the record of a conversation of our Lord with Nicodemus in which He defines the future instrument of the new birth as " water and the Holy Ghost," and we have abundant reason for refusing to consider the words of Christ reported in the Fourth Gospel as destitute of historical basis.

However, without resting our case on single passages or on conjectures, the original prophecy of John the Baptist coupled with the record of the Acts, indicating the undisputed position of baptism from the first, suffice to warrant the belief that Jesus Christ took over the ceremony of washing, freed from animal sacrifices and circumcision, from the Jewish Church as the ceremony of initiation into the New Israel, henceforth to be accompanied with the new power of the Spirit which belonged to the Messiah.

But the evidence that Jesus instituted the sacrament of His body and blood in the bread and cup of the Last Supper is much more direct and indisputable. I have already contended [2] that there is no reasonable ground for doubting that the portion of St. Paul's original teaching at Corinth on this subject, which he recalls to the memory of the Corinthians in his First Epistle (xi. 23 ff.), was, like the formulated account of the Resurrection and the appearances of the risen Jesus which he also recalls (xv. 1 ff.), something which he had " received " at his conversion. Therefore it was already the formulated tradition

[1] The command to baptize is also implied in [Mark] xvi. 16.

[2] *Belief in Christ*, p. 99, note A. I have also there spoken (p. 101) about the shorter text of St. Luke

of the Church a very few years after the Crucifixion. I need not repeat the argument here, which seems to me convincing.

St. Paul's words are very familiar: "I received from the Lord [as its source] that which also I delivered unto you, how that the Lord Jesus in the night in which he was betrayed took bread; and when he had given thanks, he brake it, and said, This is my body, which is for you [on your behalf]: this do in remembrance of me. In like manner also the cup, after supper, saying, This cup is the new covenant in my blood: this do, as oft as ye drink it, in remembrance of me." The accounts in St. Mark's Gospel and St. Matthew's, though doubtless later in date, are substantially the same. If they do not contain the words "This do in remembrance of me," they must imply them. St. Mark must have been fully alive to the practice of the churches of St. Paul's foundation and others. He must have taken it for granted that the rite, as instituted by Christ, was, as St. Paul specifically says, intended for subsequent observance by the Church. Thus I think it is arbitrary in a high degree to doubt that our Lord did institute this sacrament of perpetual memorial for His new Israel.[1]

But some more attention must be paid to these mysterious words "Take ye: this is my body which is for you. This is my blood of the covenant, which is shed for many." If we try to imagine the scene, we see that what we are witnessing is a rite of communion or "sharing together." That was the unmistakable meaning of the distribution of the one loaf and the drinking of the one cup. And it is a sacrament that is being instituted, in the sense that the purpose of the institution is the imparting

[1] On the force of τοῦτο ποιεῖτε, etc., see Dr. Lock in *Theol.*, November 1923, p. 284, "This is the passover which ye are to keep in memorial of me."

not of physical nourishment, but of something which the bread and cup symbolize and with which they are somehow identified. So St. Paul interprets the rite : " The cup which we bless is a sharing together in the blood of Christ. The bread which we break is a sharing together in the body of Christ." It is sometimes suggested that "the body of Christ" may have been understood by St. Paul as the Church, which he calls the body of Christ. But this suggestion wholly breaks down before the parallelism of "the body" with "the blood." The body and the blood together must describe Christ's sacrificed humanity as that which is being imparted under the figure of bread and wine. I cannot see any possible source of this language except in the sacrificial system of the Jews. Christ is speaking of His body as being given in sacrifice for the people, and His blood as being shed in sacrifice for them—the 'blood' meaning 'the life,' as in the case of the animals sacrificed under the ritual law, according to the saying in Leviticus [1]: " The life [soul] of the flesh is in the blood: and I have given it to you upon the altar to make atonement for your souls: for it is the blood that maketh atonement by reason of the life [soul]."

Now, there were recognized in the Jewish law many distinct classes of sacrifice, and of these one was the peace offering; and the characteristic of this large class of sacrifices was that the substance of the sacrifice was shared by the worshippers in a sacrificial meal. (This kind of sacrifice holds, as we know, a very important place, perhaps the chief place, in the institution of sacrifice as it appears all over the world.) What our Lord must have meant then by His words to His disciples, at once affirming the

[1] xvii. 11; cf. ver. 14, " As to the life of all flesh, the blood thereof is all one with the life thereof: . . . the life of all flesh is the blood thereof"; cf. Gen. ix. 4," Flesh with the life thereof, which is the blood thereof."

sacrifice of His body and blood, and calling upon them to feed upon it, was that His sacrifice of Himself was of the nature of the peace offerings in this respect, that it was to be shared by the worshippers, though in its purpose it was an atonement for sin. We shall remember that in the Epistle to the Hebrews the writer implies that the one atoning sacrifice for sin, offered on the cross and at the heavenly altar, is also to be partaken of by the worshippers. The members of the Christian Church in this respect have a higher privilege than belonged even to the priests under the law.[1]

There are many people who appear to resent the very idea that Christ should thus by the institution of the eucharist have connected the New Israel with the Old, as in other respects, so also in respect of the institution of sacrifice. But it is noticeable that our Lord, while He denounces the tradition of the Scribes and Pharisees and exalts the moral law above ceremonial observances, yet never by word or act shows any sign of disrespect to the temple worship. An attempt has been made to treat His 'cleansing of the temple' as a repudiation of the principle of animal sacrifices; but the attempt has no justification. And He appears to have attended the feasts and kept the passover; and He is recorded to have spoken with reverence of the altar, like a pious Jew.[2] Presumably He regarded the animal sacrifices as a divinely sanctioned institution which demanded fulfilment, and to which He Himself was to give fulfilment.

And if He intended His disciples to learn at the Last Supper that in some mysterious sense they were to receive into themselves His body and blood

[1] Heb. xiii. 10 f., with Westcott's notes. Also the Jews under the law were by no means to partake of the blood of the victim in any case.

[2] Matt. xxiii. 18, cf. v. 23; Mark i. 44; Luke xvii. 14.

as spiritual nourishment—and this cannot be denied without violence to the evidence—then it is surely probable that the disciples had been prepared for this startling announcement, and that the discourse of St. John vi. rests on a historical basis. It is probable that the background of that discourse, as St. John gives it us, is sacrificial—that is to say, that when our Lord speaks of His "flesh" as not only to be the bread of life given *to* the world but also as given "*on behalf* of the life of the world,"[1] He is, as at the Last Supper, speaking of it, or of Himself, as to be offered in sacrifice. But, whether this is or is not the case, the whole point of this startling chapter is to insist that His flesh[2] and blood, which means His humanity—which can mean nothing else—is to nourish His people for eternal life; and the explanation of a thought so startling is at last offered by the instruction that they are not to think of His material flesh as they now see it, but of what He will be when He has returned to His heavenly state, and His flesh and blood will be "spirit and life."[3]

But—to sum up—however much or however little the disciples at the Last Supper had minds prepared for the institution of this sacrament of Christ's body and blood, I cannot see what reasonable ground there is for doubting that Christ instituted it; also I cannot see what other interpretation can be put upon it than what St. Paul puts upon it, and that too in such terms as suggest that it was the accepted interpretation which he had no need to do more than recall to the minds of his converts—"The cup of blessing which we bless, is it not a sharing together

[1] John vi. 51.

[2] I do not think *much* difference can be assigned to "flesh" as distinguished from "body," because both alike are put side by side with blood.

[3] John vi. 61–4; cf. Burney, *Aramaic Original*, p. 108, who translates *τὰ ῥήματα ἃ ἐγὼ λελάληκα ὑμῖν*, "The things about which I have been speaking to you." Cf. my *Dissertations*, App. C.

in the blood of Christ? The bread which we break, is it not a sharing together in the body of Christ?"; and, finally, I cannot see to what other source we can refer for the interpretation of this language of Christ about eating His body and drinking His blood except to the Jewish institutions of sacrifice, which were akin to those which prevailed all over the world, and which recognized as one at least of the purposes of sacrifice the feeding upon the victim by the whole group of worshippers or offerers, though by identifying Himself as the victim He gave to the ancient symbols a new and spiritual meaning. 'I am to become your sacrifice: by my body broken in death and my blood shed you are to be redeemed; and upon that sacrifice you are to feed: my sacrificed manhood is to be your spiritual nourishment.'

It is now often argued that the idea of feeding upon the flesh and blood [1] of Christ must have been derived from the Hellenistic mystery religions; and this is part of a much larger suggestion which we shall be considering in the next chapter. But—to anticipate what we shall be seeking to prove—as regards the institution of the sacrament of Christ's body and blood, it will not help us. The idea of eating a sacrifice was indeed familiar to the Hellenistic world, as it also was to the Jews. And so long as men were able to believe that a plant or an animal was a god, they could entertain the idea of securing the divine virtue of the god by eating it. But the mysteries had long passed out of such a barbaric stage. Their religions were now anthropomorphic. And

[1] It has been matter of endless contention whether the Eucharist can rightly be called a sacrifice. I suppose that for the ancient world, Jewish or Greek, it would have been a sacrifice, simply because it was a feeding upon a sacrifice. That was one at least of the essential elements of sacrifice. And that we may feed on Him, Christ is there presented to us as sacrificed, in His body offered and His blood shed—"The Lamb as it had been slain."

there is nothing discoverable in classical literature to lead us to suppose that the idea of *eating* any one of their divine heroes or saviour gods would have been tolerable to them. It would seem that our Lord must bear the burden of the startling language He chose to use alone. And it admits of no other interpretation than that He who was to inaugurate a new covenant with His people by the sacrifice of His life was also to be their spiritual food.

Before we leave this subject let us remind ourselves that that which seems so difficult, if approached as an intellectual problem, has seemed quite otherwise to the hearts of Christians in all generations. It is not a barbaric instinct to which these words have appealed, but the highest spiritual aspirations of men, and " the Holy Communion " has created and nourished in all generations of Christians the sense of " Christ in us the hope of glory."

I do not think, then, that on a review of all this evidence there is any room for doubting that Jesus Christ did—not indeed found the Church, for it had been long in existence, but refounded it under a new covenant, and under new government, that of the apostles, and empowered by a new life, that of His own Spirit, instructed anew by His teaching and His death and resurrection, and equipped with certain outward rites or sacraments which, with the Scriptures, marked its continuity with the Old Israel.

Four remarks may be added in conclusion.

1. The faith of the first Christians in the guidance of the Spirit, as being really the guidance of Christ, was so intense that we should suppose they were not much inclined to distinguish in value between what was " ordained by Christ Himself " during His life on earth and what He was still ordaining from heaven. Nevertheless the things that Jesus began to do and teach while on earth remained determinative.

He could not have changed. Thus, before the Gospels were written, the greatest stress was evidently laid on His acts and words on earth. This is especially apparent in the writings of the apostle who had not companied with Him on earth. And the oral record of what Jesus had done and taught lies behind the written Gospels. Between A.D. 29 and A.D. 70 the conservative feeling radiating from those who were "eye-witnesses and ministers of the word" must have been a very stern restraint on the inventive power of the religious imagination.

2. The relation of the Church to the Kingdom of God is most easily understood when we view the Church, as historically we should, as in direct continuity with ancient Israel—as being in principle the same theocratic society, only refashioned and renewed. For the constant idea of the prophets of the Old Testament is that Israel is God's kingdom, the society in which God is the real king. Nevertheless there was a good time coming when God would manifest His kingdom in all the world and Israel would be glorified. This is what is meant in the New Testament by the coming of the Kingdom.

Only it appeared in the course of the apostolic experience that this coming was not to be one single act, or the matter of a single moment. In one sense Christ implied in His teaching that the Kingdom was already among men in virtue of His presence. In another sense it appeared that it was to come in His resurrection and glory and in the mission of the Spirit. In this sense the Church is even identified with the Kingdom, as already appears to be the case in the parable of the drag net and in the words of Christ to Peter, "I give unto thee the keys of the kingdom of heaven."[1] In

[1] Surely it is only so far as the Church *is* the Kingdom that Peter can have its keys. He can admit into the Church. But surely in the wider and final sense of the Kingdom the admission into it lies only in the judgement of God.

another and fuller sense the Kingdom comes only with the final and universal triumph of God in Christ—" His appearing and his kingdom." Thus "*non adhuc regnat hoc regnum.*" The Church now in the world represents the Kingdom and in a real sense *is* it ; but still it must pray " Thy kingdom come "; and when that Kingdom comes in glory, the Church will pass into it as into something much greater than itself. This double feeling about the Church—as being, and also as not yet being, the Kingdom of God—accounts for the way in which from the first Christians both laboured to develop and organize the Church on earth, and yet eagerly expected the manifestation from heaven of something much vaster and more glorious.

3. In the argument of this chapter I have appealed simply to historical considerations. But there is an appeal also open to us to common sense and universal experience. How can any spiritual movement due to the initiative of an individual—teacher or prophet—hope to maintain itself in being ? There are two chief means. The one is to embody the teaching in a book. This way of proceeding Jesus Christ did not adopt. The only book with which He left His Church was the, now confessedly imperfect, book of the Old Testament Scriptures. which had its value because it was prophetic, not because it was adequate. The other way of proceeding is to found an institution to embody and perpetuate the idea. Jesus Christ indeed did not need to originate an institution, for He found it in being—the Church of God which was the people of Israel ; but He needed profoundly to modify and refound it. This, we have sought to show, He did do in fact. But may we not say He *must*, as a wise man and wise teacher, have done something of the kind ? Can we imagine that He could have left His doctrines to float, so to speak, loose in the world ?

And in support of this argument I will not appeal to a theologian. I will appeal to Seeley's *Ecce Homo.* If anyone is disposed to doubt whether Christ is responsible for the Church—whether with the deepest deliberation He founded or refounded it—I could wish nothing better than that he should read this remarkable book; and the conviction which I think it will generate in him is not only that He did found it, but that as a wise master-builder He must have done so.

4. I suppose that the whole tendency of modern enquiry into the religions of the world is to prove their "group origin." They belong to the tribe or nation; and whatever personal religion they are capable of nourishing grows up under the shelter of the social institution. This was certainly so among the Jews. Thus if Jesus had made no provision for the future of His disciples, it may very rightly be argued that as Jews, believing themselves to be the believers in the true Messiah, they must have organized themselves as a Church; and that the natural tendency to organization, bred of their Jewish origin, would have been deepened, as Gentiles were incorporated, by the equally strong tendency to form religious organizations which characterized contemporary Hellenism. There is in fact no justification for putting the idea of Christ having instituted the Church into antagonism to the idea of natural circumstances having favoured its formation. Those who believe in Christ as God, believe also that God is at work in the processes of natural human development. The supernatural influence would have worked in with "the natural inclination which all men have unto sociable life." But contemporary critics have been seeking to persuade us that the genesis of the Church was purely natural, and that Christ neither provided for it nor was interested in it. And the object of this chapter has been to show that the

evidence condemns such a representation, not by any means to deny that the natural tendencies of the period, both Jewish and Gentile, promoted its development.

APPENDED NOTE A (see p. 38)

IS THE NEW TESTAMENT INTERPRETATION OF PROPHECY SUBSTANTIALLY ERRONEOUS ?

In the *Church Quarterly* for April 1923 the Rev. W. Maurice Pryke has an interesting but surprising article in which he contends that the ascription to the Hebrew Scriptures of the prophecy of a suffering, dying, and then glorified Messiah, an ascription which in the Gospels is constantly attributed to our Lord Himself, and in the rest of the N.T. to the apostles, is quite unjustified by the facts. " Let us then admit unreservedly that no single passage of the O.T., whether from prophet or psalmist, can rightly be produced as a prediction, conscious or unconscious, of the sufferings, death, resurrection, exaltation, and return to judgement of the Messiah " (p. 125 ; cf. p. 127, " So far the Jews were in the right "). But it is astonishing that Mr. Pryke gives no consideration to Isa. liii. Certainly (see *Belief in Christ*, pp. 60 ff.) one main feature in the teaching of Christ was the importance given to the " suffering servant " as constituting an element of the greatest importance in the Old Testament picture of " him who was to come." Certainly our Lord took the " suffering servant " of Isaiah (and also the glorified form " like unto a son of man " in Daniel vii.) into His conception of the Christ. He regarded it as moral blindness to omit the figure of the sufferer from the picture. And undoubtedly the intensely individualized picture of Isa. liii. does describe one who redeems by suffering and death and passes through contemptuous rejection and death to glory. (See Driver's *Isaiah*, in " Men of the Bible," pp. 177–8 and 152 ff., quoted in *Belief in Christ*, pp. 59 f.) And round this passage group themselves a number of other pictures of suffering servants of God, in the Psalms especially (xxii. and lxix.), which emphasize the idea that the true servant of God must expect rejection, suffering, and ignominy in the fulfilment of his mission. In a few of the Psalms I do not think it is possible to doubt that the idea is presented of the faithful servant living through death (see an article by Dr. E. H. Askwith in *Expositor*, January 1923, "The Hope of Immortality in the Psalter" and Dr. Briggs's Notes on Ps. xvi. 10–11, xvii. 15, xlix. 15, lxxiii. 23 f.). The question whether the contention of our Lord and His apostles, that the death and resurrection and glory of the Christ was prophesied in the Old Testament, was justified in fact, depends *in the main* on the question whether Isaiah liii., and the Psalms which group themselves round this central conception, really ought to be taken into the picture of "him who was to come," that is, the Christ.

APPENDED NOTE B (see p. 46)

THE RELATION OF ST. PETER TO THE OTHER APOSTLES

This is a subject which has been blackened with controversy, so that it is difficult to gain or keep a free mind about it. The Roman Church has appropriated the Petrine texts, in much the same way as Protestant tradition has appropriated the Epistle to the Galatians. Yet on consideration we do not find either that the Roman contention is supported by the New Testament as a whole or the Lutheran individualism by St. Paul's Epistles.

1. The prominence of Peter and his leadership of the apostles must surely be admitted. But, apart from any question of his office, his prominence is due to what one may call his forthcomingness. When our Lord asked the great question, "Who do ye say that I am?" Peter was forward to answer for all. He was their spokesman. Immediately after his confession, followed in St. Matthew by Christ's startling words of benediction, he again was forward in vehement deprecation of the Lord's prophecy of His rejection and crucifixion. Accordingly to him

also was addressed the tremendous rebuke, "Get thee behind me, Satan." But it was not meant for him alone. All the rest probably shared his mind. Again, it was he who was forward in professions of loyalty just before the passion, which accounts for two solemn warnings addressed to him personally—"Simon, Simon, Satan hath desired to have *you*, that he might sift *you* as wheat; but I made supplication for *thee*, that *thy* faith fail not: and do thou, when once thou hast turned again, strengthen thy brethren" (Luke xxii. 31–2). "Simon, sleepest thou? couldest thou not watch with me one hour?" (Mark xiv. 37). In the event he alone denied his Lord, but they all forsook him and fled. Then when, in Galilee after the Resurrection, he is solemnly cross-questioned by the Lord as to his love for Him, and solemnly restored to his pastoral function or apostolate—for surely the Fathers are right in so interpreting the scene [1]—he is still a representative man, representative of the others with whom he shares the pastoral commission, both in their weakness and in their penitence.

We should notice that the *representative* character of St. Peter is a great point with the Fathers—"gerebat personam ecclesiae," as St. Augustine says. (See Denny, p. 60.)

2. But also he is the leader among the apostles. If this is more obvious in St. Matthew than elsewhere, that is perhaps because the tendency of the Jewish Christian to exalt St. James into a "bishop of bishops" had to be rebuked. But there can be no mistake about his leadership. The disciples are called "those about Peter" in the uncanonical ending of St. Mark's Gospel, and "the disciples and Peter" is in Mark xvi. 7 the name for the whole group. Also his leadership after the Ascension is obvious in the Acts. But nothing can have happened, we must remember, to prevent James and John from seeking the foremost seats of honour in the day of Christ's glory (Mark x. 37), or the whole group discussing "which of them is accounted to be greatest" (Luke xxii. 24). The commission promised,

[1] See *Roman Catholic Claims*, chap. v, pp. 80, 81; and with much greater fullness, Denny's *Papalism*, § 16, pp. 65 ff.

not given, to Peter alone, in Matt. xvi. is very impressive. But it must be remembered that the commission actually given in John xx. to the whole group is in substance the same. The keys to open and shut and the authority to bind and loose (which go together) are both involved in the commission to absolve and retain sins. The Fathers seem to hold it as unquestionable that the power of the keys is nothing else than the power to bind and loose and to absolve and retain sins, and that it was given to all the apostles: see Denny, p. 57. Still we ask, Is not the stewardship given to Peter something unique and personal, like the stewardship of his Old Testament prototypes, Eliakim and Shebna? And in St. Luke xii. when Peter asks the question, "Speakest thou this [about the stewardship] to us, or even unto all?" though our Lord's reply is addressed to them all ("I say unto *you*"), yet it has been suggested that the stewardship is still spoken of as the office of a single person. There is something that is ambiguous in the Gospels, and we naturally go to the Acts and the Epistles for elucidation of the ambiguity.

3. And the Acts and the Epistles, it seems to me, negative the idea that any special office, other than a leadership among equals, belongs to St. Peter. In St. Paul's the "stewardship" belongs to all the apostles (1 Cor. iv. 1), or indeed to all the presbyter-bishops (Tit. i. 7). His language about St. Peter seems positively to exclude any recognition on his part of any authority belonging to him which he himself and the other apostles did not share equally. He ranks "James, Cephas, and John" together as "they who were reputed to be pillars." He sees Peter twice at Jerusalem with some others "reputed to be somewhat," but "they added nothing to him." His own apostolic authority he has received neither "from men nor through man." He rebuked Cephas to the face when he stood self-condemned for inconsistency at Antioch (Gal. i. and ii.). When he is speaking about the Corinthian parties "of Paul, of Apollos, of Cephas" (1 Cor. i. 12), there is no hint of superiority of one to the other. All the apostles had, it seems, the same authority under Christ the head. The idea of a headship on earth appears to be excluded.

Under Christ are " first apostles," etc. (Eph. iv. 9–16). It is the " holy apostles and prophets " who are the foundation stones of the Church (Eph. ii. 20), as in the vision of John in the Apocalypse the wall of the New Jerusalem has " twelve foundations, which are the twelve apostles." There is no room left for any Petrine authority, except that which he shared with all the others. Nor is there any suggestion of more than an original leadership in the Acts of the Apostles. When the Church " sent down " Peter and John to Samaria, they are sending seemingly two equal officers to complete what Philip could not complete. Peter opens the door to the Gentiles, but Paul bears the brunt of keeping it open. He appears to eclipse Peter, just as the apostolate to the Gentiles which belonged to Paul and Barnabas was so much more important than the apostolate to the circumcision which was allotted to James, Cephas, and John. In the Council at Jerusalem, Peter gives crucial testimony, but James presides and gives the verdict. And there is no hint of special authority in St. Peter's Epistle.

4. The later witness of the Fathers (which I have sought to summarize in *Roman Catholic Claims*, but which is to be found much more fully in Denny, *op. cit.*, and in Puller's *Primitive Saints and the See of Rome*) is not at all favourable (if one excludes the testimony of Rome itself) to the Romanist interpretation of the Petrine texts. This is not the place to speak of the claim made for the transmission of power supposed to be Peter's to his successors in the see of Rome, of which, of course, in the New Testament there is no hint.

APPENDED NOTE C (see p. 47)

THE AUTHORITY OF AN APOSTLE

The authority of an apostle, as St. Paul represents it, is the authority (ἐξουσία) of a regular officer of an organized society. As being such, he can claim support for himself and his wife, if he is married, in the churches of his foundation; and that by the ordinance of Christ

(1 Cor. ix. 1–14; 2 Thess. iii. 9). His mission, given him by Christ, is to preach the Gospel (1 Cor. i. 17) and to "edify" the churches, but also, where necessary, to exercise sharp discipline (2 Cor. x. 8, xiii. 10). Apostles are "ministers of Christ, and stewards of the mysteries [revealed secrets] of God" (1 Cor. iv. 1). St. Paul also speaks of his ministry in sacerdotal terms. "I have written to you," he says (Rom. xv. 15), "with a certain freedom in virtue of my commission as a priest of Christ Jesus to the Gentiles in the service of God's gospel."[1] In effect, then, the office of the apostle is the full pastoral office to feed and to govern the flock of Christ, with the special qualification of a founder or initiator; and it is essentially a world-wide office, though practically arrangements have been made that some apostles should go to the Jews and others to the Gentiles. It authorizes St. Paul to judge and excommunicate an offending Christian—if possible in union with the local church to which the offender belongs—and to absolve another who has repented—"in the name of the Lord Jesus" or "in the person of Christ" (1 Cor. v. 3; 2 Cor. ii. 10). St. Paul, we observe, does not like exercising mere authority, but prefers to work by persuasion. Thus he tells Philemon (ver. 8) that he "exhorts" him to do the right thing by Onesimus, but that he has full authority in Christ to command him.

The apostolate is the chief office in the Church, set there by God or by Christ, the head of the Church. He gave "some as apostles"—"first, apostles" (Eph. iv. 11, 1 Cor. xii. 28). It is "neither from men, nor through man, but through Jesus Christ, and God the Father" (Gal. i. 1). St. Paul himself received his apostolate from the glorified Christ in heaven, whom he saw. But he was appointed "out of due time." There were "apostles before him" who had been apostles when Christ appeared to them after the Resurrection, and must therefore have been appointed during His life on earth (1 Cor. xv. 5–8; Gal. i. 17).

Words could not express more simply or clearly than those of St. Paul that the authority of the apostolate did not accrue to it by the voice of the Church, or under

[1] Dr. James Moffat's translation.

the pressure of circumstances, or by personal influence. It was an original institution in the Church, of Christ's creation, the same in the case of St. Paul as in that of the original Twelve.

In the Acts we perceive that it is the function of the apostle to convey to the baptized the gift of the Holy Spirit by the laying on of hands [1]; and in the Acts and the Pastoral Epistles it appears to be also the function of an apostle—in some kind of undefined co-operation with the local presbyter-bishops—to perpetuate the ministry in the Church, again through the laying on of hands, viewed sacramentally as a means of conveying a special gift of the Holy Spirit. But about this we shall have occasion to speak in a later chapter.

APPENDED NOTE D (see p. 49)

THE COMMISSION IN ST. JOHN XX. 21–3

The general sense of this passage seems strongly to suggest that it is an *apostolate* which is being conferred, which is a continuation of Christ's apostolate. Cf. the earlier commission to the Twelve (St. Matt. x. 16; cf. Luke ix. 2), " Behold, I send you forth," and the words in the prayer of our Lord before His passion, " As thou didst send me into the world, even so sent I them into the world " (John xvii. 18). In a sense the commission is to the Church as a whole; but the sending of men into the world as evangelists is especially applicable to the apostles, though the Seventy may have shared their mission. In the latter part of St. John, however, " the disciples " appears to mean the Twelve [2]; and the nature

[1] If Dr. Swete is right in interpreting Gal. iii. 5 (" He that supplieth to you the Spirit and worketh miracles among you ") of the apostle, not of God directly, then we should have a reference to " confirmation " ; but I do not feel sure that Dr. Swete is right. We notice that in the Bezan text of Acts xi. 17 Peter protests : " Who was I that I could withstand God, that *I should not give them the Holy Spirit* when they believed on him ? " Cf. p. 132, n. 2.

[2] Cf. Westcott on St. John xxi. 1, " By the disciples is meant in all probability the apostles." Cf. *The Church and the Ministry*, p. 207, n. 2

of the commission strongly suggests administrative officers and not merely ordinary members of a society.

Apparently there were other people present (Luke xxiv. 33), but the special apostolic commission may very well have been given in the presence of others. The commission in St. Matt. xxviii. 16 is specially said to be given "to the eleven disciples" (cf. [St. Mark] xvi. 14–15), but it must probably be identified with the appearance "to above five hundred brethren at once" recorded by St. Paul.

Dr. Hort, whose great name is chiefly quoted for making the commission general, seems to me, as to Dr. Mason, in his posthumous work on *The Christian Ecclesia* (Macmillan, 1897), greatly to underrate the evidence that the apostles were understood from the beginning to be the divinely appointed rulers of the Church. See *The Church and the Ministry* (Longmans), App. Note M, p. 379. But it should be noted that in respect of the apostolic commission recorded in St. Matthew and St. John, Dr. Hort speaks very hesitatingly. "Doubt is possible"; "Granting that it was probably to the Eleven that our Lord directly and principally spoke on both these occasions (and even to them alone when He spoke the words at the end of St. Matthew's Gospel), yet it has still to be considered in what capacity they were addressed by Him." My contention is that it is plainly as officers of the future community and not merely as witnesses or disciples. I think the free and easy manner in which it is commonly taken for granted that the commission was given to the Church as a whole augurs a considerable amount of wilfulness of mind.

CHAPTER III

CHRISTIANITY AND THE MYSTERY RELIGIONS

So far what we have done is this: we have found in the Acts and Epistles of the New Testament a religion of the Spirit which is also a religion of the Church—for the only recognized sphere of the Spirit's action is the Church of the believers in Jesus as the Christ and Lord. And the Church we found to regard itself as no new foundation, but as the ancient people of God—the Israel of the prophets—reformed on the basis of faith in Jesus as the promised Christ, and admitting Gentile and Jew on equal terms into its fellowship. And we saw convincing reason to believe that Jesus Himself did regard His disciples as the only true Israel, and that He was at pains to re-equip this renewed Israel, this new "household of God," with certain stewards or officers in the persons of the Twelve and with certain symbolic rites or sacraments of incorporation and fellowship. Thus the religion of the Spirit in the Church appears in the New Testament as the culmination of the religion of Israel. "Salvation is of the Jews." This is undoubtedly the account which the New Testament gives of itself and its origin.

We must not, however, altogether exclude the notion of the incorporation into the religious development of Israel of elements from the religions of other nations. The truly original features of the Jewish religion, i.e. the prophetic doctrine about God and man, and the social and religious life based upon it, did in fact grow in the heart of a Semitic tribe or group of tribes more or less possessed already of the common Semitic type of religious ideas, traditions, and institutions. What we discern in the Old Testament is that the prophetic doctrine succeeded in transforming and correcting these ideas, traditions, and institutions, and so making of them a quite new thing. And later, when the developed religion of the prophets was brought into close contact with Babylonian, Persian, and Greek influences, it appears to have incorporated elements from them, such as appear in the later Jewish teaching about angels and about Satan, and in the doctrine of the Divine Wisdom immanent and operative in all nature, but not to such an extent as to imperil the distinctive character of the prophetic doctrine.[1] We may find indeed among the Jews such an amalgamation of the prophetic faith with alien features as seriously to corrupt the tradition. Thus we may stand in doubt whether the Essene communities, contemporary with our Lord, were not more Oriental than Jewish in their religion[2]; or whether some of the Apocalypses do not seriously pervert the expecta-

[1] Thus we may take it for granted that the later Jewish teaching about angels was due in part to Persian influences, yet it was held on a basis of belief in the unique majesty of God, due to the prophetic teaching, so that no "worship of angels" (Col. ii. 18) could be tolerable to a Jew who knew his Bible. And the later doctrine of Satan as a rebel angel who had by his rebellion become the adversary of God, as compared to the earlier doctrine of Satan as one among the sons of God (see A. B. Davidson's *Theol. of the O.T.*, pp. 300 ff.), was really an inevitable outcome of the fuller recognition, under the stress of the prophetic teaching, of the divine goodness, which made it impossible to think that the adversary and the tempter could be among the agents of God's will (see Jas. i. 13). And the idea of "the Wisdom" of God—the "immanent God"—learned in part from the Greeks, was an outcome of the teaching of the divine omnipresence as seen in Ps. cxxxix. The assimilated ideas maintained the prophetic teaching and in no wise corrupted it.

[2] Hastings, *Dict. of the Bible*, s.v. "Essenes."

tion of the prophets.[1] But this was not the case with the religion of the Old Testament as we see it passing into the New. That is essentially the religion of the prophets, and of the ceremonial and civil law as reconstructed under the leadership of the prophets.

When we have passed from the Old Testament to the New we find certainly a similar process of assimilation going on. Confessedly Christianity 'borrowed' from Greek philosophy,[2] and the process is already beginning in St. Paul and the Epistle to the Hebrews and St. John, and is still more marked in the early Apologists (to go no farther). Again the question arises—how far did the process go? Is the Christianity of the Epistles really in all its substance the religion of the prophets, consummated in Jesus Christ and realized in the mission from Him of the Holy Spirit, as it obviously claims to be, or is it an amalgamation of Jewish and Hellenistic elements in about equal proportion? In particular, is all that has been associated with the religion of the Spirit in the Church—the idea of the Spirit of God, or Christ by the Spirit, indwelling the community and its individual members, they in Him and He in them, the idea of the sacraments as channels or instruments of spiritual grace, accomplishing man's regeneration and re-creation by incorporation into Christ and feeding upon Him, and the idea of a priestly ministry divinely appointed to teach and to safeguard divine mysteries,—is all this group of ideas which has largely constituted the substance of Catholicism, as it appears in history from St. Paul downwards, really *not* due to the prophets or to Jesus Christ or to Hebrew tradition at all, but to Hellenism? Was it even the case that the spirit of Hellenism passed in such full flood into the first Christian communities outside Palestine, with the

[1] See *Belief in Christ*, pp. 21–5.
[2] See above, pp. 18 f., 31 f.

influx of the Gentiles, as really to transform the religion of Jesus substantially into a mystery religion on the Hellenistic pattern ?

This I suppose to be at the present moment the most formidable of the proposed 'explanations' of Christianity and, owing to its elusiveness, the most difficult to deal with. We have always been accustomed to see in the Gnostic sects, in marked distinction from the early Catholic Church, amalgamations of Hellenism with Jewish and Christian ideas—a group of amalgamations in which Hellenism had a substantial victory. But is it after all the case that as between the Gnostic sects and the orthodox Church, even the Church as St. Paul expounded it, it is only a question of more or less—that even the Church as St. Paul expounded it is substantially Hellenistic, and so far quite alien to the mind and intention of Jesus of Nazareth ?

In part we have had to face this theory already—as when it would attribute the title "Lord" as applied to Christ to Hellenistic influences, assimilating Christ to Serapis or Adonis or the like 'saviours,' and we found the attribution really quite groundless.[1] Again, we had to consider the attempt to detach from Christ the institution of the sacrament of His body and blood, and to present it as an element of contemporary mysticism which passed into St. Paul's mind in a vision—a communication which he believed to be from the Lord Jesus, but which was really due to the 'sacramental' atmosphere of the Hellenistic world ; and this interpretation again we found we must decisively reject.[2] But it does not suffice to deal with this theory of the Hellenizing of Christianity piecemeal. We must seek to envisage the position as a whole. It presents itself from two sides: from the side of the anthropologists or students

[1] See *Belief in Christ*, pp. 102 ff., Note B.

[2] See *op. cit.*, pp. 99 f., Note A, and in this volume see pp. 54 f.

of comparative religions, as represented, for instance, by Sir James Frazer in *The Golden Bough*; and from the side of students of the Hellenistic movements and literature, amongst whom Reitzenstein is the most conspicuous.[1] And we will consider Sir James Frazer's position first.

I

Sir James Frazer is among the most distinguished of the anthropologists who have devoted themselves to the study of comparative mythology; and after thirty years of laborious investigation, which began from the legends connected with the priest of Nemi and has spread over the whole of our globe, he has recently condensed into a single volume the evidence, reasonings and conclusions of the twelve volumes previously published, under the general heading of *The Golden Bough*.[2] Perhaps the most interesting feature of these widespread enquiries is the disclosure of the deep impression made on primitive man, in widely separated portions of the world, by the seeming death of nature in the autumn and its revival in spring, or in tropical countries by its death under the tyranny of the sun and its revival with the rains. Sometimes we see men apparently afraid that nature, on whose bounty their life depended, was in real danger of death, and devoting themselves by 'sympathetic magic' to keeping it alive or renewing its life. Then, as the regular recurrence of the seasons made this fear absurd, we see them none the less impressed with the constant spectacle of Mother Nature living by dying, and conscious also of their own kinship with nature in this respect. Thus in some forms of barbaric nature worship, some animal

[1] See *Belief in Christ*, p. 133.

[2] *The Golden Bough*, a study in magic and religion, by Sir James George Frazer, F.R.S., F.B.A., Abridged Edition (Macmillan, 1922).

or plant, which is the representative of nature, is worshipped as a divine being, and some individual specimen of the proper species is consecrated and eaten by its worshippers as a religious act, in the belief that its life and strength will so pass into them. So we get religion associated with sacrifice and 'sacramental' feeding.[1] And as by a nearly universal instinct men either shrink from death and desire to perpetuate their lives, or believe that the human spirit does in fact survive death, so the hope grows that by eating their god who lives by dying—the corn-spirit, for example—they can secure themselves against death or win a happy state of existence after death. This outcome of nature worship seems to be proved in certain cases and is very interesting.

Then when religion passes into an 'anthropomorphic' stage, that is when the gods are figured in quasi-human forms, we have the same fundamental fact of the death and revival of nature figured in myths of the death and recovery of some divine or semi-divine man, beloved of a goddess (Mother Nature). Thus Tammuz, whom the Greeks called Adonis, beloved of the Babylonian goddess

[1] There is good evidence for this "sacramental" feeding in the ritual of the Aztecs (see Frazer, *op. cit.*, pp. 488 ff.) and in some tribes of Northern Europe. But in Frazer's chap. L, on "Eating the God," most of the examples are very questionable. We remember that when the Jews ate their peace offerings, they attached no such idea to the eating. "Upon data so fragmentary and uncertain," Frazer remarks in one instance (p. 491), "it is impossible to build with confidence." The same remark might be often repeated. He quotes from Cicero (without a reference), p. 499: "When we call corn Ceres and wine Bacchus we use a common figure of speech; but do you imagine that anybody is so insane as to believe that the thing he feeds upon is a god?" Cicero would have spoken differently if he had had any idea that the common people did so believe or ever had so believed. There is no evidence that when the worshippers of Attis ate out of a drum and drank out of a cymbal they had any such belief, or when the votaries of Eleusis absorbed the sacred drink (κυκέων). But the kind of belief may have been widespread wherever the god was *identified* with an animal or plant: see further App. Note, pp. 105 f.

Ishtar or Aphrodite, and Attis, beloved of the Phrygian Cybele, and the Egyptian demi-god Osiris, beloved of Isis, were beautiful young men killed by accident, or self-mutilation, or murder, and then in some way brought back from death or made lords of the dead. In each case there were solemn rites commemorating the divine hero's death, as you read in Ezekiel of the idolatrous women in Jerusalem "weeping for Tammuz," and the sorrow of the devotees was turned into joy in the contemplation of his life renewed and the power that was now his. And there were 'mysteries' or secret cults[1] associated with these divine couples by which the initiates were assured that they too would pass through death to life. Thus one of the sacred hymns of Attis said, "Take courage, O ye initiates, because the god is saved; so to you also after troubles shall be salvation"; or a hymn of Osiris said, "As truly as Osiris lives, he also shall live; as truly as Osiris is not dead, shall he [the initiate] not die; as truly as Osiris is not annihilated, shall he not be annihilated." And these mystery-cults were celebrated with an imposing or frenzied ritual, and were in charge of special priesthoods.

The cults just named were oriental in origin; but there were like cults, which were of very old standing in Greece. Thus the divine Dionysus or Zagreus had been murdered in the form of a bull and raised to life again by his father Zeus, and in the festival of his commemoration the frenzied worshippers tore a live bull to pieces with their teeth and perhaps

[1] Perhaps the best and most trustworthy source of information on these cults is Cumont's *Religions orientales dans le paganisme romain* (*Oriental Religions:* Engl. trans., 1911, Chicago Open Court Publishing Co., and Kegan Paul, Trench, Trübner & Co., London). Dr. Percy Gardner's *Religious Experience of St. Paul,* chap. iv (Williams & Norgate), is also suggestive; and indeed the subject is now one of widespread interest among the learned and is becoming popularized.

originally believed themselves to eat their god.[1] And, in spite of the savage origin of this cult, a man as refined as Plutarch can comfort his wife over the death of their infant daughter with the hope of immortality assured to them by the mysteries of Dionysus into which they were both initiated.[2] And the mysteries of Eleusis, besides incorporating the Dionysus myth, were based upon the story of Persephone who was carried off by Pluto to Hades, and won back again, at least for two-thirds of the year, by her mother Demeter (Mother Earth). And there seems to be no doubt that all these gods or semi-divine beings, Oriental, Egyptian, or Greek, rescued from death and promoted to glory, were, in more or less thinly-veiled disguise, the corn-spirit or god of vegetation in some form. It is the death and resurrection of nature which lies at the root of all these worships.

Acquaintance with these mystery religions shows that their ideas and rites were at bottom barbarous and obscene.[3] Nevertheless, as the established State religions of Greece and Rome became discredited and abandoned, these mystery religions took their place in the affections of the people, and, in spite of official resistance, became the fashion among religious-minded people, and even among the later philosophers. The mood of the world had become a mood of pessimism. Men were oppressed with a sense of overhanging fate and with a feeling of the

[1] See, however, below, p. 105.

[2] *Consol. ad ux.*, 10 : τὰ μυστικὰ σύμβολα τῶν περὶ τὸν Διόνυσον ὀργιασμῶν ἃ σύνισμεν ἀλλήλοις οἱ κοινωνοῦντες.

[3] And in great part they remained so: see Strabo (born about A.D. 64), *Geogr.*, xii, 2, 3, and xii, 3, 32, and 36, as to the accompaniments of the worship at Comana in Cappadocia, and Comana in Pontus, and Corinth. The degrading effect of the myths and rites upon the mass of men is also admitted in one of the few classical books about the mysteries—Plutarch's *de Iside et Osiride*. He wishes to give the myth and the ritual alike a philosophical meaning; but he is quite explicit about the actual facts: see capp. 20, 35, 68 (end), 70, 71.

pollution of physical life. In this atmosphere all sorts of superstitions flourished, and a wide welcome was given to mysteries which promised their associates release and immortality, and fellowship with a divine being through the medium of initiations and symbolic rites, even though their origins might be barbarous and degrading.

It is easy to use language which assimilates these mythological mystery religions to the Christian creed and rites. Thus Frazer, though he has abandoned an extreme form of the mythical theory which at one time he put forward to account for the crucifixion of Jesus,[1] does not scruple to use this kind of language abundantly. Thus—"The god [Osiris] who annually died and rose again from the dead"; "As Osiris died and rose again from the dead, so all men hoped to rise again like him from death to life eternal"; "He gave his own body to feed the people; he died that they might live"; "The fast which accompanied the mourning for the dead god [Attis] may perhaps have been designed to prepare the body of the communicant for the reception of the blessed sacrament"; "A man-god slain to take away the misfortunes of the people"; "The good god [Saturn] who gave his life for the world." And of course the virginal conception of Jesus is regarded as a feature in this assimilation. "His [Attis'] birth is said to have been miraculous. His mother Nana was a virgin." Again a parallel to Christian ideas is found in the remoter East. "Thus through the mist of ages the tragic figure of the Pope of Buddhism—God's vicar on earth for Asia—looms dim and sad as the man-god who bore his people's sins, the good shepherd who laid down his life for the sheep."[2] Besides all this, Frazer is constantly pointing out how the popular observances

[1] See *Golden Bough*, vol. ix of the original work, p. 412.
[2] See *op. cit.*, pp. 325, 347, 367, 376, 351, 586, 347, 574.

of Christian festivals show obvious connexion with the ancient pagan feasts which they superseded.

How all this language of Frazer's impresses people is shown from an incidental remark of Mr. Bertrand Russell [1]: " Sir J. G. Frazer in his *Golden Bough* has shown that most of the elements of Christianity are derived from worship of the spirit of vegetation, the religion invented in the infancy of agriculture to insure the fertility of the soil."

I will give one more instance of this assimilation—from Loisy.[2] He thus summarizes St. Paul's conception of his Lord. " He was a saviour-god, after the manner of an Osiris, an Attis, a Mithra. Like them he belonged by his origin to the celestial world ; like them he had made his appearance on the earth ; like them he had accomplished a work of universal redemption, efficacious and typical ; like Adonis, Osiris, and Attis he had died a violent death, and like them he had been restored to life ; like them he had prefigured in his lot that of the human beings who should take part in his worship, and commemorate his mystic enterprise ; like them he had predestined, prepared, and assured the salvation of those who became partakers in his passion." This suggested assimilation of Christian beliefs and processes to those of Oriental mysteries—which is just now very popular—we must attentively examine. But first of all let us make four important concessions to those who make such suggestions, if " concessions " is the right word to describe what is very cordially made.

The first is that, if we believe in one God—the common Father of all—who has all through human history been at work in the heart of man and has nowhere left Himself without witness, we shall not

[1] *The Prospects of Industrial Civilization*, p. 47.
[2] *Hibbert Journal*, October 1911, p. 51. The foundations of such a theory are laid in *Les Mystères païens*, etc., referred to later.

be surprised to find all the world over ideas in the minds of even barbarous tribes which we shall recognize as akin, even if remotely akin, to the ideas of incarnation and atonement and divine fellowship which we associate in their highest form with Jesus Christ and His redemption of man. So far from being shocked to find anticipations of such ideas even in the religion of savages, we ought to be eager to recognize them, (1) as evidence of the unity of the human race, and (2) as a sort of prophecy. (1) No one can read the evidence of the beliefs and customs of primitive men all the world over, as Sir James Frazer has accumulated it, without being deeply impressed with the sense of identity in human sentiment and aspiration everywhere, and feeling how naturally religion in all parts of the world takes on a 'sacramental' form, that is, expresses itself in rites and ceremonies which are believed to convey some sort of spiritual influence. Certainly, we feel, we are "of one blood" even with Aztecs and Australian bushmen. (2) No one can believe that God has a purpose for man, which is ultimately to be realized in and through Jesus Christ, without welcoming the signs that, even in a savage form, aspiration was being evoked which was one day to find satisfaction in a form from which all savagery had been purged away. Thus we should examine the connexion of Christian ideas and institutions with those of the pagan world quite without prejudice. And I think that anyone who takes an unprejudiced view of the circumstances of early Christianity will admit that the 'mystery religions' of the empire created a sort of widespread spiritual appetite which Christianity showed itself better able than anything else to satisfy: but of this I shall say something more before I have done.

Secondly, we shall (with St. Chrysostom) recognize that Jewish institutions—such as temple and sacrifices and festivals and sacred dresses and taboos—had their origin in the common stock of Semitic customs or ideas. The evidence of this is clearly to be found in the study of the earliest layer of the Old Testament literature ; and as the Christian institutions or ideas were based upon the Jewish, so they were, even in virtue of their Hebrew origin, very remotely based upon the common stock of human religions.

Thirdly—in view of Frazer's tendency to argue from the dates and observances of the Church festivals—let it be recognized that when Christianity came out into the world and was making its way to become the established religion, it found certain annual festivals in possession of mankind, such as the festival of the winter solstice, the spring festival, and the midsummer festival, associated with moments in the annual course of the sun or of the crops. These were natural festivals, corrupted no doubt with much superstition and vice, but too dear to the hearts of the people to be easily suppressed. No wonder then if the Church, having its own spring festival, with its date determined by the Jewish Passover, instead of entering into rivalry with the old festivals, sought to superimpose the new Christian feast upon the old and let the new Christian ideas banish the old vices and superstitions. So in England they identified the Paschal festival with the old pagan spring festival of "Easter" and even retained the old name—as Bede says, "giving to the old feast a new consecration." So the festival of St. John the Baptist was used to give a new meaning to the old midsummer celebration. So, it may be (but this is not at all certain) the date of Christmas was fixed to correspond with the festivals of the winter solstice.[1]

[1] See Duchesne, *Christian Worship*, pp. 256 ff.

Fourthly, there can be no doubt that, when Christianity became the religion of the Empire and began to be the only safe religion to profess, and a little later was accepted by barbarous races in mass at the bidding of their chiefs, a great deal of pagan superstition passed inside the Church. With such corruptions of the tradition we are not yet concerned. For some three centuries Christianity had been kept relatively pure by the danger of professing it. And it is only with the religion of the early centuries, and especially with the religion of the New Testament, that we are concerned.

But when due account has been taken of all this, it must be admitted that Frazer and Loisy are behaving very unscientifically in relying upon similarities of language—and sometimes, it must be added, very forced similarities—as an argument for similarity of origin, without any real regard to the source of the language in each case.

Thus though, remotely hidden, the origin of the Jewish festivals of the Passover and Pentecost and Tabernacles may lie with a Semitic nature worship, based upon the decay and revival of nature, such origin appears to have been utterly forgotten by the Jews, who for centuries before Christ had retained no traces of nature worship, but held it in abhorrence. And the Jewish belief in the resurrection of the dead had not arisen in any connexion with the life of nature, but out of the belief in God and His justice and the relation of the soul to God.

And when the belief in resurrection among the Jews received its confirmation in the death and resurrection of Jesus of Nazareth, the belief in His resurrection was wholly alien from any idea of 'corn-spirits' or gods of vegetation. Nor do the anthropomorphic legends of Osiris and the rest suggest the conception of resurrection as the Christians understood it. Some of these wholly mythical hero-gods [1] were returned from the world of the dead by the decree of Zeus for part of the year, like Adonis and Persephone; and the fragments of the murdered and dismembered Osiris, re-collected by the loving search of Isis, were remade into an Osiris who became the Lord of the dead. The Christian word "resurrection" with its very concrete associations can hardly be properly applied to such vaguely conceived returns of souls from the world of the dead or glorifications of a dead hero in Hades.

Again, there is no suggestion in any of these myths, as the ancients give them us, of a "redeemer-god" or a "saviour-god" who had come from heaven to save mankind by the sacrifice of his life. These myths are concerned (for instance) with beautiful youths, loved by goddesses, who were put to death by a wild beast or by suicide or murder, and were themselves saved and rescued from death by one of the higher gods, yielding to the importunity of the divine lover. There is not a trace of the Saviour-God who came down to earth and sacrificed Himself that men might live. The passage in Frazer in which such a rôle is assigned to Saturn is exceedingly forced, and based on a more than precarious idea that Saturn in a certain rite of the Saturnalia was regarded as sacrificed apparently to himself.[2] As for the strange sentences about the Thibetan Lama,[3] one has only to read the preceding pages to realize how little they are based upon. There was indeed in the Prometheus myth, as Aeschylus treated it, the idea of the self-sacrifice of a semi-divine hero for the good of men, side by side with that of the jealousy and cruelty of the higher gods, but it inaugurated no cult and had no apparent influence.

[1] Plutarch, we notice, *de Isid. et Osir.*, cap. 11, repudiates with horror the idea of the myth being true—*δεῖ μηδὲν οἴεσθαι τούτων . . . γεγονὺς οὕτω καὶ πεπραγμένον.* Cf. capp. 21 ff.

[2] Frazer, *op. cit.*, p. 586. [3] p. 574.

Nor, again, is there any justification for language which finds in these nature mysteries a counterpart to the Christian idea of communion in the body and blood of Christ. There is nothing to suggest the eating of the god, except at the stage of religion where the plant or animal is crudely believed to be a god. But this stage had long been outgrown in the anthropomorphic myths, and there is nothing to suggest the " man-god " feeding his people with his own substance.[1]

Finally, it is true that the mother of Attis is said to have " conceived by putting a ripe almond or pomegranate in her bosom " ; and there are of course multitudes of legends of " miraculous births " by the intercourse of gods with women, but they suggest nothing in the Bible except the single fragment of unassimilated mythology in Gen. vi. 1–6. And if the presence of this passage in the sacred books of Israel has any purpose, it must be to make it plain that all such ideas could be associated only with what was disastrously evil, and could enter in no wise into the purpose of God. We must agree with Harnack about the virginal conception of Christ—that " the conjecture that the idea of His birth from a virgin is a heathen myth which was received by Christians contradicts the entire earliest development of the Christian tradition."

II

Now let us recall to our minds the distinctive qualities of the Christian religion, as it appeared in the first churches of apostolic foundation, and especially, where we know most about it, in the

[1] See Appended Note A, p. 105, where this is discussed at some length.

churches of St. Paul—the distinctive qualities of the religion, which both kept it separate from all the religions of the empire in a jealous aloofness which was the cause of their hostility to it, and also force us to recognize its uniqueness as a historical religion.

There was nothing in the Hellenistic world to be compared to the Jewish theology of the One God, the Creator, either in its definiteness of teaching or clearness of outline. It was a doctrine which in the race of Israel had struggled for centuries against the native tendencies of the people, and finally, through the depth of a seeming failure, had passed into control of the nation and all its concerns, as the one and only word of God. Then on the basis of this definite self-revelation of the one God (as it claimed to be) the religion of Israel had assumed still more definite content in Jesus the Christ. Here was one who was unmistakably man, the Son of Man, who had recently lived a human life, and proclaimed a certain teaching, maintained in careful remembrance, and had died a malefactor's death at the will of His misguided people and at the hands of a recent Roman magistrate, but had been vindicated by God in His resurrection from the dead, of which the Apostles were the witnesses, and been recognized, on the basis of his own language about Himself, as the Son of God, the real and only manifestation of the one God in human nature, coming in order to enlighten the world and save it from sin and redeem it from all evil.

All this message was definitely concrete and historical. It knew exactly what it appealed to and on what grounds it based its confident and exclusive claims. We can easily familiarize ourselves with its tone in the New Testament. It is unmistakable. Then we contrast with this the vague and shifting and formless character of the 'theology' and tradition of the mysteries.[1] The god of one mystery fades into the god of another. They betray their origin as vague symbols of nature. They have no character or history. Thus in the best and most intelligible account of initiation into any of the mysteries which classical literature presents to us—the *Metamorphoses* of Apuleius—Isis, whose rites are being celebrated, declares herself identical with the Phrygian Mother Goddess, with the Athenian Minerva, with the Venus of Paphos, with Diana, with Proserpine, with Ceres, with Juno, with Bellona, with Hecate.[2] So again the originally distinct divine mothers of Asiatic worship merge into one another. So the legends of Demeter and Persephone become inextricably mixed up with the legend of Dionysus in the Mysteries of Eleusis. So in Egypt Amon of Thebes was identified with Ra of Heliopolis and again with Min, who was later identified with the Greek Pan. Plutarch makes a great point of this identity of the divine under the veil of different names. Everything is vague and shifting and nebulous and unhistorical.

Again, the Christians derived from the ancient prophets a profound belief that God has a purpose in all history. This gives an importance in their eyes to history and to facts which is quite alien to the mythology of the Hellenistic world.[3] *There* was to be found no hope for the redemption of the world—no idea of a world-wide purpose with which men were called to co-operate—but only a method of escape for the individual from corruption and misery. It is the sense of what God has actually done for

[1] Aristotle is quoted by Synesius as saying that those who partook of the mysteries did not learn anything but were the subjects of an impression—*οὐ μαθεῖν τι δεῖν ἀλλὰ παθεῖν καὶ διατεθῆναι*, Synesius, *Dion.*, 10.

[2] Apuleius, *Metamorph.*, bk. xi, cap. 5; cf. Plut., *op cit.*, cap. 61.

[3] On this prophetic doctrine see *Belief in Christ*, pp. 11–19, and *Belief in God*, p. 132, n. 1.

men in historical fact, coupled with the sense of what He is pledged to do—the gospel of the Kingdom, which accounts for the sense of joyful strength in the early Christian Church and their assurance of coming victory over the religions of the idols, which are "vanity" or "nothing at all" or "demons" impotent against God. Certainly, then, the theological and historical content of Christianity suggests no debt at all to the mystery religions.

Again, the Christianity of the New Testament inherits the sternly ethical tradition of the prophets. To these prophets we owe what to us seems inevitable and obvious, but was quite strange to the nature-worships of antiquity or the myths they generated—the intimate association of religion with morality. This intimate association is deepened in the teaching of our Lord and His apostles. It is the commonplace of St. Paul. "This ye know of a surety, that no fornicator, nor unclean person, nor covetous man, which is an idolater, hath any inheritance in the kingdom of Christ and God. Let no man deceive you with empty words: for because of these things cometh the wrath of God upon the sons of disobedience. Be not ye therefore partakers with them; for ye were once darkness, but are now light in the Lord: walk as children of light . . . ; and have no fellowship with the unfruitful works of darkness, but even reprove them; for the things done by them in secret it is a shame even to speak of."[1] St. Paul is conscious of the danger, incurred by the Christian communities, that the influx of Gentiles might weaken their moral sense. St. Jude's Epistle and the letters to the Seven Churches in the Apocalypse reveal a sense of fearful peril. But there could be no doubt what Christianity stood for, and it did in fact weather the storm and carried into the empire its great tradition of moral purity and of the spirit

[1] Eph. v. 5–12.

of unselfish fellowship. Much more than on its theological doctrine, it relied on its moral witness to convince "those without."

But in all this the basis and the tradition of the first Christian Church was in marked contrast to that of the mysteries. *Their* origin lay in what is barbarous and obscene; that is their character in classical literature. It is true that nothing could suppress them. They became the popular religions of the empire. They appealed to a craving for deliverance from fate and the contaminations of physical life, and for immortality, and for fellowship with the divine. They learned to use lofty language, and produced, no doubt, a profound impression even on educated people. But their appeal was emotional rather than moral. One of our few really luminous witnesses to the meaning of initiation into one of the mysteries is Apuleius (an author of the second century), who records at great length the initiation of his hero, Lucius—who represents himself—into the mysteries of Isis.[1] He describes magnificent and imposing processions, and a solemn period of preparation in the temple precincts, and sacrifices and mystical objects exhibited by the priests, and a ceremonial purification and a long abstinence, and white robes; and then, going as far as he dares in describing what may not be revealed, he says of the actual service of initiation, "I drew near to the confines of death, I trod the threshold of Proserpine, I was borne through all the elements and returned to earth again. I saw the sun gleaming with bright splendour at dead of night, I approached the gods above, and the gods below, and worshipped them face to face. Behold I have told thee things of which, though thou hast heard them, thou must yet know naught."

[1] *The Metamorphoses, or "Golden Ass,"* bk. xi, Engl. trans., 1910, vol. ii, pp. 138 ff. (Clarendon Press).

All this is very solemn. It may be intended to hint at some dramatic ceremonies or at a process of hypnotism. It is declared to result in a life of dedication to the goddess. Then two other initiations follow—the description including sly intimations of the important place held in these processes by the demands of the priests for fees and banquets. Lucius (or Apuleius) was clearly a person of a high emotional sensibility; but the book, which concludes with these experiences and narrates the previous adventures of the hero, is full of lewdness, and the character of himself which Apuleius gives us in his *Apologia* does not suggest moral seriousness at all. The mysteries, we should gather, cultivated and in part satisfied the religious emotions of very many people. But there is no evidence that they were likely to effect a permanent moral reformation.[1] Christianity in its later history adopted an impressive ceremonial, and sometimes relied dangerously on appeals to the dramatic emotions, but it was not so at all in the early centuries,[2] and certainly in its methods of appeal it had in its early days learned nothing from the mysteries, which it viewed with horror on account of their immoralities.[3]

[1] See Gardner, *Religious Experiences of St. Paul*, p. 87: "We have no reason to think that those who claimed salvation from Isis or Mithras were much better than their neighbours."

[2] Tertullian, *de Baptismo*, 2, as we have seen, contrasts the bareness and puritanism of the Christian rites with the splendour of the ritual in the mysteries.

[3] I have said nothing about Mithraism, to which M. Loisy alludes in the passage quoted above, partly because it is so astonishingly unlike Christianity in its theology and in the picture which it offers of the adventures of its hero, partly because its influence, which was very great and widespread from the second century onwards, does not appear to have been felt at the formative period of Christianity in the regions where it took shape. See Cumont, *op. cit.*, pp. xix, xx, and 140, 148. No doubt at the middle or end of the second century Justin and Tertullian see in the mysteries of Mithras a satanic imitation of the Christian sacraments (Justin, 1 *Apol.*, 66; Tertull., *de Praescript.*, 40). We should prefer to say that there is a sacramental instinct in all religions which may

III

Neither then in respect of its theology, nor of its morals, nor of its ritual, did the Christian Church owe anything to the mysteries at its origin. But a more plausible case can be made out for its sacramentalism. It must be admitted that the Christian Church, as it appears in St. Paul, shared with the mysteries in some sense the habit and principle of attributing a sacramental value to symbolic ritual acts. It must be admitted also that sacramentalism was not a characteristic of the Jews. The Jews regarded their sacred rites as divine commands, elements in a covenant of God of which they were the subjects. They were circumcised because it had been so commanded, that they might remain within the covenant, into which as Jews they were born.[1] They offered sacrifices because they were the divinely appointed means for maintaining or renewing their good relations with Jehovah. But they did not regard them as instruments of spiritual grace. Even in Philo, in whom the mystical sense is strongly developed, it shows itself only in interpreting historical events and scriptural phrases in a spiritual sense. But in St. Paul's language about baptism and the eucharist, and in the Gospel accounts of the institution of the eucharist, we already see the sacramental sense proper in unmistakable exercise.[2] Did it, we ask,

express itself in ceremonies of purification and sacred meals. But to acknowledge similarity is not at all the same thing as saying that both have a common origin.

[1] Such phrases as "Circumcise therefore the foreskin of your hearts" (Deut. x. 16, xxx. 6) are not properly sacramental; i.e. they do not attribute to circumcision of itself any spiritual effect. The only suggestion of sacramental effect ascribed to a religious rite that I can think of is that "the spirit of wisdom" in Joshua is attributed in Deut. xxxiv. 9 to the laying on of Moses' hands. But not so in Num. xvii. 18.

[2] In the next chapter we shall examine St. Paul's sacramental position with care.

enter the Church from the Hellenistic atmosphere around them? I think the answer must be in the negative, on historical grounds.

As we have seen, a new and powerful outpouring of the Spirit of God was associated in Jewish prophecy with the coming of the Messiah. John the Baptist had contrasted his baptism with that of "him who was to come" in the sense that "he shall baptize you with the Holy Spirit." And when, by what seems to have been the direction of Christ, baptism with water was taken over from the Jews by the Christian Church, we find attached to it, in association with the laying on of hands—also a rite familiar to the Jews—a sacramental value as a spiritual cleansing (not merely an admission to membership in the New Israel), and as the instrument for the reception of the Spirit.[1] This, St. Luke tells us, antedated the conversion of St. Paul, and also any influence of Gentile mysteries that can reasonably be imagined. It directly attaches itself to John the Baptist's words and the Old Testament prophecy of the fruit of the Messiah's coming. The rite of washing and the laying on of hands had thus become more than symbolical. It had become spiritually effective or properly sacramental.[2]

Once more we have seen that the precise account of the institution of the eucharist which St. Paul gives us must be accepted as part of what he "received" at his conversion only a few years after the crucifixion of Jesus, like the formulated account of the appearances after the Resurrection. It must be accepted as a historical account of what actually happened, which is repeated in almost the same terms by St. Mark. And we must interpret it in the

[1] Acts ii. 38, viii. 18, xix. 5, 6. See below, chap. iv

[2] This belief was no doubt confirmed among the disciples by outward signs. The newly incorporated members spoke with tongues and prophesied

light of the sacrificial system of the Jews.[1] The New Covenant, like the Old, is being inaugurated in sacrifice—the self-sacrifice of Christ—and the disciples of Jesus, the members of the New Israel, are to feed upon the sacrifice. The bread and the cup are to be the instruments of a real spiritual nourishment. The manhood in which Christ offered Himself—His body and blood—are to be imparted to them under those material forms. They are sacramental.

All this sacramentalism of the New Covenant has its roots, then, in properly Jewish soil, and derives its materials thence; and the sacramental belief is already there before contact with Hellenism can reasonably be imagined to have taken place. Moreover, we must not exaggerate the resemblance of these rites and beliefs among the Christians to anything which was to be found in the Gentile religions and mysteries. The Syrian religions and mysteries in particular appear to have been notoriously corrupt,[2] and most unlikely to furnish models for the Christians. It is true that washing has been all the world over a religious or symbolic rite; and also religious or sacrificial meals have been common. But they were also Jewish institutions of immemorial antiquity with

[1] The phrase "the table of the Lord" used by St. Paul in connexion with the eucharist (1 Cor. x. 21) has, as St. Paul implies, analogies among the heathen in what he calls "the table of devils." Both alike are sacrificial feasts. There is a celebrated papyrus from Oxyrhynchus in which a certain Cheremon invites his friend to be a guest "at the table of the Lord Serapis in the Serapaeum to-morrow." But it is also the case that "the table of the Lord" was an old Jewish phrase for the altar of sacrifice (Mal. i. 7–12; Ezek. xli. 22, xliv. 15, 16). We should take note that the idea of the papyrus is that of having the god for host at a banquet. That is not the idea suggested in the New Testament for the eucharist; there the function of Jesus Christ is not that of host, but rather (in whatever sense) that of victim and food.

[2] See Apuleius, bk. viii, cap. 24 to ix, cap. 10, for the reputation of the "Dea Syra" and her priests and holy emblems (ix, 4). These chapters are interesting because, revolting as the priests and their rites are, they attract the reverence of the "chief citizen" of a Thessalian city "who had a religious disposition" (viii, 30).

specially Jewish associations. The heathen mysteries dealt in imposing ceremonial and hypnotic influences and frenzied excitement. Their barbaric origin was still prominent. There was nothing of this sort among the Christians. As to the 'sacramental' banquets among the Gentiles and the ideas attached to them, we know practically nothing. And we must not argue from the altogether unknown, when the known supplies us with all we need to account for the origin of the very simple and deeply ethical Christian sacrament.

Finally, we must consider the suggestion made by Reitzenstein and others [1] that in particular the whole complex of ideas associated with "the religion of the Spirit" in St. Paul's and St. John's writings is part of a common stock of ideas which was pervading the Hellenistic world more or less abundantly, having their origin in great part from Egypt; and that in their Christian form they can be best explained by Hellenistic influence. By "the complex of ideas" about the religion of the Spirit is meant such as the following: that a man may become possessed by divine spirit and thus become a "new man" or be "born again," and pass from the defiling and transitory life of this world into life eternal and divine; that he will experience conflict between the spirit and the flesh or between spirit and soul (natural life); that the spirit will triumph and that he has even now concealed within him a spiritual body, immortal and indissoluble, waiting for liberation from the incumbrance of the present gross material body; and, finally, the idea of the inspiration of particular individuals by a divine spirit, so that they are taken out of themselves and speak supernatural truths.

This proposal of Reitzenstein's to find a new source for Christian ideas is very elusive—partly because there are confessedly many ideas concerning spirits

[1] See *Belief in Christ*, p. 133.

and spiritual influences which are common to men of many traditions and races; partly also because the dates of many of the documents which are relied upon by Reitzenstein and those who think with him are profoundly uncertain. Thus in some cases where some connexion between the non-Christian and the Christian documents appears to be unmistakable, it may be, not that the non-Christian document has influenced the Christian, but the other way. This uncertainty especially affects the Hermetic documents, which have generally, and it would seem rightly, been reckoned to exhibit the same sort of influences from Hebrew religion as the Gnostic theories and documents undoubtedly do.[1] Under these circumstances of uncertainty the most satisfactory method of argument is to start from the clearly known—that is, the influence of the Old Testament upon the first Christians, and their own experience in the school of Jesus the Christ, and to ask how far this accounts for all the ideas about the religion of the Spirit which we find in the New Testament; and also to note not only the resemblances but the differences which undoubtedly exist between the New Testament ideas and those to be found in Hellenism, and consider whether they reach the point of making any fundamental influence of the latter on the former improbable.

1. Let us then have it clearly present to our imagination that the idea of 'spirits' and consequently of 'spirit' is approximately universal among men. It seems to be derived from the sense of breath in men and animals. There is something clearly tenuous and invisible but yet real in men's bodies

[1] See Dr. H. A. A. Kennedy, *St. Paul and the Mystery Religions*, pp. 144 f., 167, etc. (Hodder & Stoughton). Critics, like the late Dr. Edwin Hatch, have often rebuked orthodox writers, and justly, for quoting documents without due regard to their precise date. I think, however, it is time for the orthodox to retaliate.

which at least in death departs from them. This is soul or spirit. Also the world of nature with all its mysterious movement and life appears to be the habitation of spirits. Such beliefs are approximately universal among men. And the conception of 'spirits' is generally that of tenuous and aerial, rather than completely immaterial, substances. Besides this belief in spirits in general, there is commonly also a belief in some more powerful spirits or gods. And inasmuch as men all the world over have passed their lives in an awful dread of these spirits greater and lesser, the acceptable religions have been those which appeared to possess control over them, or which taught men how to keep on the favourable side of them. There is also almost universal in the world the conception of the inspired man—that is, the man possessed by a divine spirit, rapt out of his own self-consciousness into trance or frenzy, and becoming thus "a new man,"[1] and perhaps the organ of a god to declare his will or to give guidance in answer to questions. All this belongs to natural religion and to the lower ranges of natural religions.

2. This traditional background is often unmistakably felt in the Old Testament, but it is kept at a distance and in restraint by the distinctive beliefs, due to the prophets, which gradually came to absorb the whole tradition of the Jews and to control all their literature—especially the belief in one God, the Creator, to whom all spirits must be absolutely subordinated, as His creatures. In St. John's Gospel our Lord is represented as saying "God is spirit"; and the expression carries with it no speculation on the divine essence. In its context it seems to mean that God is absolutely raised above all the limitations of place, and knows things as they are, and values them by moral, not material values. It was in fact

[1] See 1 Sam. x. 6, where Samuel says to Saul, "Thou shalt be turned into another man."

along the lines of the unity, the moral perfection, the omnipotence, and the omnipresence of God, and the absolute distinction of the Creator from His creatures, and not by any philosophical speculation, that the Jews reached the idea of God as "pure spirit."

But they attached to the spirituality of God—at least in the literature of the Bible—no idea of aloofness. God is intensely active in the world. And this universal activity in creating and sustaining is called His spirit. As we have seen, however, the idea of the spirit of God came to be almost reserved for the action of God in the redemption of Israel, and through Israel the whole world, including the sanctification and transformation of individual souls. And it was in this reserved sense that it passes into the New Testament. There the gift of the Holy Spirit is found pre-eminently in Christ and then passes as His gift from Him upon His Church. So concentrated is the thought of the New Testament writers upon "the Holy Spirit," the Spirit of the Father and of Jesus, as something of which they have personal experience, that, though they continue to talk of evil spirits, they speak no longer of good spirits, but only of the one Spirit of the one God and the one Lord, and of the human spirits, which He comes to enrich.[1] There is nothing in any religious tradition with which the first Christians could have come into contact at all resembling this overwhelming belief in the one God and the one Lord and the one Spirit, and no one would suggest that this belief could come from any source but one.

The philosophic world did indeed believe in some sense in one God (though not in such a sense as to

[1] We hear in the New Testament of angelic beings of many grades, but they are never called "spirits," unless in the quotation from the Psalms in Heb. i. 7, where R.V. translates "winds." In 1 John iv. 1–3 "spirit" seems to be used impersonally, almost as we talk of the 'spirit' of such and such a movement: see my *Epistles of St. John*, pp. 168–9.

exclude the many gods of popular belief), and they spoke much of the divine as immanent and operative in the world, under terms such as 'logos' (reason or law or force) or 'nous' (mind). But they did not commonly use the term 'spirit.' Even in Plotinus, when philosophy had come to be so deeply occupied in what we call 'the spiritual life,' the term (πνεῦμα) 'spirit' is of rare occurrence and without importance in his system.[1] In English books this is not always made apparent, because there is a habit, which Dr. Inge warmly commends, of translating *nous* (mind) by 'spirit.' But the fundamental ideas are essentially different. *Nous* is fundamentally intellectual and static, and *pneuma* is dynamic. *Nous* is concerned with thinking, and *pneuma* primarily with acting. They must not be confused. Thus upon Philo, Jew though he is, the Alexandrian influence is so strong that the idea of "the Spirit" is almost absent except with regard to prophets rapt into trance. The only field of Greek speculation previous to Christianity[2] where 'spirit' was much heard of was Stoicism, where the all-pervasive God, conceived of as elemental fire, was spoken of as the *sacer spiritus*; but the writers of the New Testament had nothing in common with this Heraclitean speculation; and though some allusions in Stoic writers to the converse of men with "the holy spirit" have a Christian sound, the underlying ideas are very different.[3] When Dr. Inge[4] speaks of "the adoption of the Stoical πνεῦμα by the Christians," he seems to me to be speaking without any regard to history. With the Christians the belief in the Spirit of God has entirely

[1] Inge's *Plotinus*, ii, 38.

[2] In some later, e.g. Mithraic, documents there is language resembling the Christian about the divine spirit, but it may well be due to an infiltration of Christian ideas.

[3] See Dr. Edwyn Bevan's *Stoics and Sceptics*, pp. 42–3. For the use of 'spirit' in the Hermetic books see App. Note B, p. 107.

[4] *Op. cit.*, p. 247.

a Jewish origin and an origin more ancient than Zeno.

It is further to be noticed that the doctrine of spirit among the Stoics is pantheistic, and with them to be identified with the spirit is to be "deified." Christians in the early centuries and later occasionally used this sort of language. But it is alien to the New Testament.[1] True, the consciousness of possession by the divine spirit carries with it the sense of fellowship in the eternal or divine life even now, with the hope of fuller fellowship hereafter; but the idea of Christians being 'made gods' or 'becoming god' would be abhorrent to it.

3. No doubt with the Jews, as with the Greeks, the idea of spirit had been very closely associated with the 'inspiration' of holy men; and no doubt, as has been already explained,[2] the idea of inspiration which lies at the basis of the Old Testament was the common idea which prevailed throughout the world, which finds the evidence of 'possession' in frenzied excitement or trance or ecstasy. The special prophets to whose inspiration we owe the religion of Israel never wholly lost this association of inspiration with trance or ecstasy. It is seen especially in Ezekiel. It is seen in St. Paul. But it comes to occupy a very small place. The message which the prophets receive both in the Old Testament and in the New is addressed by the Divine Spirit to their own alert consciousness and will.[3] Thus when Philo, under the alien influences of Alexandrian Hellenism, identifies inspiration with trance and ecstasy, and declares that the reason and intelligence of the prophet must be utterly extinguished while he is under the divine influence—

[1] The nearest approach to it is in 2 Pet. i. 4, "partakers of the divine nature."

[2] *Belief in God*, chap. iv.

[3] See *Belief in God*, p. 87.

"The mind in us is expelled at the arrival of the divine spirit and returns to its home at its removal"[1] —he is departing definitely from the higher ground of Jewish prophecy on which Christian prophecy continued to stand. "The spirits of the prophets," says St. Paul, "are subject to the prophets."[2] No doubt the psychical perturbation common in the Gentile world, which was attributed to possession by spirits, was seen among the Christians especially in the phenomenon of "the tongues." Such psychical phenomena, unaccompanied with intelligence, have occurred in connexion with all sorts of religious movements. St. Paul does not deny their divine origin,[3] but he ranks them low among spiritual gifts; and, even so, if "the tongues" among the Christians are compared with the phenomena of 'possession' among the Gentiles, they appear restrained and sane indeed.[4] Thus there is indeed some connexion between the phenomena of inspiration or possession in the Jewish-Christian world and in the world of Gentile religions. But the characteristic development of the gift, and conception of the gift, in the former is markedly different, and the result on the whole markedly distinct. The Christian Church of the second century was quite right when it repudiated the Montanist conception of prophecy (in which the prophet was deprived of his senses) as pagan and not Christian.

4. The more we study the Hellenistic lore of 'the spiritual life,' the more, I think, we feel that it is not

[1] Sanday, *Inspiration*, p. 74; Swete in Hastings, *D. of B.*, ii, 405.

[2] 1 Cor. xiv. 32.

[3] I should speak more strictly if I were to say "divine or diabolic."

[4] Cf. the account in Apuleius, *Metamorph.* viii, 27, of the gesticulations and self-macerations of the priests of the "All-Mother": "One of them raved more wildly than the rest . . . as though he were filled with the breath of some divinity."

fundamentally ethical. "The holy faith" and "the glorious faith" of which Apuleius speaks in connexion with different mysteries,[1] the ceremonial "purity" demanded, the temporary asceticism required, the "salvation" which is the goal, do not really have the same meaning as the same words would have in a Christian document. To be holy means to be dedicated to a divine being, who may, like the goddesses worshipped at Ephesus and Corinth, be quite indifferent to morality; the salvation is deliverance from the pollution and transitoriness of physical life; the purity is ceremonial rather than moral; the asceticism is based on the conception of certain things as essentially evil—that is, on an essential dualism.[2] On the other hand, there runs through the whole Bible the healthy sense that the beginning and end of true religion is moral, and is to be seen in our dealings in common life; that all created things are in themselves good; that the blame for sin cannot be laid on the body or on fate, but must be borne by the will; that when the will is once set right all the whole nature will follow; and that sacraments are not charms nor substitutes for change of character. Certainly our Lord or St. Paul was very unlike a Hellenistic hierophant, with his secret tradition and his magical charms.

St. Paul has been accused of regarding the body and the flesh as essentially evil. He does use language which looks like it. But he is speaking of the body as it is enslaved to sin. That is what he means by "the body of sin"; and by "the works of the flesh" he describes the kind of life which men live when their lower nature is allowed to dominate their higher. On the whole, he leaves no room for mistake. It is our whole nature, bodily and mental, which, under the control of the converted will and by

[1] Apuleius, *Metamorph.*, viii, 28, xi, 11.
[2] This is very obvious in Plutarch, *de Isid. et Osir.*

the power of the indwelling Spirit, is to be first sanctified and then glorified; and the goal of redemption is for the whole of our nature and not only for souls.[1]

5. Finally, we must not be misled into supposing that the use of certain terms by St. Paul means that he used them in the same sense as the votaries of the mysteries. They talked of course about mysteries, meaning rites handed down in a secret tradition and not to be revealed to the profane. But before St. Paul's time the word had passed into meaning generally "a secret," and is so used in the Greek Bible. St. Paul uses it to mean a "secret," and once apparently as meaning a "symbol"[2]; but his most characteristic use of it is to mean a secret purpose of God now revealed, which it was the business of the messengers of the Gospel to proclaim to all the world. This is very far off its meaning in the Greek mysteries. No doubt the mysteries had created a vocabulary which no one who used popular Greek could quite avoid. "Perfect" with them meant "fully initiated," and in St. Paul's use of it there is a trace of such a meaning, but he much more often means by it complete or "full grown."[3] He once says "I have been initiated" (μεμύημαι, Phil. iv. 12), but it is only into the secrets of how to use both poverty and wealth; his use of "wisdom" and "knowledge" is what the Old Testament would suggest. One word which Christianity really had in common with the

[1] See 1 Cor. vi. 19, 20; Rom. xii. 1, viii. 11, 21; Phil. iii. 21. It is not apparently certain whether any belief in a "spiritual body," other than a ghost, was current in Hellenistic circles before St. Paul's day. But it is, I think, certain that St. Paul's idea of the spiritual body is based on what he believed about the risen and glorified body of Christ. See Kennedy, *op. cit.*, p. 184.

[2] Eph. v. 32. For St. Paul's use of "mystery," see especially Dr. Armitage Robinson's *Ephesians*, pp. 234 ff.

[3] See especially 1 Cor. ii. 6, where τέλειοι = πνευμάτικοι (iii. 1) and is put in contrast to νήπιοι; cf. xiv. 20.

mysteries—"rebirth"—occurs only once in the Pauline letters.[1]

On the whole, I dare to think that the answer to the problem with which this chapter began is fairly plain. Christianity, the religion of the Spirit, is in its whole original substance derived from the Jewish root and from Christ. From these sources comes the idea of the one Spirit, and the conception of the Church of God as His home, and the beliefs about the sacraments of initiation and communion, and the conception of life in the Spirit, and of the destiny of the body. The Christian idea of inspiration is essentially Jewish and not Hellenistic; and the absence of secrecy in the early days about the doctrines and rites of the Church, and above all its sturdy moralism, betoken an origin different from the mysteries.

The mysteries, then, played no part in the origin of Christianity. But they surrounded the Church when it went out into the Gentile world and were an important element in the atmosphere in which it lived. They do not appear to influence the New Testament in any important particular. But when we find the later Church calling baptism and the eucharist "mysteries," and mysteries not to be disclosed to the profane, we do feel their influence; and it was not always for good. Still, on the whole, they may be said to have created a temper of mind in the world which made the Christian message of redemption and salvation irrespective of class or race

[1] Tit. iii. 5. For the whole subject of "St. Paul's relation to the Mystery terminology" see Dr. Kennedy, *op. cit.*, chap. iv. Some uses of the idea of "rebirth," in connexion with Mithraism, and elsewhere, were very likely influenced by Christianity; but the idea itself—the idea of a man being possessed by some divine *afflatus* and becoming "another man"—is so natural that no borrowing of one religion from the other can be established on the ground of the common use of it.

acceptable and familiar; and, by those who believe in a divine providence, the prevalence of the mysteries in the Roman Empire will certainly be regarded as part of the divine preparation for the spread of a universal Gospel. Indeed the ideas and needs associated with the mysteries appear to be so fundamental in humanity, that no religion could really have claimed to be the religion for mankind which was not able to appreciate and to satisfy them.

APPENDED NOTE A (see p. 86)

THE PAGAN MYSTERIES AND THE EUCHARIST

M. Loisy in *Les Mystères païens et le Mystère chrétien* and Dr. Farnell in his *Cults of the Greek States* (vol. v, under the head of the Dionysus worship) would have us believe that in the worship of Zagreus or Dionysus (and in the Orphic mysteries) the worshippers believed themselves to *eat their god*; and on this ground M. Loisy assimilates the Eucharist to the mysteries. Sir James Frazer, as we have seen, does the like. It has indeed become a commonplace to do so. But the evidence quoted by Loisy and Farnell does not support this idea. I am allowed to quote the following passages from a letter of Mr. Edwyn Bevan, who writes on Hellenistic matters with an authority I could not claim:

"I have looked up what Loisy says about the sacramental eating of the slain god in the Zagreus cult. Apparently the Zagreus worshippers did eat, as a religious ceremony, a living bull, tearing it to pieces 'à belles dents' (p. 32), and Loisy says that the rationale of this was that the bull was regarded as an embodiment of the god and that the worshippers conceived divine virtue to be communicated to them by the sacrament. He says (pp. 34, 35):

"'Sauf que la participation s'établit dans le sacrifice chrétien moyennant le pain et le vin, non par une victime animale, l'économie du mystère eucharistique est conçue de la même façon que celle du mystère dionysique.'

"But in the passages which Loisy cites in the footnotes I cannot find any statement to the fact to the effect that the bull was regarded as identical with the god or that the worshippers derived divine virtue from eating. One passage is from Firmicus Maternus; it says that the Cretans devoured the bull in *memory* of Zagreus' being devoured by the Titans 'crudeles epulas annuis commemorationibus excitantes'—nothing about divine virtue being derived from eating. The second passage is from Arnobius; it says that the Bacchae devoured goats, not in order to *get* divine virtue, but in order to show (i.e. by doing something superhuman) that they *were full* 'dei numine ac maiestate.' Loisy's interpretation seems therefore a merely conjectural reconstruction of the theory underlying the rite. It looks as if (supposing it is true that the idea had originally been that the god himself was eaten) the rite was not understood in this sense at the time to which the statements of Firmicus and Arnobius refer.

"Loisy also tries to prove the same thing with regard to the Orphic mysteries. His data seems to be: (1) That it 'paraît certain' (a suspicious phrase always) (p. 46) that the Orphics practised ὠμοφαγία. The evidence he adduces is a fragment of Euripides (footnote, p. 44). (2) The Orphic formula ἔριφος ἐς γάλα ἔπετον (the meaning of which, I believe, is very doubtful). Putting these two together, he concludes (p. 47) that 'l'initié régénéré, était sauvé en s'assimilant le chevreau mystique, en mangeant la chair de la victime qui représentait, qui était toujours d'une certaine manière, pour la foi, Dionysus Zagreus, en devenant ainsi lui-même "chevreau," en s'identifiant à Bacchus.' But if Loisy has no data for this beyond those he quotes, they would seem a very inadequate foundation for his beautiful description of the Orphic sacramental belief, which seems to be taken out of his own head."

I entirely concur in Mr. Bevan's judgment. And of the passages cited by Dr. Farnell in his notes on the Dionysus worship none support the supposition that the frenzied worshippers believed themselves to be eating their god. He cites a passage from Clement of Alexandria which says something quite different: *ὠμὰ γὰρ ἤσθιον κρέα οἱ μυόμενοι Διονύσῳ δεῖγμα τοῖς τελουμένοις τοῦ σπαραγμοῦ ὃν ὑπέστη Διόνυσος πρὸς τῶν Μαινάδων.* That is to say, they ate raw flesh as a memorial of the mythical incident. I have already quoted Cicero's saying which shows that he at least thought the idea of "theophagy" too absurd to be even suggested.

I have only been able to find one reference at all contemporary with, or within the area of, nascent Christianity to eating a god, and that is Plutarch's description (*de Isid. et Osir.*, cap. 72) of how neighbouring cities in Egypt would provoke one another to war by contemptuously eating the god of their neighbours. Thus the inhabitants of Cynopolis ate the fish which was the god of Oxyrhynchos, and the Oxyrhynchites retaliated by sacrificing and eating a dog. And the Lycopolites ate a sheep, saying that was the way of *their* god. This does not look as if to eat your god was a form of devotion, even where edible animals were gods.

The conclusion to which I would ask adhesion is that, though it is possible the bull who was torn to pieces in the mysteries of Dionysus may in a remote past have been identified with the god, yet the evidence shows that this was so no longer.

NOTE B (see p. 99)

ON THE USE OF 'SPIRIT' IN THE HERMETIC BOOKS

These books, which appear to be of Egyptian origin, are a sort of manual of the spiritual life, as it was understood in the third century in some non-Christian—mainly neo-Platonist—circles. There does not appear to be any good reason for assigning to those 'chapters' which we possess an earlier date: see *Belief in Christ*, p. 134. In them 'spirit' is mostly conceived of as an element in nature—the principle of physical life. It is coupled with fire or air or light: "The spirit is in the body and penetrates the veins and arteries and blood and moves the living being" (see cap. i. 9, 16 [reading πυρός for πατρός], 17, ii. 6, 8, iii. 1, iv. 1, ix. 9, x. 13). But in cap. xiii the creator god is called 'spirit bearing' and a higher position seems to be assigned to spirit. Certainly there is nothing in these books suggesting any connexion with the N.T. doctrine of the Holy Spirit.

CHAPTER IV

THE HOLY SPIRIT IN THE CHURCH

IN the two previous chapters we have freed ourselves from certain doubts which some influential modern writers have been instilling into us. Not only particular passages and texts of the New Testament, but the whole historical setting in which Jesus is presented to us, as the Christ who was to fulfil the vocation of Israel, has reassured us in believing—not that He founded a Church, but that He refounded the Church, the true Israel henceforth consisting of those who believed that Jesus was the Christ, or the Christ was Jesus ; and that in the persons of the twelve apostles He re-equipped it with a body of officers in the place of those who had lost their position by their absolute rejection of " the counsel of God "; and that He sanctioned and instituted in baptism and the eucharist certain rites of spiritual fellowship for the observance of the Church, which were to be safeguards of its unity. The extreme apocalyptic view which would regard all this as impossible, because Christ anticipated no future for the world, we have set aside as arbitrary, resting its case as it does on a one-sided emphasis on part of the evidence and rejection of the rest. Moreover, the purely " apocalyptic " conception of Christ cannot account for the earliest Church, as we see it in St. Paul's Epistles and in the Acts, organizing itself from the first to deal with a developing situation. It is quite true that our Lord gave few specific directions to His Church, and left it in the main to organize itself, under the guidance of His Spirit. Nevertheless, when He left the world, He left behind Him a certain rudimentary organization already in being.

We have looked steadily at the mystery religions, as providing in great part the Gentile atmosphere in which the Church spread. It is a study of absorbing interest; and we have recognized there a world of religious societies, bound together by secret rites into the fellowship of gods whose patronage was relied upon to save their votaries from the present world of change and dissolution, and translate them into a world beyond, free from death and corruption. We have recognized how much the prevalence of these mystery religions, as in some sort religions of redemption, facilitated the spread of the religion of the Church, and also the danger the Church ran of assimilation to these truly superstitious associations. But we have seen the best of reasons for rejecting the modern suggestion that either the fundamental doctrines or characteristic ideas or rites of the primitive Church were derived from these pagan mysteries. On the one hand, the doctrines and ideas and rites of the Christians of the New Testament are accounted for by the tradition and Scriptures which they inherited from old Israel, interpreted in the light of the new and overwhelming experiences through which they had passed in the fellowship of Jesus and in the receiving of His Spirit—experiences which antedated any immediate contact with the world of Hellenism. And on the other hand, the attitude of St. Paul in his epistles and St. Luke in his history towards the Gentile "idolatries" makes the notion of their imitating the practices or assimilating the ideas of the heathen in a high degree improbable. Moreover, we have been led to feel that those who would assimilate the Church to the mysteries are apt greatly to exaggerate the resemblances in idea and rite and language and to ignore the differences.

So we are left believing the New Testament record that Jesus Christ did intend to perpetuate His work in the world for a period which He refused to define, and did refound and refashion Israel to be His organ for this purpose, and did really inspire into it His own and the Father's Spirit; and our next task must be to examine more closely the religion of the Spirit and the Church, as we see it in our earliest records.

I

All that Christ did in the world, He did in and by the Spirit which possessed Him wholly, and when from His throne in heaven He poured out His Spirit, which is also the Spirit of the Father, upon His Church, it was in order that all the rich endowment of humanity which had been found in Him might be transmitted to the Church which is "His body." Thus, if in one sense the ascension of Christ represents an end and a climax, as it is the fulfilment of humanity on the throne of God, in another sense it is but the beginning. For that humanity of Jesus is the fountain-head of a new race in which all the attributes of that New Man are to be perpetuated and manifested, as it gathers within its compass men of all nations and tribes and kinds. Thus the Holy Spirit comes not so much to supply the absence of Christ as to accomplish His presence in the world as its Saviour and New Life.

This is the developed doctrine which we find in St. Paul's Epistles, and with substantially the same implications in St. John.[1] But doubtless, like St. Paul's doctrine about Christ's person, it was not realized at once.

All the whole matter of the New Testament referring to the Holy Spirit is carefully and fully analysed by Dr. Swete in *The Holy Spirit in the New Testament.*

The Synoptic Gospels tell us a good deal about the Holy Spirit in Christ,[1] and they all of them reproduce the assurance of John the Baptist that it was to be the function of 'Him who was to come' to baptize men with the Spirit. But, as has been remarked, they say singularly little about any preparation given by Christ to His disciples for the reception of the great gift. St. Luke, however, in the beginning of the Acts represents our Lord as referring to teaching about the Holy Spirit which He had given them. "Wait," said He, "for the promise of the Father, which ye heard from me: for John indeed baptized with water; but ye shall be baptized with the Holy Ghost not many days hence."[2] This interprets the saying recorded at the end of Luke's Gospel, "Behold, I send forth the promise of my Father upon you: but tarry ye in the city, till ye be clothed with power from on high."[3] This "promise of my Father"—this gift of "power from on high"—is the Holy Spirit. We cannot but think of the words ascribed to our Lord in the Fourth Gospel, "The Helper, even the Holy Spirit, whom the Father will send in my name."[4]

It is, I think, very difficult to imagine that our Lord did not give His disciples some such preparatory teaching about the gift of the Holy Spirit as is conveyed in His last discourses before His passion according to St. John. And the teaching of these discourses is at once so original, so profound, and so singularly well adapted to the situation of the moment, that we are led to believe that it is not an imaginative construction by the evangelist, but a real memory. The Holy Spirit really brought to his remembrance all that Jesus said to them.[5] Still, it would not appear that the full meaning of the Spirit's presence,

[1] See above, pp. 10 f.
[2] Acts i. 4, 5.
[3] Luke xxiv. 49.
[4] John xiv. 26.
[5] John xiv. 26.

any more than the full meaning of the person of their Master,[1] was realized by the first disciples or by the Apostles immediately after Pentecost. I do not indeed think that it is true to say that in the Acts the gift of the Spirit is associated in any exclusive sense with the extraordinary gifts of 'tongues' and prophesying, or with the miraculous in general.[2] It is true that St. Luke lays stress on the wonderful signs which marked the sudden arrival of the Spirit on, or just before, the day of Pentecost,[3] and on the similar signs which marked the first bestowal of the gift upon the Gentiles, Cornelius and his companions, and again on the twelve men who had been disciples of John the Baptist and were now led on into the faith of Christ.[4] And he delights to recount the miracles of healing wrought by the apostles. But also courage in speaking the word, and wisdom, and faith, and large-hearted goodness are associated with the Spirit's presence,[5] and He is recognized not only as the inspirer of the prophets of old, but also as the present and personal guide and helper of individuals, and of the assemblies of the Church, in all their ways.

Nevertheless it is to St. Paul that we owe in the first instance, as the theology of the person of Christ, so also the theology of the Spirit. From him first

[1] See *Belief in Christ*, pp. 76 ff.

[2] I think Harnack, for instance, is unfair when he says (*Luke the Physician*, p. 141 (Williams & Norgate): "We cannot repress the suspicion that with him (Luke) everything is concentrated in the magical efficacy of the Name of Christ. . . . Miraculous healing is the essential function, and forms the test, of the new religion." Dr. Anderson Scott remarks that this was a tendency which appears specially in the early stages of the Acts and diminishes as it proceeds. See his essay in *The Spirit* (ed. Streeter), p. 131. Later the emphasis comes to be rather on prophetic insight and guidance as the characteristic marks of the Spirit's presence.

[3] See Appended Note A, p. 148, on the Pentecostal gift as described in Acts.

[4] Acts ii. 4, x. 46, xix. 6.

[5] Acts iv. 31, vi. 3, 5, xi. 24.

we get that subtle and profound conception of the Holy Spirit as distinct—I can only say personally distinct—from the ascended Christ, while yet so intimately one with Him that His presence involves the presence of Christ, so that "in the Spirit" means also "in Christ."[1] We cannot speak with any confidence as to how precisely this conception was formed in St. Paul's mind. I suppose that the actual experience of the Church, before St. Paul came on the scene, had given the apostles and their companions an intense sense, as of the personal Christ now glorified in the heavens, so also of the personal Spirit, the Spirit of Jesus, guiding them from within. I suppose also that from the first they must have realized that the Holy Spirit was something more than the substitute for a now absent Christ. We cannot regard it as doubtful that in "the breaking of bread" they had from the first repeated the words, "Take, eat, this is my body," "Drink ye all of this, this is my blood," and had known themselves to be sharers together in Christ. It may have been by an internal revelation that St. Paul's subtle theology of the Spirit in His relation to Christ came to form itself in his mind. But it is the same theology that we find in St. John's Gospel, especially but not only[2] in those last discourses spoken by Christ immediately before His passion. There, too, the Spirit is distinguished sharply from Christ Himself as "another Helper," but also so intimately involved with Him and with the Father that His coming is the coming back of Christ and the presence of the Father. And I continually find myself asking whether such words of Christ as "He will give you another Helper," "The Helper, even the Holy Spirit,

[1] See *Belief in Christ*, pp. 237–40 and 253 f. I should wish to emphasize what is there said of the distinction of the Holy Spirit from the glorified Christ in St. Paul's conception.

[2] For we must not forget iii. 5–8, vi. 63, vii. 39, xx. 22.

whom the Father will send in my name," "I will send you another Helper," "I will come unto you," "We will come unto you" (i.e. the Father and I), were not already in the memory of the Church even before St. Paul's activity began.

And this intimate theology of the Spirit brought to the front in St. Paul's teaching the central moral purpose of His coming and presence in the Church and in all its members. As has been said, there is no doubt in the Acts a tendency, though not an exclusive tendency, to emphasize the action of the Holy Spirit in connexion with extraordinary or miraculous gifts. St. Paul recognizes these among the endowments of the Spirit, but depreciates them by comparison with those we should call moral and normal. All that we identify with the humanity of Jesus—enlightenment, sonship, moral liberty, self-control, love, the consecration and sanctification of body as well as spirit—all this it is the function of the Spirit to bring to be enwrought into the texture of our sin-defiled nature. All the "knowledge" which St. Paul so passionately prays for for his converts is relative to this practical end. It is not philosophical or speculative endowments that he desires. The work and purpose of the Spirit coincides absolutely with the work and purpose of Christ. St. Paul does not identify the Spirit with the ascended Christ,[1] but Christ comes to us only through the Spirit, and to be "in the Spirit" is to be "in Christ."

Superficially considered, such a conception of the Spirit's work would be compatible with regarding the gift of the Spirit as a gift to separate individuals. And it is for St. Paul a glorious truth that the Holy Spirit's presence does deepen and intensify the sense of individuality and the value and responsibility of the individual. But it is a sure sign of shallow thinking to put individuality in man into antithesis

[1] See *Belief in Christ*, pp. 253 ff.

to his corporate and social life. Tyranny, it is true, depresses individuality, but corporate life intensifies it. Certainly the gift of the Spirit in St. Paul's teaching is a gift to the 'holy community'; and the life of the individual recipient of the Spirit is not otherwise conceived of than as that of a "member" which lives by its incorporation in "the body." If the bodies of individual Christians are "temples of the Holy Spirit," it is because they belong to the greater temple which is the Church.[1] We shall see that St. Paul has a vivid sense of the sacraments as means of grace to the individual, but an equally vivid sense that they are social ceremonies by which the individual is bound to the Church. So the principle is established that fellowship with God is not otherwise to be won or maintained than in the fellowship of men, and by faithful recognition of the obligations of membership. The Christian ethic, as St. Paul expounds it, is a predominantly social ethic; and the most characteristic expression of the meaning of life in the Spirit is with him to be found in the words 'love' or 'communion,' which means sharing together—the "communion of the Holy Ghost."[2]

We shall come back upon these thoughts shortly. But we must delay for a little in order to consider how far St. Paul's theology of the Spirit is also that of the other New Testament writers; and first of St. John.[3]

Modern critical writers on the New Testament are,

[1] 1 Cor. vi. 19, iii. 16–17.

[2] It must not be forgotten that though St. Paul speaks of the gift of the Spirit to the Church and its members as already abundant, yet it is only a pledge or foretaste of a greater abundance in a world yet to come. 2 Cor. i. 22, v. 5; Eph. i. 13–14.

[3] Like other people I have recurrent difficulties about the authorship of the Fourth Gospel, but on the whole I am always forced back upon the belief that John the son of Zebedee must be, in the real sense, the author of it and of the Epistles which bear his name. And the historical value of the Fourth Gospel seems to me always increasingly certain.

I cannot but think, too much intent on discerning and emphasizing differences between the writers of the New Testament, and ignoring substantial identities,[1] while at the same time they emphasize superficial similarities of language between the Christian and the pagan writers, ignoring profounder differences. Thus it is true that, in the last discourses of our Lord to His disciples as reported by St. John, the Holy Spirit whom they are to expect is described as "the Spirit of truth," and the fruit of His coming is to be an accurate recollection and clear understanding of their Lord's words, and a vigorous witness to Him[2]; and that in the Epistles of St. John it is still this true and trustworthy knowledge which is emphasized as the result of the Holy Spirit's unction[3]; but it has to be remembered that the discourses of our Lord were addressed to the disciples at a moment when they were, and were confessing themselves to be, utterly bewildered in their mind as to the meaning of their experiences and of the words of the Master.[4] What they needed above all was the assurance that, when He was gone, they would understand His meaning and be able to deliver their message to the world. It has to be remembered also that the Spirit is elsewhere in this Gospel described by our Lord as the Spirit of regeneration or a new life, and as the life-giver, and as the living water of eternal life, and the power enabling the Twelve to continue the apostolate of Christ.[5] And in the discourse following the Last Supper, in spite of the special references to the Holy Spirit as the Spirit of truth, something more general is implied in the term "the Paraclete" (or Helper), in whose

[1] I find myself as I read some modern critical or hypercritical books murmuring the words of the son of Sirach, "There is an exquisite subtilty, and the same is not just."

[2] See xiv. 17, 26, xv. 26–7, xvi. 7 f.

[3] 1 John ii. 20, 27.

[4] John xiii. 36, xiv. 1, 5, 8, 22.

[5] iii. 5–8, vi. 63, vii. 38–9, xx. 22–3.

coming Christ is to come back to them. This leads us to think that all that is implied in the figure of the vine—("Because I live, ye shall live also," "Abide in me, and I in you")—is to be realized by the coming of the Holy Spirit to abide in them. And as regards St. John's First Epistle, if it is only the witness of the Spirit to Jesus that is actually spoken of, and the secure perception of truth conveyed by His anointing —a reminder which the intellectual disturbances of the time made specially opportune — yet it is gratuitous to suppose that St. John was unconscious of the connexion of "eternal life" in all its aspects with the Holy Spirit. What a man says in a particular letter is not all he has in his mind, but what the circumstances of the moment require.

St. Peter in his First Epistle speaks of the Spirit of Christ specially as the Spirit of ancient prophecy and the inspirer of the Gospel message.[1] But he also calls Him generally "the Spirit of the Glory" (Christ) and the Spirit of sanctification,[2] and when he speaks of the diverse 'charismata' bestowed on members of the Church, he doubtless would have us recognize them as gifts of the Spirit.[3]

In the Epistle to the Hebrews, once more, there is very little about the Holy Spirit, but what there is implies much. The writer affirms His inspiration of the writers of the Old Testament, and His concern in the details of the ritual law—that was essential to his argument; but also among the privileges of Christians he mentions "having been made partakers of holy spirit," and he speaks of apostasy from Christ as an insulting of the Spirit of grace, and he alludes to the variety of the Spirit's gifts.[4]

[1] 1 Pet. i. 11, 12. [2] iv. 14, i. 2. [3] iv. 10 f.

[4] Heb. iii. 7, ix. 8, vi. 4, x. 29, ii. 4. In the Epistle of Jude (ver. 20) we have the remarkable expression "praying in holy spirit," and in St. James (iv. 5) probably "the Spirit which God made to dwell in us." In the Apocalypse our thoughts are directed almost wholly to the Holy Spirit as the inspirer of prophets.

It is thus in St. Paul, St. Luke, and St. John that we specially find the Gospel of the Spirit. But we must be on our guard against supposing that rareness of mention in the other writers necessarily implies either ignorance or disparagement. It is something difficult to account for, almost all down the history of the Church, that the Holy Spirit is comparatively little spoken of except at a few moments of controversy. This strikes us especially in the theology of the Middle Ages; and yet if we think of the three hymns *Veni sancte spiritus*, *Veni creator spiritus*, and *Nunc sancte nobis spiritus* (the hymn for the third hour), and of their influence, we shall be restrained from supposing that the comparative silence in the region of theology means an ignoring of the supreme gift in the spiritual life. So the fact that we have only passing allusions to the Holy Spirit's action by the author of the Epistle to the Hebrews and by St. Peter and St. Jude should not suggest to us that their belief was different from St. Paul's and St. John's.

II

The compass of this book will not allow of our pursuing the teaching of the Church concerning the Holy Spirit down the centuries. I must almost content myself with what has been already briefly said in the volume on *Belief in Christ*, under the heading of the origin and development of the doctrine of the Holy Trinity.[1] And I yield to this necessity with the less reluctance because Dr. Swete has given a full and, as far as I can judge, an impartial account of the history of opinion and definition on this subject in his treatise on *The Holy Spirit in the Ancient Church*.[2] But there are certain points in the development of the doctrine which may be noted. The credit for its formulation lies especially with the

[1] Chap. viii. [2] Macmillan, 1912.

Cappadocians of the fourth century, Basil and his brother Gregory of Nyssa, and perhaps principally Gregory of Nazianzus. In the fifth of his great theological orations (A.D. 380)—that on the Holy Spirit—the last-named Father gives a gloomy view of the confusion which had prevailed on this subject within the Church. "Of the wise men among us some considered the Spirit as an activity, some as a creature, some as God; and some have not known which of these opinions to choose, in reverence, as they say, for Scripture, as if it made no clear declaration."[1] This, we can venture to say, with the writings of the earlier centuries in our hands, gives an exaggerated impression. Nevertheless, confusion there certainly was, and, more markedly even than confusion, there was an ignoring of the importance of the subject, due to the preoccupation of men's minds with the controversies about the person of Christ. Gregory pathetically remarks that people have been "nauseated" by the controversies on this latter subject and left without any taste for embarking on any other.[2] "Nevertheless," he adds, "with the Spirit's help the argument shall run and God shall be glorified." And we cannot but feel that the definition which was so largely due to Gregory, according to which the Holy Spirit was determined to be both personal and essential to the being of the one God, was the definition which "the simple and untechnical language of Holy Scripture" (as Basil beautifully calls it) really requires. But about this something more must be said when we come to speak about the development of Christian doctrine. Here I confine myself to noting in the briefest way some points in the theology of the Fathers of the fourth century to whom (with the earlier Origen) we owe the definition.

The first is their extreme unwillingness to go

[1] *Orat. Theol.*, v, 5. [2] *Op. cit.*, 2.

outside the language and spirit of Scripture in theological definition. They at least are quite free from intellectualism, or the love of definition for its own sake. Thus "It is impossible," says Athanasius, "for created beings, and especially for us men, to speak adequately about things which transcend language. And this being so, it is specially audacious to devise on these subjects newer and unscriptural[1] terms."

Secondly, their profound sense of the practical value of belief both in the personality and in the Godhead of the Holy Spirit. They keep their arguments close to the common experience of Christians.

Thirdly, their refusal to limit the action of the Holy Spirit (or of the Word) within the barriers of the Church. Wherever God acts, they insist, it is through His Word and by His Spirit.

Fourthly, the equipoise they successfully maintain between the conceptions of unity and variety as evidences of the Spirit's presence in the Church. Their doctrine is of course the common Catholic doctrine about the unity of the Church and the sin of schism, but they really deserve the title of Broad Churchmen. They love to insist on the variety which characterizes the work of the Spirit, who is the giver of life as in nature, so in the supernatural life of the Church. He is set to nourish and not to suppress individuality. His presence is marked more by exuberance of vitality than by monotony or uniformity.

III

We must return to our records of the origins of Christianity, especially to examine as carefully as

[1] Athan., *Ep.* i., *ad Serap.*, 17. The words are παρὰ τὰς γράφας. παρά, as Lightfoot said (on Gal. i. 8), may mean "contrary to" or "besides." And in the particular case it is difficult to decide precisely which is meant. The latter meaning would appear to condemn the *Homoousion*.

possible the conception of sacraments which we find there. But though it should appear that the sacraments are viewed as ordained instruments and recognized channels for the action of the Spirit, yet it certainly also appears that "the life in the Spirit" was not a life of special occasions only, such as the administration of sacraments, but was the whole of life, lived under a new impulse and in a new power. Christians are to "walk in the Spirit." This is what gave to the earliest Christian life its peculiar characteristic of joy—"joy in the Holy Spirit." "Be not drunken with wine, wherein is riot, but be filled with the Spirit, . . . singing and making melody with your heart to the Lord."

It was the presence of the Holy Spirit in the Church and all its members which was to make practicable a perpetually prayerful mind—"praying in the Holy Spirit." That Holy Spirit, as St. Paul reminds the Roman Christians, is Himself, in His own person, the constant intercessor "according to God"; and, though our intercessions are blind and weak, behind them, to sustain them and to interpret them to God, is the Spirit who perfectly understands the divine purpose.[1] Here indeed is a ground of encouragement in whatever depth of adversity. So it came about that thankfulness and joy become the notes of life in the Spirit. If we pass a generation or two down below the apostolic age, we still find the emphasis on these notes. Thus the prophet Hermas in his *Shepherd* writes:

"Put off grief from thyself, for it is the sister of doubt and all ill-temper. . . . Dost thou not understand that grief is the most evil of all the spirits, and most to be dreaded by the servants of God, and more than all spirits it destroys man and obliterates the Holy Spirit? Put off, therefore, grief from thyself and do not vex the Holy Spirit which dwells in thee. . . . Clothe thyself in the

[1] Rom. viii. 26 ff.

gladness which always has favour with God and is acceptable to Him, and delight thyself in it; for every glad-hearted man does and thinks good things and despises grief."[1]

And there is hardly a period of Christian history where illustrations of the same temper could not easily be found.

Further, this sense of the presence and activity of the Holy Spirit in the Church was quickened and made enthusiastic by meetings such as those of which St. Paul gives us such a vivid picture at Corinth—where the "gifts" had special exercise and indeed showed signs of running riot. Let me quote Duchesne[2]:

> "If the Church took over *en bloc* all the religious services of the Synagogue, it added thereto one or two new elements. . . . I refer to the Supper, or sacred repast, and the spiritual exercises.
>
> "After the Eucharist,[3] certain inspired persons began to preach and to make manifest before the assembly the presence of the Spirit which animated them. The prophets, the ecstatics, the speakers with tongues, the interpreters, the supernatural healers, absorbed at this time the attention of the faithful. There was, as it were, a liturgy of the Holy Spirit after the liturgy of Christ, a true liturgy with a real presence and communion. The inspiration could be felt—it sent a thrill through the organs of certain privileged persons, but the whole assembly was moved, edified, and even more or less ravished by it and transported into the divine sphere of the Paraclete."

I think exception might be taken to certain details of this picturesque account—as that it makes "preaching" more prominent than St. Paul's words, which are practically our only authority,[4] would warrant. St. Paul seems to complain of the lack of it. It

[1] Hermas, *Pastor*, Mand. x, 1, 3.
[2] See *Christian Worship*, pp. 48 f. (S.P.C.K.)
[3] I do not know what the authority is for these words.
[4] 1 Cor. xiv.

was ecstatic "tongues"—a kind of unintelligent and unintelligible thanksgiving or prayer—that was more in evidence. Also Duchesne seems to assume that the scene described at Corinth would have been found in the churches generally. But St. Paul does not suggest this, though it may be true. He does not say, in seeking to introduce more order into these assemblies, as he does in the matter of marriage, "And so ordain I in all the churches."[1] Nor does he suggest that there was public healing of the sick on these occasions. Nevertheless this enthusiastic cultivation of ecstatic gifts in a public assembly of the Church, this "liturgy of the Spirit," was a very highly valued part of public worship at Corinth and very likely elsewhere. That it was easily liable to abuse is apparent. St. Paul's intimation, "The rest will I set in order when I come," given in connexion with scandals at the love-feast and eucharist, may have struck a chill into the hearts of some enthusiasts; and we do not know how soon these spiritual exercises were "regulated away" like the love-feasts. No doubt in the second century the excesses of the Montanist enthusiasts bred in the Church a deeper repulsion from ecstatic spiritual gifts. Nevertheless the Corinthian meetings afforded an opportunity for unofficial persons to exercise spiritual gifts. We cannot help wondering whether the ordinary excuses for officialism were not allowed too lightly to abolish them. We recall the revivalist meetings and free prayer meetings which before and after the Reformation the Church has frowned upon, but which, with all their admitted excesses and absurdities, have nourished and exhibited a real and intense spirituality. We assent to St. Paul's demand that such manifestations of the Spirit should be kept within the bounds of Church order, but it is difficult to restrain the feeling that in one form or another they ought never

[1] 1 Cor. vii. 17

to have been abandoned, and that a good deal of the freedom of the Spirit was lost, when they ceased to hold their place among the methods of the Church, and only officials of the Church could lead the public worship.

IV

It does not seem to me to admit of question that St. Paul, in his earlier Epistles, and in the Epistle to the Ephesians, and (if we may quote them as St. Paul's in substance, if not in words) in the Epistles to Timothy and Titus, shows himself a genuine sacramentalist.[1] It is a poor plea that St. Paul does not say much about sacraments, when what there is is so plain in the sense it conveys. That comparatively little is said about them means probably that there was no controversy about them. Nor can we admit—in the light of St. Paul's plain statements about the efficacy of baptism—that the words " Christ sent me not to baptize, but to preach the Gospel " are intended to disparage baptism by the side of preaching. They mean no more necessarily than that St. Paul regarded baptism as something to be left to his companions, or later to the local presbyters. And he sees a positive advantage in this arrangement, because it hindered the false impression from arising that he was founding a sect of adherents to himself—" Lest any man should say that ye were baptized in my name." But let us consider his sacramental teaching positively.

1. The language he used about baptism is quite plain in its implications. The rite viewed externally

[1] Let us use this word to express one who believes in spiritual gifts being really bestowed through the external forms ; and keep " Sacramentarian " to its proper historical use as another name for those who, in opposition to Luther, held a merely symbolical view of the eucharist—Carlstadt, Bucer, and Zwingli. " Sacramentarian " means the opposite of "sacramentalist." If this distinction is not observed, books about the Reformation become misleading.

is symbolical. The going down into the water and being immersed in it and rising out of it is an acted representation of life through death, the dying to an old life and being buried and rising again to the new life ; but it is more than a symbol. It effects what it symbolizes. It is the transference of a man into a new spiritual sphere. It is baptism "into Christ" or "into the one body"—the Church, which St. Paul calls the body of Christ, or even Christ Himself, the Christ consisting both of the head and the body. And it is the Spirit who effects this transference—"By one Spirit were we all baptized into one body"; and the spiritual effect is regarded as following always on the outward action—"All we who were baptized," "as many of you as were baptized into Christ did [then and there] put on Christ."[1] In the *Ephesians* St. Paul regards the "one baptism," which he enumerates among the bonds of unity, as a cleansing applicable to the Church as a whole, and he seems to distinguish the matter of baptism, i.e. the water, from what is later called "the form," or accompanying words—"having cleansed it by the washing of water with the word."[2] The idea of the effect of baptism

[1] Rom. vi. 3; 1 Cor. xii. 12, 13; Gal. iii. 27; Col. ii. 12. We should note that in writing to the Romans, whom he had never visited, St. Paul assumes that they must as a matter of course understand what baptism means. "Are ye ignorant" means "Ye cannot surely be ignorant."

[2] Eph. iv. 5, v. 26: see Dr. Armitage Robinson *in loco*: "It is plain that the phrase ἐν ῥήματι indicates some solemn utterance by the accompaniment of which the washing of water is made to be no ordinary bath, but the sacrament of baptism." And he continues: "In the earliest times, however, baptism appears to have been administered 'in the name of Jesus Christ' (Acts ii. 38, x. 48, cf. viii. 12) or 'the Lord Jesus' (Acts viii. 16, xix. 5). And on the use of the single formula St. Paul's argument in 1 Cor. i. 13 seems to be based. . . . It is probable then that the ῥῆμα here referred to is the solemn mention of the name of the Lord Jesus Christ in connexion with the rite of baptism either as the confession made by the candidate or as the formula employed by the ministrant." I have expressed disagreement with this in the past, but I desire to retract the disagreement. I think the evidence is fairly convincing that at the beginning only the single name was

conveyed in these phrases is the same as that conveyed in the Epistle to Titus—"according to his mercy he saved us, through the washing of regeneration and renewing of the Holy Ghost, which he poured out upon us richly, through Jesus Christ our Saviour."[1]

Incorporation into Christ or His body, the being invested in a new spiritual nature which is Christ, "cleansing" from defilement mediated by washing, a new birth into a new spiritual status—all these phrases convey the same idea, and the process thus variously described is assigned to the same agent, the Holy Spirit, with the same external rite as its instrument. There is then in baptism an outward and visible sign and an inward and spiritual gift, and the two appear to be inseparably connected. The same conception of baptism as a spiritually effective rite is suggested by St. Peter's strong phrase "Baptism (as the reflection of Christ's descent into Hades) now also saves you,"[2] though the words which follow are ambiguous, and by the phrase of the Epistle to the Hebrews[3] "Having our hearts sprinkled from an evil conscience, and our body washed with pure water."

In the Acts also baptism is regarded as effecting

used. Down to the time of the Schoolmen this view prevailed, see S. Thomas Aq., *Sum. Th.*, 3ª, qu. 66, a. 6. It would appear (see Dr. Brightman in his essay on "the terms of communion" in *The Early History of the Church and the Ministry*, pp. 344–5: Macmillan, 1918) that in the Roman Church for some centuries there was no baptismal formula pronounced by the ministrant, but only the threefold question of the ministrant, "Dost thou believe," etc., followed by the threefold reply, "I believe," and the threefold affusion. The Church by its "binding" and "loosing" power later settled the precise conditions of valid baptism.

[1] Tit. iii. 5; cf. 1 Cor. vi. 11: "Ye were washed, ye were sanctified, ye were justified in the name of our Lord Jesus Christ, and in the Spirit of our God."

[2] For the reading and meaning see Dr. Bernard's *Studia Sacra*, pp. 26 ff. (Hodder & Stoughton). I think the words ἐπερώτημα εἰς Θεόν are probably suggested by Ezek. xx. 1, 3 (LXX. ἐπερωτῆσαι), to "enquire of God"; cf. xiv. 7.

[3] Heb. x. 22.

the great transition from the world of sin to the world of righteousness. So Cornelius is represented as explaining its meaning to Saul on his conversion. "Arise, and be baptized, and wash away thy sins, calling on his name" (the name of Jesus).[1] And from the beginning the emphasis is on absolution or being set free. "Repent, and be baptized every one of you in the name of Jesus Christ unto the remission of your sins; and ye shall receive the Holy Spirit."[2] That is, baptism is represented from the moment after Pentecost as an ordinance which the Apostles are commissioned to require, its efficacy lying in absolution and cleansing from sin, and in opening the door to the gift of the Spirit, which, however, is specially connected in the Acts with the following rite of the laying on of hands. And in interpreting the phrases in the Acts and the Epistles we recall of course the words in our Lord's discourse with Nicodemus in the Fourth Gospel, "Verily, verily, I say unto thee, Except a man be born anew" (or "from above"), "he cannot see the kingdom of God. . . . Verily, verily, I say unto thee, Except a man be born of water and the Spirit, he cannot enter into the kingdom of God."

Modern critics, then, such as would assimilate the Church to the mysteries, are quite right in affirming that St. Paul (and the other New Testament writers) believed in baptism as acting *ex opere operato*,[3] if by that is meant simply that he believed a real change of spiritual status to be wrought in all cases through the visible rite. In this we must agree with Dr. Kirsopp Lake against Dr. Kennedy[4]; but when he goes on to suggest that "the attitude which regarded Christianity as a 'mystery religion' inevitably must have led men to exaggerate and misinterpret

[1] Acts xxii. 16. [2] Acts ii. 38.
[3] See Dr. K. Lake, *The Earlier Epistles of St. Paul*, p. 385.
[4] See *St. Paul and the Mystery Religions*, pp. 232 f.

the Pauline doctrine of freedom, to regard the cleansing from sin gained by the Christian as giving him permission henceforth to do as he liked without incurring guilt, and to consider baptism as an *opus operatum* which secured his admission into the kingdom apart from the character of his future conduct," he is going beyond his evidence. There was a perilous tendency to antinomianism among the Gentile converts, as was natural enough considering their antecedents. But the evidence of St. Paul's language in combating their grievous error would indicate that it was excused by an appeal to the doctrine of free forgiveness greatly misunderstood, or to the triumph of grace over law, or to 'liberty,' rather than by any appeal to the efficacy of the sacraments.[1]

Some of the later books of the New Testament are heavy with anxiety caused by the spread of an immoral idea of religion, coupled with a false asceticism, and worthless speculations about the unknowable and unprofitable. Such a spirit the mysteries would have nourished. But the Church would have none of it; and it succeeded in weathering the storm, and on the whole maintaining for centuries a splendid level both of personal and social morality. It was true to the heritage of ideas which it had derived from the prophets of Israel that religion and morality were strictly indissoluble and that there was no fellowship with God possible except by the way of righteousness. At a certain moment of controversy with the Judaizers, St. Paul used language which might easily be perverted. But about his real meaning there is no mistake. He was as sound on the one end of religion as St. James. In the process of redemption, faith, which opens our hearts to the promises of God and commits our whole life to His

[1] Rom. vi. 1, 15: cf. 1 Cor. vi. 12, x. 23, "All things are lawful for me"; cf. 2 Pet. ii. 19, "Promising them liberty."

will, has a supremely important place: so has baptism, which actually and spiritually introduces us into the covenant of grace and the fellowship of the Spirit; but both alike are relative to the one end. Three times St. Paul states the essentials of religion from three different points of view in controversy with the Judaists. " Neither circumcision," he says, " availeth anything, nor uncircumcision; but faith working through love." " Circumcision," he says again, " is nothing, and uncircumcision is nothing, but a new creature." Finally, " Circumcision is nothing, and uncircumcision is nothing; but the keeping of the commandments of God." [1] Faith, and the recreative act of God, in which baptism holds its great place, are essentials as means; but there is only one essential end, which is actual conformity with God in character and conduct.

When we turn from St. Paul to St. John we find that to him the gift of regeneration is so indissolubly associated with the life of practical goodness into which it serves to admit men, that he speaks as if regeneration and complete moral victory were one and the same thing. " Whosoever is begotten of God doeth no sin, because his seed abideth in him: and he cannot sin, because he is begotten of God." " Whosoever is begotten of God overcometh the world." [2] Elsewhere, even in the immediate context of these words, he shows that sin is sadly possible in Christians [3]; but he is unwilling even to speak of regeneration except as seen in its proper fruits.

The early discipline, and the early ceremonies of baptism, must have impressed deeply upon every convert the moral meaning of being baptized; and there is no subject on which the Christian writers appear to draw on a more profound spiritual experience. But the Christian rites were, of course,

[1] Gal. v. 6, vi. 15; 1 Cor. vii. 19.

[2] 1 John iii. 9, v. 4.

[3] v. 16, i. 8.

designed for adult converts; and when Christianity became a matter of course, and infant baptism the almost universal rule, it ran a great risk of losing its moral power by being treated almost as a charm. I must say a word therefore on the baptism of infants.

It is probable that the Church from the beginning took over from the Jews the practice of baptizing the children of proselytes—" the little proselytes "—with their parents.[1] The phrases in Acts xvi. about both Lydia and the jailer at Philippi—" he was baptized, he and all his," " she and her household "—suggest it. Our Lord's words " Suffer the little children to come unto me " would have encouraged the practice then, as in later ages. St. Paul appears to address children as already " in the Lord " (Eph. vi. 1), and, since he speaks of the children of two parents, only one of whom had become Christian, as " holy " (or consecrated to God—1 Cor. vii. 14), he would probably think of them as fit subjects for baptism. Nevertheless this would have been because the allegiance to Christ of the parent or parents provided a pledge that the child would be educated in the principles of Christ. All the moral circumstances of baptism in early days sharply differentiated it from a charm. It involved for the adults a most definite choice, and such a separation from the old life as made the choice a real adventure of faith. And all the early lore about baptism, and the early ritual, emphasize the element of solemn and deliberate choice—the " dying to live." This situation continued on the whole for some three centuries. Thus the homes of Christians would have been for their children normally nurseries of faith. The real disaster happened when Christianity became the established religion and baptism became really indiscriminate. " Baptism doth represent unto us our profession "—it is the profession of

[1] See Taylor's *Teaching of the Twelve Apostles*, pp. 55–8, and Sabatier's *La Didaché*, pp. 84–8.

discipleship; and it seems to me that no departure from the principles of Christ has been so serious as that which allowed membership of the Church to become a matter of course. But upon this we must return.

2. Our aim is to make it plain that the sacramental principle was acknowledged in the Church from the beginning, and to indicate the solemn rites in which the principle was recognized. One of these was the laying on of hands. We should gather from the Acts that baptism prepared for the gift of the Holy Spirit, but the laying on of the hands of the apostles was the normal instrument of its bestowal.[1] It has recently[2] been suggested that the narrative in Acts viii. may be interpreted as a kind of experiment, made because the Samaritan Christians had not, as a consequence of their baptism, showed the signs of the possession of the Spirit which were expected—the speaking with tongues. But if this had been in the mind of the writer, he would surely have made it more evident. And it is quite inapplicable to the narrative in chap. xix. I think it must be admitted that St. Luke intends us to understand that the normal ceremony of initiation was baptism followed by the laying on of hands, and that it was so from the beginning. In the Epistle to the Hebrews, when the writer is enumerating the elements of the first teaching of converts, he speaks of the "teaching of baptisms, and the laying on of hands." And they were joined together in the early Christian tradition[3]; the rite

[1] Acts ii. 38, viii. 17–18, xix. 6. Dr. Chase, *Confirmation in the Apostolic Age*, p. 34, says: "The imposition of hands after baptism is represented as the natural act of the apostles after baptism. No explanation of the origin of the practice is given. . . . Short of an express statement to that effect, we could have no more convincing proof the apostles were following a command which they had received from the Lord Himself."

[2] In *The Acts* (Clarendon Bible), p. 166.

[3] Tertull., *de Bapt.*, 6: "Not that we receive the Holy Spirit in the waters, but cleansed in the waters, we are prepared for the Holy Spirit. . . . Then the hand is laid on us, by benediction invoking and inviting the Holy Spirit."

of baptism, as commonly spoken of, *included* the laying on of hands. And though the words of Christ, according to St. John, attach the action of the Holy Spirit to baptism with water, and St. Paul's words confirm this—"By one Spirit were we all baptized into one body"—yet to the laying on of hands was attached that full indwelling of the Spirit which equipped each "member" to play his part in the royal and priestly body.

There is no mention of what we call "confirmation" in the New Testament except in the Acts and the Hebrews [1]; but it is suggested by St. Paul's habit of referring to the reception of the Holy Spirit as having occurred at a definite moment of the convert's life.[2] Certainly it is St. Paul's teaching that the Spirit was from a definite moment in their lives lodged in their heart and body, and he never suggests that Christians should ask for the Spirit as if they did not already permanently possess Him.

The laying on of hands was hardly regarded in early days as a second sacrament—rather it was regarded as the completion of baptism; and in the tradition of the early centuries it was restricted to the bishop.

3. For the interpretation given to the eucharist in the earliest days of the Church we depend mainly upon a few passages in St. Paul's First Epistle to the Corinthians, for special abuses, which arose at Corinth alone, caused him to write about what elsewhere he

[1] Unless we agree with Chase in interpreting 2 Tim. i. 6 of confirmation. See below, p. 143, n. 1.

[2] See Chase, *op. cit.*, pp. 52 and 150, and Swete, *The Holy Spirit in the N.T.*, pp. 202, 204. The latter interprets Gal. iii. 5, "He therefore that supplies to you the Spirit and works miracles among you," of the apostolic minister, rather than of God, pp. 202–3. Cf. Acts xi. 17, acc. to the Bezan text, "Who was I that I should withstand God, *that I should not give them the Holy Spirit when they believed on him?*" But I doubt if these additional words can be authentic.

can take for granted. Nothing can make us feel the insecurity of the "argument from silence," or of the habit of measuring the importance of a subject by the number of references to it, more than the accidental way in which St. Paul is led to refer to the original teaching which he had given at Corinth, and which no doubt he gave in all the churches of his foundation, about both the institution of the eucharist at the Last Supper and the meaning of the rite. Up to a certain point these references are very explicit, and they are most suggestive. They put in the most startling contrast the remarkably domestic and, as we may say, casual character of the celebration with the awful spiritual realities enshrined in it. Here you have a vivid glimpse of "the breaking of the bread," the common meal of fellowship, or "agapè," as it was later called, for which the Christians met daily or at the opening hours of the First Day, i.e. our Saturday evening. It was a quite natural meal, intended to express brotherhood, but capable of being misused, as it actually was at Corinth, to the strangely contrary ends of class distinction and excess. But to such a meal—so unguarded in its circumstances—was attached the commemoration of Christ in the bread broken and the wine cup blessed, which He Himself had appended to the Paschal meal. And the strange words which He had then spoken, "This is my body," "This is my blood," St. Paul would have us interpret with a tremendous realism.

The body of Christ, offered for them in sacrifice, and the blood outpoured is really present under the humble forms of bread and wine. It is present to be their spiritual food. The cup which they bless is a sharing together in the blood, and the bread which they break is a sharing together in the body of Christ. The one bread and the one cup are the symbols and the instruments of their unity. But prior to reception the heavenly realities must be by their faith recognized as present. To fail to "discern the body"[1] is to fall under judgement. To eat the bread or drink the cup unworthily is to be guilty of the body and blood of the Lord. And those who have been content with taking the bread and drinking the cup without discernment of the unseen reality have been in fact punished with sickness and sometimes with death.[2]

The particular phrases which St. Paul uses have been scrutinized with more strictness than human language, quite unscholastic human language, will bear. I think we need to trust more than critics and theologians are apt to do to the general impression they make on our imagination. St. Paul's language, I think, gives us a vivid impression of the "breaking of the bread" as it was practised at Corinth, and shows us a fraternal meal easily liable to abuse—not such as we should naturally associate with anything specially sacred. Then into the middle ot this scene he introduces the most tremendous spiritual presences. The earthly and the heavenly, the natural and the supernatural, are brought into the most startling proximity. This is sacramentalism indeed. Here we are presented with an institution of Christ for His Church in which, with a divine boldness, the highest things are offered to us under the most familiar earthly forms and conditions. In the subsequent history of the Church we begin to see very soon different schools of interpretation of the words of Christ forming themselves, and later in history controversy has raged about them again and again. But it does not seem to me open to question that St. Paul takes it for granted that there was a

[1] In the context I cannot conceive that "the body" can mean anything but Christ's own body, which is put in conjunction with His "blood" (or life).

[2] 1 Cor. xi. 20 ff., x. 16 ff.

real presence of the body and blood of Christ in the elements blessed in the eucharist, such as should strike his converts with an awful dread of a careless approach to them.

No doubt steps were taken by St. Paul to make impossible the particular scandals he was confronted with. We know that very soon the eucharist proper was separated from the love-feast. But for a long time, especially, it would appear, in the Church of Rome, the natural basis of the sacrament in a fraternal meal remained evident. In an *Ordo* of the eighth century we have a description of the single Mass celebrated in Rome on the Sunday by the bishop for his assembled flock. What would have struck us, if we could have been present, would have been what followed the solemn reading of the Gospel—the gathering from the assembled multitude of their offerings, a great store of bread and wine, and "the spreading of the table-cloth" on the altar to receive the oblations; then when the eucharistic prayer had been said by the bishop and the gifts in great part consecrated, we should have seen them returned to the whole congregation which had offered them, in bags and flagons, now made to be the divine food which was to sanctify them as one people in Christ.[1] Surely we may say that St. Paul would approve of no ritual of the Christian sacrifice which did not leave its social nature apparent. "We, the many, are one bread, one body: for we are all partakers of the one bread."

With the sacrament of ordination I am to deal immediately. What I am seeking to do in these pages is only to make evident that the Church from its origin was unmistakably and deeply sacramental—

[1] I have described the service in more detail in *Reservation* (by the Bishops of Oxford and Chelmsford: Robert Scott, 1917). I would refer also to *The Body of Christ* (John Murray), where I have dealt with eucharistic doctrine more at length.

10

that it certainly believed in divine gifts ministered through earthly rites; and I have illustrated this from the three instances of baptism, confirmation, and the eucharist. Harnack, in his brilliant work on *The Expansion of Christianity*,[1] describes, and in part parodies, the sacramental religion of the early Church. Then he adds, "*Ab initio sic non erat* is the protest that will be entered. 'From the beginning it was not so.' Perhaps. But one must go far back to find that beginning, so far back that this extremely brief period now eludes our search entirely." It is true that it entirely eludes our search; but the question is whether we have any justification for believing that it ever existed.[2]

V

The outward unity of the Church, the body of Christ, as it appears in the New Testament and in the subsequent history of the Church, was guarded against the disruptive tendencies of humanity especially by three bonds: first, by the authority of the common faith or word of God, of which we are to speak in the chapters which follow; secondly, by the need to seek the gifts of God in the sacraments of the society; thirdly, by the obligation of adherence to the apostolic ministry.

Elsewhere [3] I have sought to examine at length the grounds for holding (1) that the principle of the apostolic succession in the ministry of the Church was one of its most uncontested principles from the middle of the second century downwards; (2) that

[1] Engl. trans., i. 293.

[2] On the "seven sacraments," see Appended Note B, p. 149.

[3] I.e. in *The Church and the Ministry* (Longmans), published in 1888 and recently republished after careful revision by Professor C. H. Turner. The Professor has also recently embodied the conclusions of his historical studies in a little tract, which can be read in a quarter of an hour, on *The Apostolic Succession* (among "The Congress Books," No. 33).

the books of the New Testament and the indications of the sub-apostolic age supply the justification for this principle. The controversy on the subject covers a very wide field and I cannot here repeat the argument. I can only ask that it be considered, as is not, I fear, often done, as a whole. Here I shall only concern myself with the evidence supplied by the documents of the apostolic and sub-apostolic period, and I shall seek to indicate the chief points on which any enquirer must make up his mind, at the same time showing the answer to which it seems to me the evidence points.

1. The root question is whether, prior to all development suggested, or rendered necessary, by circumstances, the Church does appear, even before Pentecost, as a body already equipped with officers holding pastoral authority by Christ's appointment in the persons of the apostles. Those who oppose this position are apt to refer to the great authority of Dr. Hort. But we must not allow ourselves to be enslaved to any single scholar or group of scholars, however eminent. We must seek to exercise our free judgement. Like Dr. Mason,[1] I find the section of Dr. Hort's posthumously published work on *The Christian Ecclesia* which deals with this subject quite unconvincing,[2] nothing else than an over-subtle scholar's paradox. As we have seen,[3] St. Paul certainly believed that authority, which must be called official, had been given by God to the Apostles, and to himself among them. He claims this authority not only in the churches of his foundation, but in the Roman Church, which he had never visited. And the same impression is made on our minds by the narrative of the Acts. That such authority was

[1] See *Early History of the Church and the Ministry*, p. 41.

[2] See *The Church and the Ministry*, Appended Note M.

[3] See above, p. 68; for the Roman church, see Rom. i. 1, 5, xi. 13, xv. 15 f.; for the Acts, above, p. 47.

solemnly and deliberately granted by our Lord is stated in the Gospels of St. Matthew and St. John, and is implied in St. Mark and St. Luke.[1] The Church from Clement of Rome downwards accepted the fact as obvious ; and I think the evidence constrains us to assent.

2. We have to ask ourselves whether the existence of such officers in the Christian society, believed to have been appointed by divine authority, and put in trust of the "mysteries of God"—and not of doctrine only, but of the ministry of grace as a whole[2] —does not involve the principle of a priesthood, whether the Greek word *hiereus* is used for them or no. The ideas attached to the particular word, whether among Jews or Greeks, might very naturally have made the Christian Church somewhat slow to adopt it. But is not the principle there ? It is indeed protected against abuse by certain safeguards : by the fullest recognition of the equal freedom of approach to God belonging to all those who share the same Spirit ; by the openness to all alike of the divine 'mysteries,' and the absence of any idea of a 'reserved' doctrine ; by the moral teaching which should have made it impossible to regard any sacraments administered by priests as charms which could be beneficial without moral response ; and by the important share in the discipline and worship of the Church assigned to all its members. Let us say that the priesthood of the Christian ministry is a representative, not a vicarious priesthood. Still, in the persons of the Apostles, it has its powers not from the people, but from God. Men must, it seems, normally seek the gift of the Holy Ghost from

[1] See above, pp. 45 ff.

[2] 2 Cor. iii. 6 and Rom. i. 11. We notice that in Rom. xv. 15 St. Paul justifies his "bold" tone to the Romans by the nature of his office. Dr. Moffat translates his words, "I have written to you with a certain freedom, in virtue of my divine commission as a priest of Christ Jesus to the Gentiles in the service of God's Gospel."

apostolic hands; and the "stewardship" of these officers, granted them by Christ, gave them powers of "binding" and "loosing," "absolving" and "retaining sins" with a divine sanction, which could not be ignored, and which appear at the last resort to inhere in their special office, though they seek to exercise them in union with the whole body of the faithful. Thus this is the question—Does not the spiritual life of the members of Christ appear in the New Testament as in manifold ways dependent upon their adherence to the Apostles and those who shared their ministry with them? If this is so, is it not the case that we cannot repudiate sacerdotalism, but only certain forms of it or abuses of it? [1]

3. The apostles had a certain function as witnesses and founders which necessarily died with them; but St. Paul plainly regards his pastoral office as one to be perpetuated, and so presumably did the others.

[1] There is nothing in the New Testament which gives any indication as to who might or who might not preside at the eucharist. The eucharist was instituted apparently in the presence of the Twelve only (Mark xiv. 17), and was entrusted to them in the words "Do this [celebrate this rite] in remembrance of me." And it was a symbol or instrument of the unity of the Church such as would naturally be in the hands of the officers of the Church. So in Clement, at the end of the first century, it is the traditional function of the presbyter-bishops to "offer the gifts"; and by Ignatius it is said, "Let that be esteemed a valid eucharist which is celebrated by the bishop or someone to whom he has intrusted it." And in the *Didaché* the election of "bishops and deacons" is made apparently specially with a view to the celebration of the "pure sacrifice" of the Church, in the absence of the apostles and prophets. And in Justin Martyr the "president of the brethren" celebrates.* Dr. Hamilton (*People of God*, bk. ii, chap. vi, pp. 110 ff.) works out the evidence for the connexion of mon-episcopacy with the 'presidency' of the eucharist. But there is nothing about the matter in the New Testament. Nothing seems to me more certain than that as regards matters of order in the Church there can be no agreement except on the basis of the belief that the legislative ordering of the Church, as it came about in course of time, has a divine sanction in proportion to its unanimity and constancy.

* Clem., c. 44; Ignat., *ad Smyrn.*, 8; *Did.*, xv, 1; Justin, *Apol.* i, 65.

And we see the process beginning especially in the Acts and the Pastoral Epistles. We see local church officers, the seven, the presbyter-bishops, the deacons, being appointed. And whether they are elected for their office by the people or designated by prophets,[1] they are in any case appointed [2] by the apostles, or later by apostolic delegates themselves appointed by the apostles, like Timothy and Titus (Tit. i. 5).[3] Towards the end of the first century Clement of Rome gives us in the simplest manner a history of the Christian ministry down to his own time.[4] "Christ," he says, "is from God and the Apostles from Christ; all took place in both cases in order by the will of God. . . . Preaching then in country and town they appointed their firstfruits, when they had tested them in the Spirit, for bishops [i.e. presbyter-bishops] and deacons of those who were about to become believers." Then he adds that "Our apostles knew, through our Lord Jesus Christ, that there would be contention about the title to the episcopate. Therefore on this account, having received perfect foreknowledge, they appointed the aforesaid [presbyter-bishops and deacons], and subsequently gave an additional injunction, that, if they fell asleep, other approved men should succeed to their ministry." And the next sentence appears clearly to interpret this "additional injunction": "They, then, who were appointed by those [apostles] or *subsequently by other distinguished men with the consent of the whole flock*, etc." The additional injunction then was the provision that, after the death of the first generation of local clergy (when

[1] Acts vi. 3, 5, xiii. 2; 1 Tim. i. 18. [2] Acts vi. 3, 6, xiv. 23.

[3] Only in the *Didaché* do we get mention of "election" without mention of any other kind of appointment. But the *Didaché* is a manual for the local church, and the ordination, if ordination there was, would have lain with the superior order of apostles or prophets of whom the book speaks. See *The Church and the Ministry*, pp. 251–2.

[4] On Clement, see *The Church and the Ministry*, pp. 273 ff.

the apostles also presumably would have gone), there should be other distinguished men who, not arbitrarily, but with the consent of the whole flock, should appoint their successors. Timothy and Titus appear to be examples of this class of 'distinguished men' or notables.

We cannot trace with certainty the apparently different processes by which the transition was effected between the state of things described by Clement and that of later Church history. Clement, we have seen, presents a state of things in which there was at Corinth a local ministry of presbyter-bishops and deacons subordinated, in respect of the appointment of their successors, to certain men of distinction, not presumably belonging to any one city. We know that, not twenty years later, Ignatius of Antioch can speak of the threefold local ministry of bishop, presbyters, and deacons as (1) an apostolic institution, (2) necessary to the constitution of a church, (3) of world-wide acceptance.[1] At the moment of his writing this last point may have been an exaggeration; but it very speedily became true. And whatever was the precise method of transition in particular cases, it seems to me that there is no good reason to doubt that it came about on the principle of succession, i.e. that the elected officers of the churches had always received their commission, in whatever grade, from those who in the generation previous had held—from apostles[2] in the first instance —not only the authority themselves to minister, but the authority also to appoint others to the ministry. This is what is meant by the phrase 'ordination from above,' by contradistinction from mere election by the members of the Church ('from below').

[1] On Ignatius, see *The Church and the Ministry*, p. 258.

[2] It must be recognized that the term "apostles" covered not only the Twelve but Paul and Barnabas, and Andronicus and Junias, and others unknown who were held to have received their commission from Christ Himself

I think the only occasion for scruple in maintaining this position lies in the problem of the prophets. There were in the Church 'prophets' and 'teachers' more or less closely associated with apostles, and of these we should suppose that the prophets at least were persons who were accepted simply because there was a divine gift of inspiration recognized in them; and the narrative in the Acts xiii., coupled with the *Didaché*, would suggest that they were recognized as priests for ministry as well as prophets for admonition. This may have been the case; but when the question is that of the perpetuation of the ministry, the only document which suggests any continuance of this kind of authority in the prophets is the *Didaché*; and, if that is a genuine document of the sub-apostolic age (as I believe), it represents a group of churches outside the main stream of Church life; and the highly dubious character of the prophets there described shows the wisdom of the Church at large in refusing to recognize them in any other capacity than as preachers, like Hermas.

4. The method of appointment to a church office is described in 2 Tim. i. 6, in an unmistakably sacramental phrase, "For this cause I put thee in remembrance that thou stir up the gift of God, which is in thee through the laying on of my hands."[1] There is no like phrase in St. Paul's 'undisputed' Epistles, nor in the Acts, as concerns ordination to pastoral office, but if you gather the references in the New

[1] I cannot doubt that this refers to ordination and not to confirmation, as Dr. Chase would have us believe. I think mention of the spirit of σωφρόνισμος (see Swete, *Holy Spirit in the N.T.*, pp. 245–6) and the whole character of the context indicate this. So also Dr. Mason and Dr. Parry. It has been usual to couple together 2 Tim. i. 6 with 1 Tim. iv. 14, and to suppose that Timothy was ordained through prophecy, indicating the divine approval, by (διὰ) the laying on of St. Paul's hand *accompanied with* (μέτα) the laying on of the hands of the presbytery. This seems to make a little too much depend on the particular prepositions used in different epistles. I should have thought both διὰ and μέτα could describe the act of ordination; and St. Paul in

Testament, so incidental in their occurrence, to the laying on of hands as the method of admission to Church office,[1] is it not unreasonable to question that it was the regular method—the more so as it seems to have passed over to the Church from the Jews, and in the Old Testament appears as a symbol of transmission from one to another of authority or status or guilt? And it would surely have carried with it the same kind of sacramental implication as the laying on of hands in confirmation. Undoubtedly in St. Paul's view, the "teachers," "helps," and "governments," whom he mentions among Christ's gifts to the Church, were as much "charismatic," as much empowered for their function by a gift of the Spirit, as apostles or prophets or workers of miracles.[2] It was the Holy Spirit made men presbyter-bishops (Acts xx. 28).

5. In Church history we constantly find the Church exercising its function of "binding" and "loosing" in matters which concern the ministry. We witness the careful delimitation of the specific functions of each order of ministers and the admission of the validity of baptism by laymen. We witness the decision—accepted at last fully in the West—of the validity of ordinations as well as baptisms conferred in heretical and separated bodies of Christians. Again, we have a controversy—never perhaps decided—as to whether the undoubted distinction of bishops and presbyters in the Church tradition was originally

one passage emphasizes his own pre-eminent part in the action, and in the other associates himself (like St. Peter) with the whole presbyterate. Harnack (*Law and Constitution*, p. 26) is very emphatic on the sacramental character of ordination from the first: "That the laying on of hands was regarded as conferring the charisma necessary to the office is obvious from the passages in Timothy, and it is improbable that these express only a later idea. The laying on of hands was thus certainly sacramental."

[1] Besides 2 Tim. i. 6, see Acts vi. 6, xiii. 3 (appointment for a particular mission), 1 Tim. iv. 14 and v. 22.

[2] See Dr. Armitage Robinson's excellent essay in *The Early History*, pp. 60 ff.

of divine or only of ecclesiastical authority. But there are two assumptions which appear always to be taken for granted in these controversies: (1) that when Christ founded or refounded the Church He instituted a ministry in the persons of the apostles which was to be continued down the course of history by a process of sacramental ordination—so that this continuous ministry was, so to speak, the backbone of the Church and the visible instrument of its coherence and continuity; and (2) that the settlement of questions of order lay with the Church, which had been granted the power of legislation in matters of discipline with a divine sanction.

Nothing seems to me more certain than that the New Testament documents give no decisive indication of the precise form the ministry was to take. But the actual peace and cohesion of the Church in each generation depends on there being decisive regulation on the subject of the functions of the different orders of ministers. If so, unity is in fact only possible if we accept the authority of the Church in such practical matters as claiming the obedience of individual churchmen or sections of churchmen, unless indeed it could be shown that there was anything in their ordinances antagonistic to the spirit of the New Testament.

VI

The object of this chapter has been to give a general view of the Religion of the Spirit as it is presented to us in the documents of the New Testament; and it has been specially directed to show that as in Jesus Christ the Word took flesh, so, when the Holy Spirit came from the ascended Christ to perpetuate His work in the world, for Him too, in another sense, a "body was prepared" which was the Church, the reformed Israel. Thus there was not from the beginning any distinction between membership of Christ and membership of His "body." And the body which St. Paul speaks of in a strain of such glorious exultation in the Epistle to the Ephesians is no other than the actual historical Church with all its imperfections—the beginnings of which are recorded in the Acts, and which found its bonds of unity in the common faith, the sacraments of fellowship, and the authority of the apostolic ministry.

Sometimes it appears as if it were hardly necessary to argue this point any longer. Luther's contention, so long prevalent in Protestantism, that the Church, of which such lofty things are spoken by Paul, was not any visible body, in which the evil is mingled with the good, like the church at Corinth, but the invisible company of the elect, who may or may not be members of any visible church and whose names are known only to God—this doctrine appears to-day almost to have vanished.[1]

Perhaps its place is taken by Sohm's theory, which would distinguish a moment in the life of the early Church—a moment which is marked more or less distinctly by the Epistle of Clement—when the *Catholic* idea of the Church, with its *official* conception of the ministry and *legal* conception of an authoritative law, overwhelmed the earlier "religious or charismatic" conception. The theory is stated and criticized by Harnack in an appendix to his *Constitution and Law of the Church*, where he points out that official authority already belongs to an apostle in St. Paul's Epistles, and the idea of a binding law is already present there, as also in the canon of the Jerusalem Council. The idea of an

[1] See above, Appended Note B, p. 32; and on "the heavenly Jerusalem," see Appended Note C to this chapter. See also *Essays on Christian Unity* (Clarke, 1923), by Dr. William Robinson, the Principal of Overdale College, chap. iii, a book which is surely a hopeful sign in the movement towards reunion.

"officer" and a "law" is already present in the original conception of the Church as the true Israel.[1]

We may take it for truth, then, that as represented in the New Testament, the New Covenant, like the Old, is with the community, not with separated individuals, and that Christianity from the beginning was the religion of a sacramental Church. The bearing of this consideration on the circumstances of the present day we must seek to consider later.

In conclusion, I will content myself with enumerating very briefly the leading considerations which commend sacramentalism to our understanding.

1. The principle that spiritual values and forces are mediated through material processes is a principle that runs through nature as a whole. I have already illustrated this by reference to the sexual method by which a spiritual (human) personality is brought into being. But it admits of much wider illustration. Truth and beauty and goodness are spiritual values and forces. But all of them within our experience arise and become effective only under material forms. And human life in all its forms of fellowship is full of natural sacraments, such as the lover's kiss and the friend's handshake and the soldier's flag, which both express and kindle the respective feeling.

2. The whole history of religions or religion, as recent investigation unfolds it to us, tends to emphasize the principle that religion is first of all a *group* consciousness or tribal consciousness, and that *individual* religion develops later and under its shelter. And the tribal character of religion everywhere expresses itself in what may be called in a broad sense 'sacramental' forms.

3. Within the Christian religion the Incarnation is

[1] I hope Dr. Armitage Robinson's essay on "The Primitive Ministry" in *The Early History of the Church and Ministry* will put an end to the vogue of distinguishing "charismatic" from official. In the New Testament the local officers are certainly regarded as "charismatic."

the central fact—but that is the mediation of the spiritual, the divine presence and grace, through the flesh. The method of the Spirit in the Church and the sacraments is thus properly called an extension of the principle and fact of the Incarnation.

4. The sacraments are social ceremonies ; and the mediation of spiritual gifts through sacraments of the society presents itself therefore as the divinely chosen means by which our fellowship in the life of God is tied to our membership in the appointed human brotherhood. We cannot become united to God in isolation or in a merely self-chosen society.

5. By the sacraments the highest gifts are made equally accessible to persons of all stages of culture. Spiritual things are hard of intellectual comprehension. In an intellectual form only the intellectual few could assimilate them. But experience shows that the youngest and the least educated can by simplicity of faith appreciate and assimilate spiritual gifts embodied in symbolical rites, such as washing, and receiving the blessing of the hand, and feeding on bread and wine.

6. Emotion is an extraordinarily powerful force in religion, and the uneducated are even more emotionally susceptible than the educated. But emotion is also variable and delusive. We are enthusiastic and cold, elated and depressed, by turns, and we know not why. In two ways the religion of Christ would direct our attention away from our emotions. Partly by making our acts, that is our will, the test of genuineness, and not our feelings. Partly also by the institution of sacraments. By sacraments, spiritual gifts, such as regeneration and reception of the Spirit and absolution, and communion with God in Christ, are imparted to us objectively, in outward acts and signs. We are assured by a divine guarantee that at a certain moment we were made members of Christ and did receive the Spirit, and were set free

from sin and did receive Christ Himself to be our spiritual food; and the injunction given us is addressed to our wills, not to our emotions. We are bidden to act as sons of God and sharers in Christ, knowing by an outward sign that we are so. Our reliance is to be on the word and act of God, while the joy of responsive emotion comes or goes.

APPENDED NOTE A (see p. 112)

THE GIFT OF TONGUES AS REPRESENTED IN ACTS II

The conception of the gift of tongues in Acts ii. appears at first sight to be in marked conflict with the conception to which 1 Cor. xiv. 2–34 would lead us. In the first passage it appears to be a gift of speaking foreign languages (ver. 11). In the latter it is a non-rational kind of utterance, alike unintelligible to the speaker and his audience—hardly what we should call a language at all. But the difference must not be exaggerated. The idea that Acts ii. describes what we commonly call a gift of using foreign languages, such as would be available for preaching, is not borne out in the text. Like St. Paul, St. Luke apparently describes the tongues as an utterance addressed to God (1 Cor. xiv. 2, 15–17; Acts ii. 11). Also he describes it as a simultaneous utterance, and an utterance which could be mockingly described as the senseless clamour of a group of drunken men (ver. 13). There is no suggestion in the Acts that "tongues" were used for preaching. On the other hand, St. Paul (1 Cor. xiv. 21) compares the "tongues" to a foreign language, the unintelligible language of strangers. There seem to be two alternative conclusions about the matter: either that the phenomenon of the day of Pentecost was really special—something like the gift of tongues as St. Paul describes it, combined with the gift of "interpretation" in the mind of the foreign hearers, so that they heard, or seemed to hear, the combined ecstatic shouts of praise, each in his own language wherein he was born; or that the account which St. Luke received and reported was not accurate in detail. We should be ready for either conclusion, but we have no sufficient grounds for deciding between them.

APPENDED NOTE B (see p. 136)

THE ENUMERATION OF SEVEN SACRAMENTS

Besides baptism, the laying on of hands in confirmation and in ordination, and the eucharist, do we discover in the New Testament any other sacraments, i.e. sacred rites of the community believed to carry a divine gift with them? Not, I suppose, in the strict sense. But the judgement and absolution of the Church, the remitting and retaining of sins, was sacramental in the sense that, though we do not hear of any outward rite in which it was expressed (as later by the laying on of hands upon the penitent in absolution), the judgement and the absolution were human acts which were believed to carry with them a divine power by the appointment of Christ. And unction as described by St. James was an outward ceremony by which a gift, though it was physical rather than spiritual, the gift of healing, was mediated. This could be described as sacramental in a sense. Finally, marriage, though there was no ecclesiastical ceremony at first attached to it, because the mutual pledge carried with it a divine sanction, might also be so described. Thus was made up the list of the seven sacraments by which the life of the Christian was surrounded from the cradle to the grave.

The enumeration of seven sacraments we first find in Gregory of Bergamo (twelfth cent.), but his list is made up of baptism, confirmation, the eucharist, ordination, marriage, Holy Scripture, and the taking an oath. There was no tradition of seven sacraments. It is Peter Lombard in the next century who gives us the seven with which we are familiar. No doubt we must maintain the pre-eminence of baptism, completed in confirmation, and the eucharist, and place ordination next to them; but the other three, though they fail to correspond to the stricter definition, may well be admitted as sacraments.

APPENDED NOTE C (see p. 145)

THE HEAVENLY JERUSALEM

The nearest approach to a doctrine of an invisible Church to be found in the New Testament is the idea of "the heavenly Jerusalem" (Gal. iv. 26; Heb. xii. 22; Apoc. iii. 12 and xxi.). In the Apocalypse it is represented as existing in heaven, but it is to be manifested on earth at the consummation. I suppose this is equivalent to saying it is the *predestined* consummation. But in the Epistle to the Galatians we are already members of it. It is already "our mother" (St. Paul appears to be quoting Ps. lxxxvi. [LXX], Μήτηρ Σειών, ἐρεῖ ἄνθρωπος). So in the Epistle to the Hebrews we are already "come to" it. I suppose the idea is that of the Church as having its ground where Christ is "in the heavenlies," and where the angels and the spirits of just men made perfect are. In this sense the Church is heavenly and invisible, but the visible churches on earth are the earthly limbs of the heavenly body or the earthly representatives of the heavenly society, substantially one with it.

CHAPTER V

THE AUTHORITY OF THE CHURCH

WE have had the opportunity of reading many books, written from different points of view, on authority and its function in society generally, and particularly in the maintenance of religion, which certainly presents itself in history not merely as an intuition of the individual, but as a social tradition.[1] And these books will satisfy most men on two points—that, on the one hand, authority must play a great and even predominant part in the maintenance of society, and of the heritage of truth in general, and of religion in particular, so that it is folly to seek to disparage authority on account of its errors and crimes, as if we could in any sense do without it ; but that, on the other hand, authority or tradition, alike in religion and in every other department of human life, is always liable to become conventional, one-sided, narrow, and tyrannical, and needs constant correction by the action of the individual conscience and reason, and by the voice of the prophets, awakening, discovering, protesting, and demanding revision ; also that the authority of conscience, when a man has done his best to open his conscience to the light, must be recognized at the last resort as supreme for him.[2] He "can do no other." Thus

[1] One of the best of recent books for opening our mind to the idea of authority and the questions arising therefrom is *Authority in Religion*, by J. H. Leckie (Clark, 1909). It is written from the standpoint of a Presbyterian.

[2] It will be remembered how strenuously Cardinal Newman vindicated the legitimacy of this principle by Roman Catholic

the traditionalist and the protestant, the conservative and the radical, the disciplinarian and the prophet, are each needed in the world and in the Church, and each in due measure have their gift from God.

So far, perhaps, we shall find common agreement. But this agreement on general principles in their abstract form is found to give us very little satisfaction. For it is not in the abstract region that our difficulties lie, but in their particular application, whether what is in question is authority constraining us to action or authority constraining us to belief.

Thus, for example, Greek literature has left us two classical pictures of incomparable power, the one of obedience, the other of disobedience to the authority of the state or ruler, both of which command our almost unhesitating admiration. The one is Plato's picture of Socrates, in the *Crito*, in prison and under unjust sentence of immediate death, earnestly implored by a venerable friend to avail himself at the last minute of an opportunity of escape, and steadfastly refusing, because, though the State is just now doing him wrong, yet it is his parent and his master, and he has entered into a covenant of obedience to it, and he will not meet wrong with wrong or break his covenant to save his life. The other is Sophocles' picture of Antigone protesting in face of the Ruler that she ought to obey God rather than man—the law of the gods which bids her bury her brother rather than the command of man which prohibits it. I say we give a whole-hearted assent both to Socrates' refusal of disobedience and Antigone's refusal of obedience to the normal authority. But we still find ourselves tortured and unenlightened, in particular cases, where the diffi-

standards in his *Letter to the Duke of Norfolk*, pp. 55–66 (Pickering, 1875), ending up with the words, "Certainly, if I am obliged to bring religion into after-dinner toasts . . . I shall drink—to the Pope, if you please—still, to conscience first, and to the Pope afterwards."

culty is to find out which principle ought to be applied. Thus, during the history of the Tractarian or Catholic movement in the Church of England, how many a clergyman, commanded by his bishop to abstain from doing or teaching this or that, which the principles of the Church, as he has come to understand them, appear to enjoin or permit, has been tormented by the difficulty of satisfying his conscience whether *in this case* to refuse obedience to his normal ruler would be wilfulness and party spirit, or whether he must stand stoutly for the higher principle and defy his ruler, saying, like the apostles confronted by their normal ecclesiastical authorities, "We ought to obey God rather than men." The difficulty lies not in the general principles, but in their balance and application.

Again, in cases where authority is asserted in order to constrain a man to belief—when he is barely told that "the Church teaches" this or that doctrine, which his private judgement tells him is lacking in evidence, which makes no appeal to his conscience, and for which he finds no support in the New Testament—he may have no doubt about the authority of the Church in general or the duty of the individual to reverence it, but he may still want to know in what sense "the Church" can be truly said to teach this particular doctrine, and also whether the authority of the Church, whether the catholic or the local Church, is of such a nature that it has the right to express itself in this peremptory and unqualified form.

For there is, especially in discussions concerning religion, and not only among people who value the name of Catholic, a great tendency to identify authority with absolute authority. People so often seem to take it for granted that they have to choose between a state of religious anarchy and an authority which is peremptory with regard to conduct and belief alike. And so much of the talk about authority is vitiated by a lack of clearness in our ideal of authority.

I think, however, that those who believe the Christian religion to be in some real sense divine—and such belief at this stage of our argument we take for granted—will find their greatest assistance in solving the perplexing questions which arise as to the nature and limits of authority in religion, not in abstract argument, but in watching the authority of the Church as it comes into being in the prophets of the Old Testament, and as it finds its culmination and centre in our Lord and its development in the administration of the apostles and in the early and undivided Church. Of course we shall be challenged to show why the principles of the early Church should be held to be regulative for succeeding ages. For the appeal to the primitive Church appears not to be in favour to-day. We shall try to meet this challenge later on.[1] But at least in Christ and His apostles, Christians of all kinds acknowledge something formative for all ages ; and if we can note certain marked characteristics in their idea and exercise of authority we shall have gained solid ground on which to stand.

I

The authority of the Church is as old as the Church —that is to say, it goes back behind the New Testament to the Old ; and its ground is the word of the Lord. The assumption on which it is based is that God, the sovereign ruler of men, can make His mind and will known to men, and has done so through His prophets. This is the word of the Lord given in many parts and many manners, which it was the

[1] See below, chap. vii, on the theory of development as applied to Christian doctrine and institutions, and chap. viii on the authority of Scripture; cf. pp. 345–6.

function of the Church of the Old Covenant to keep in memory and to obey, and of the authorities of the Church to uphold and interpret. "What was the advantage of the Jew (over the Gentile)? Much every way. First, that to them were intrusted the oracles of God." [1] And this self-revelation of God was essentially dogmatic; that is to say, it was presented not by way of argument or as a conclusion of reasoning, but as the word of God, not to be gainsaid.

And the next point that we notice about it is that it was primarily moral—a challenge to the *conscience* of men and a strict requirement that they should conform their life, social and individual, to its demands. It involved indeed intellectual propositions about God—as that there was only one God, one object of worship, one almighty creator and sustainer of all that is, and one ultimate judge of all rational beings; and that this one God has moral character—that He is righteous and good—in such sense that no ritual service of Him has in His sight any value whatever, if it be not also moral service—the conformity of human life to His justice, goodness, purity, and truth. It involved also certain propositions about man's nature—as that he is a free and responsible being; and that he is sinful and needs to be redeemed; and certain propositions concerning the purpose of God—as that He has a glorious purpose for men which is ultimately to find world-wide accomplishment, but which at present has Israel for its channel and lays upon them special privileges and special obligations.[2] These dogmas are constantly

[1] Rom. iii. 1, 2.

[2] It is very well worthy of notice that these fundamental doctrines, which are implied in the message of God to Israel and which pass from Israel to the Catholic Church, are, intellectually speaking, the most difficult dogmas. I cannot doubt that so long as men continue to believe that God is one and the Creator of all that is, and that God is love, and that man is really free and responsible, they will not in the long run find much difficulty about what are called the "specifically Christian" doctrines. On the contrary,

and more and more clearly implied in the progressive self-revelation of God in the Old Testament. Nevertheless they are always given by way of supplying the motive for what remains the primary appeal—the appeal to men to live a certain kind of life and to conform their private and common conduct to a certain moral requirement.

All this "word of God" our Lord, when He came "not to destroy, but to fulfil," accepts and takes for granted, and makes it the foundation on which He builds. Accordingly He accepts and recognizes the authority of the ancient Church of which He was a member. He is even recorded to have said, "The scribes and Pharisees sit in Moses' seat: all things therefore whatsoever they bid you, these do and observe: but do not ye after their works; for they say, and do not."[1] Nevertheless, His recognition of the authority of the contemporary Church—and the recognition of it which He claimed from His disciples—was very far from being unconditional. He revised the substance of the old law; and that He alone could do—that was not within the competence of the successors of Moses. But what they ought to have attended to was that their authority reposed upon "the word of God," and ought to have been kept true to its norm. In their precepts about the Sabbath, and their religious requirements generally,[2] they had forgotten its great principles. In their zeal for detail, and for the maintenance of their own

the dogmas of the Incarnation, the Atonement, the Holy Trinity, the Church, the sacraments, and life eternal are really the necessary intellectual corollaries, supports, and justifications of the fundamental doctrines that we inherit from Israel. It is very suggestive that St. Peter should describe the purpose of the atoning death and resurrection of Christ as being "that your faith and hope might be in God" (1 Pet. i. 21). The most important articles of faith must not be confused with those that have been most disputed, or the subject of ecclesiastical definitions.

[1] Matt. xxiii. 2, 3. This saying, as reported, must be interpreted in the light of xv. 1–14.

[2] See Matt. xii. 1–13, xv. 1–14.

dignity, they had neglected "the weightier matters of the law, judgement, mercy, and faith." They had made the word of God of none effect by their tradition. They had looked to precedent and not to moral principle. It is for this reason that they fell under His scathing condemnation.

I cannot but think that in Christian history the maintenance of ecclesiastical authority has in general given very much less attention than was its due to our Lord's startling attitude towards the existing ecclesiastical authority, the legitimacy of which He recognized. It is not merely that He criticizes the lives of the persons who hold the authority. It is that He criticizes the nature of the authority they thought it their business to exercise—they ignored the ground of all true authority in the word of God, which is above all else the expression of a moral will. Certainly Christ re-established in the renewed Israel which is the Church the legislative and judicial authority which He criticized, and entrusted it afresh to constituted officers, and gave it a fresh spiritual sanction. These points have been argued already. No doubt also He promised to be with His Church all the days and endowed it with the Spirit, so that the first council of the Church dared to ascribe its decision to the Holy Spirit co-operating with them. But I see nowhere any ground for believing that the officers under the New Covenant would be protected from error, if they should behave like the officers of the Old.[1]

But let us advance from the Old Covenant to the New. The Inaugurator of the New Covenant speaks with more than prophetic authority. Sometimes indeed He argued; and we shall come back upon our Lord's use of argument. But in the main certainly He did not argue. He affirmed as one who

[1] See, on the infallibility of the Church, the Appended Note, p. 205.

had a right to affirm infallibly. Sometimes, as we shall see, He gave men glimpses into divine mysteries which became the basis of Church doctrines. But there can be no question that in the main His teaching was moral. He presented a way of life to men's hearts and wills. The critical matter in His eyes is the opening of their hearts to the light and the surrender of their wills to obey. The constant assumption is that "he that willeth to do God's will, shall know of the teaching, whether it be of God." [1]

Thus when the Church of the New Covenant went out into the world, the first name for it was "The Way." [2] Its primary function was to exhibit among men a new way of life—a new kind of fellowship with God realized in a new kind of fellowship of men. People talk disparagingly of a "merely ethical gospel," and contrast it with the Gospel of the New Testament. Quite rightly. The new law for the Church was warmed and inspired by a gospel about God and redemption—about Father and Son and Spirit—which made it something very different from a mere code of ethics. But nevertheless it was primarily as a way of life to be lived by a community, claiming to be both the true Israel and the New Humanity, that the religion of Christ went out into the world and converted men. The bulk of the New Testament is ethical teaching. It describes and enforces "the Way." Even in the most doctrinal epistles this will be found to be surprisingly true.[3]

Now, this primacy of the moral appeal in the message of the Church has been lamentably forgotten or its nature lamentably distorted. I suppose it was on

[1] John vii. 17.

[2] See Acts ix. 2—men of *the Way*; xix. 9, 23; xxiv. 22; cf. ii. 28—the ways of life; xvi. 17—the way of salvation; Luke xx. 21—the way of God; John xiv. 6, "I am the Way"; 2 Pet. ii. 21—the way of righteousness.

[3] See Appended Note, p. 183.

the whole kept well in view so long as the Church was so unpopular a body that it cost men much to declare themselves Christians. So long the situation of the Church guaranteed the moral seriousness of its members.

But various causes combined to imperil this supremacy of the moral claim. Theological controversy, fascinating and absorbing the Greek intellect, tended to give the Church the appearance of a great society primarily claiming assent to theological propositions, precisely formulated and balanced. Also the new position of the Church as the religion of the Empire brought with it an enormous peril. Henceforth it cost men nothing to profess the Christian name. Nay, after a short interval it cost them very much to profess anything else. Hence the average standard of living in the Church declined with astonishing rapidity. The "standard of the saints" survived in religious houses and elsewhere. But the average moral level of Church membership became deplorably low—"secular and grovelling," as Frederick Denison Maurice called it. And the Church for long ages has acquiesced in this double standard: an ideal for saints and a requirement for men of the world of all classes—a minimum of conformity necessary for salvation. But it is hardly possible to imagine anything more contrary to the moral claim of our Lord than this kind of compromise on the largest scale with the spirit of the world.

Let us recall the scathing estimate of the average moral standard of English churchmen given by William Law in the opening chapters of *The Serious Call.* In particular we discern in the compromise two main surrenders to the spirit of the world: first, that it recognized a distinction between disreputable sins, which are offensive to society, and respectable sins, which must be taken for granted, such as pride, love of money, exclusiveness, and uncharitableness ; whereas in our Lord's eyes the latter are at least as incompatible with the Kingdom of God as fornication or violence. Secondly, it allowed the Christian moral aim to become a process of selfish soul-saving, and abandoned or threw into the shade the claim of brotherhood and the equal spiritual worth of all human souls—the claim of the Kingdom—which was the central motive of original Christianity. Thus the vast organization of modern industrial society grew up—almost without protest from the Church—on a basis which can only be described as frankly anti-Christian, and the accepted relations of nations, in what still called itself Christendom, hardly retained a trace of Christian principle.[1]

The seriousness of this declension in the moral standard and witness of Christendom it is impossible to exaggerate. But I think the situation in the world of to-day gives the Church an opportunity of repentance and constitutes a call of almost unexampled urgency. The tendencies of contemporary thought and feeling are largely anti-Christian ; and the hostility is almost more marked towards the Christian moral standards than towards its theology. On the other hand, a very large number of the best people of all classes are feeling that nothing can save our civilization or their own souls except those very principles of self-control and brotherhood for which Christianity stands. Thus I believe that the most pressing call upon the Church to-day is to remember that its authority and mission rest simply upon the word of God, and that this is first of all the challenge to a new life—a difficult but glorious life. It is called to direct its chief attention to making the Christian doctrine of the Kingdom of God again understood,

[1] What is here very briefly sketched is treated at greater length in an " Essex Hall Lecture "—*Christianity Applied to the Life of Men and Nations* (Lindsey Press, 1920).

and summoning men with a fresh understanding to live the life. It will be a very difficult task. But only so can we hope to get men to understand the truth about the authority of the Church; for this doctrinal and sacramental authority is strictly relative to its moral and social mission. And only by giving this the first place in importance does there seem to me to be much hope of restoring the understanding of what the Church is for.

II

But the "word of the life"—"the life that is life indeed"[1]—with which the Church was entrusted was a message rooted in and depending upon a certain doctrine concerning God and human nature and destiny. Such doctrine is the ground and explanation of the life to be lived, alike in the Old Testament and in the New, as it has been the purpose of the volumes preceding this to show.[2] Nor could it have been otherwise. The rule of life in Buddhism, aiming as it does at an escape from life itself, is quite consistent with positive atheism or indifference to the existence of God. But the whole idea of the Christian life is that of active correspondence with a God, believed in as essentially love, and as having shown His love in the redemption of the world. The life draws its motives and its support from this theological doctrine, and could not subsist if its motives and its support were gone.

And alike in the Old Testament and the New the doctrine concerning God's will and nature is not presented as a conclusion from reasoning, but as a positive revelation and self-disclosure of God—a word of God which commends itself to the conscience of men, but is to be received in faith. There can be

[1] 1 John i. 1; 1 Tim. vi. 19.
[2] See, for instance, *Belief in Christ*, p. 315.

no question about that either in the Old Testament or the New. Thus the religion of Christ is in its very essence an authoritative religion based upon the word of God, and the Church is authoritative because it is the commissioned carrier of the message.

What we have now to do is to look a little more closely at the nature of the authority which the New Covenant claims for its message; and first at our Lord's use of authority.

Certainly our Lord teaches with authority and with the note of infallibility. He certainly regarded men as in a pitiable position if they have not trustworthy spiritual guides. They are as "sheep not having a shepherd," or "blind men led by the blind." And in training the Twelve He is training them to understand and deliver His Gospel—that is assuredly an authoritative message. In our Lord's judgement, mankind cannot do without religious authority to guide and enlighten them. Only the word of God can set them or keep them on the right way.

Also He lays great stress on the childlike temper which knows how to trust and believe. This accounts for His language about the privileged classes—for privilege generally means pride and self-sufficiency. So He saw in wealth an obstacle to belief, and also in learning. They minister to self-sufficiency. And our Lord's religion is to be a religion for common men who feel the burden of life and know their need of help and guidance. This He deliberately makes a matter of thanksgiving. "He rejoiced in the Holy Spirit, and said, I thank thee, O Father, Lord of heaven and earth, that thou didst hide these things from the wise and understanding, and didst reveal them unto babes: yea, Father; for so it was well-pleasing in thy sight." [1]

[1] Some modern critics who dispute the attribution to our Lord of this saying of Luke x. 21–2, and the addition to it in the parallel

But we must not forget who "the wise and understanding" of our Lord's day and country were. "Woe unto you lawyers!" He said, "for ye took away the key of knowledge: ye entered not in yourselves, and them that were entering in ye hindered."[1] The "wise and understanding" of our Lord's time were in fact bigoted traditionalists. If true learning means openness to the light, whencesoever it comes, certainly they were no learners. And our Lord constantly warns men against moral and intellectual obsession, and insists on the love of the light. We remember that great leaders in science, like Francis Bacon and Pasteur, have loved to insist, like our Lord, on the necessity for the childlike mind, because it is docile and free from obsession; so that we must not misunderstand our Lord's seeming depreciation of learning and wisdom. It is the wisdom of self-sufficiency that is the enemy.

We note that when our Lord argues with opponents and questioners, He shows a singular desire to stimulate thought and enquiry. As has been already remarked, we have several striking examples in His recorded arguments of His seeking to impart no positive teaching, but only to make men feel the obligation of consistency with their own professed principles.[2] And, above all, it would seem that our Lord, as conspicuously as Socrates, though by a different method, was at pains to stimulate thought in common men like the Twelve, such as are without any special education, and believed in their capacity to think freely and truly.

The word of God, which He taught, might indeed

passage of St. Matthew, are disposed to find the origin of it in Ecclus. li. This is strange. For the supposed author of the saying must have had deep powers of spiritual intuition and would hardly have gathered this depreciation of "wisdom" from a book in praise of wisdom, and the sort of wisdom of which the artisan is incapable (xxxviii. 24—xxxix. 11).

[1] Luke xi. 52.

[2] See *Belief in Christ* pp. 186 ff.

sound at first hearing paradoxical and impracticable; but He seemed to assure men that if they would listen in a candid, open-minded spirit they would "recognize the truth as a friend" by the light that was in them. We cannot imagine our Lord giving a dogmatic lesson about the Trinity or about any subject remote from the conscience and thoughts of His hearers, and forcing it upon their acceptance by a miraculous proof. When, later, the doctrine of the Trinity came to the Church, it came, as we have seen, as something which in the course of their experience had emerged into light. It became evident as a doctrine because it was the interpretation of experience. And in our Lord's teaching the faith on which He makes so profound a claim is not by any means passive acceptance, but the movement of an inward guidance towards the light.

There can be no mistake about this. Though He saw so plainly men's need of religious authority, though His nearest disciples and friends were so spiritually dull, and though He seemed to have in Himself a fount of spiritual knowledge, yet He very rarely uses the dogmatic method of imparting mysteries. People, including His disciples, are constantly asking Him plain questions, and He so rarely gave them plain answers. Sometimes He replies with another question to make them think.[1] He behaves as one who dreads to dwarf or crush the minds of His disciples by dogmatic words, and strives by every means to stimulate and develop their thinking. This is the point of His teaching by proverbs and parables, which express spiritual truth in a challenging and provoking form, never so as to satisfy a questioning spirit. It was characteristic of our Lord that He should have left His disciples to reach their own conclusion as to the secret of His person—

[1] See Luke xiii. 23, xxi. 7, John xiii. 36, xiv. 5, 22, xvi. 19; and with His adversaries, Luke xx. 2.

"Who say ye that I am?" And if Peter and John are really the authors of the Epistles which bear their names,[1] as the evidence justifies us in believing, they are certainly classical instances of plain men trained to realize the deep things of God, not in the main by dogmatic dictation, but by the leadings of a wonderful experience which a divine Teacher had helped them to interpret.

It must be admitted that there is in the Fourth Gospel more of the dogmatic method than in the Synoptists. There you have more positive and plain disclosures made by our Lord of divine mysteries, as about regeneration, and about Himself as the Christ and as the Bread of Life, and about His pre-existence. I have argued that such disclosures must have been really made in some form by our Lord, if we are to account for the confident beliefs of the Church. But as to the *manner* of our Lord's teaching, I think we cannot doubt that it is more truly represented by the Synoptists than by St. John. Nevertheless, in his Gospel also we find the complaint that He does not teach plainly enough. "How long dost thou hold us in suspense? If thou be the Christ, tell us plainly."[2]

III

We shall find the study of St. Paul's conception and use of authority give us a good deal of illumination. There is no doubt that to him the Church is simply based upon a message of authority, and the apostles and later ministers of the Church are the carriers of it. Thus he writes, "When ye received from us the word of the message, even the word of God, ye accepted it not as the word of men, but, as it is in truth, the word of God."[3] We can see a

[1] I refer to the first Epistles of Peter and John.
[2] John x. 24.
[3] 1 Thess. ii. 13.

certain change of emphasis in St. Paul's message, as, for instance, about the immediate coming of Christ. But in its main substance there is no evidence of change. He found himself entrusted with a divine message about God the Father, and His only Son, who was incarnate in the fullness of time, Jesus Christ, and lived as man, and died a sacrifice for our sins, and was raised the third day from the dead, and ascended into heaven, and is to come as the final judge in the day of the Lord; and about the Holy Spirit and the Church and the sacraments, and our resurrection. Of all this, and of the moral ideal and standard in which it was to find expression, St. Paul was set in charge. And though he was the first to give the message intellectual consistency, the elements of it were ready to his hand [1]; and, as we have seen, there appears to have been no controversy among the leaders about his interpretation or formulation of the message. This was the authoritative "tradition" or "teaching whereunto men were delivered," [2] and there was no other.

Thus there is no room to doubt that for St. Paul the basis of the mission of the Church is a message of divine authority committed to it, and especially to the apostles. There can, again, be no room to doubt his conviction that the apostles, and he among them, were endowed with disciplinary authority as rulers.[3] Also he is convinced that only by such an

[1] Such, I mean, as these: the tradition of the words of the Lord about His divine sonship (see *Belief in Christ,* pp. 86 ff.); the belief in His resurrection, ascension, etc., and in the efficacy of His sacrifice "for our sins"; the belief in the Holy Spirit, in the Church as the New Israel, in the spiritual cleansing and absolution conveyed in baptism, and the gift of the Spirit to the members of the Church conveyed in the laying on of hands; the belief concerning the eucharist conveyed in the formulated tradition; the belief in the apostolic commission and authority; the beliefs about the resurrection of the dead and judgement to come. All these materials and elements of belief were in the Church before St. Paul.

[2] Rom. vi. 17.

[3] See above, p. 68.

authoritative message could the spiritual needs of men be met. The " wise men "—Jewish or Greek—might mock at the message ; but St. Paul, like his Master, exults in the triumph of the divine folly over human wisdom. I need not quote the very familiar words. The summary of them is in the thought—" Seeing that in the wise providence of God the world through its philosophy could reach no sufficient knowledge of God, it was God's good pleasure through the preaching that the ' wise men ' mock at to save them that believe." [1]

Certainly, then, St. Paul would not have us put " the religion of the Spirit " into contrast with " the religions of authority." The primary work of the Spirit had been to inspire men to speak the word of God, and the word of God had reached finality in Jesus Christ. The religion of the Spirit was based upon this authoritative message. Moreover, the religion of the Spirit was membership in a society which had authoritative rulers. Both in matters of doctrine and in matters of conduct St. Paul would have the members of the Church recognize that they are under authority. Where he sees wilfulness and individualism, such as would break up the common life, he speaks very sharply. " We have no such custom, neither the churches of God." " What? was it from you that the word of God went forth? or came it unto you alone ? " When he sees grave sin, such as would annul the moral witness of the Church, he makes an uncompromising demand for the excommunication of the offender. " Put away from among yourselves the wicked person." Nay, he himself intervenes to do it in the name of Christ.[2] The examples shown us of the exercise of discipline are chiefly in cases of moral conduct and church practice. But where St. Paul detects a new teaching which is fundamentally destructive, as in the case

[1] 1 Cor. i. 21.

[2] 1 Cor. xi. 16, xiv. 36, and v 13.

of the Galatian Judaizers, he speaks with a like sharpness and decision. "Though we, or an angel from heaven, should preach unto you any gospel other than that which we preached unto you, let him be anathema. As we have said before, so say I now again, If any man preacheth unto you any Gospel other than that which ye received, let him be anathema."[1] St. Paul, then, is a strong authoritarian, and the "spirit of discipline" in the Pastoral Epistles is certainly no good argument against St. Paul's authorship. Nevertheless this is only half the truth.

1. To St. Paul, authoritative action is tolerable only at the last resort. He has a dread of legislation and what he calls "dogmas," that is, ordinances.[2] He would have the life in the Spirit show itself in free and loving obedience without external regulation. He dreads ordinances as leading to legalism.[3] He is also very tolerant of minor differences among Christians. One has his mind in this way and another in that. "Let each man be fully persuaded in his own mind," and let the Church learn to tolerate differences in matters which are not vital. "Receive ye one another [with all your differences], as Christ also received you."[4]

2. Moreover he is far from suggesting an opposition between faith and the free exercise of reason. There is a wisdom of the world, indeed, which stumbles at the doctrine of the Cross and can only come to naught. But when once the soul is grounded in the faith in Jesus Christ he would have it in all cases grow up into a full rational understanding. "We received . . . the Spirit which is of God; that we might know the things that are freely given to us by God." "In mind be ye grown-up men."[5] Like his Master, St. Paul has the greatest respect for the average man's intelligence if he is spiritually minded.

[1] Gal. i. 8–9. [2] Col. ii. 16–23. [3] Gal. v. 1
[4] Rom. xiv. 5–xv. 7. [5] 1 Cor. ii. 12, xiv. 20.

Nothing can be further from his mind than to praise the passive acceptance of dogma. "Quench not the spirit; despise not prophesyings; prove all things."[1] His Epistles are full of a generous attempt to make every convert in the churches of his foundation understand the mind of God and the meaning of his religion. "Teaching every man in all wisdom, that we may present every man perfect in Christ," i.e. full-grown or fully initiated. He would have a joyous sense of freedom in the truth possess the Church, and not a breath of obscurantism could blow from his quarter. "He that is spiritual judgeth all things, and he himself is judged of no man."[2]

3. He is always anxious to represent the whole body of the Church, and not only its officers, as the organ of the Spirit. It is misleading to describe the Church as St. Paul represents it as a democracy, because it is much more manifestly a theocracy.[3] It looks up for its authority to Christ and the Spirit, and it has a positive revelation which controls it. But it is true that the early churches cultivated a democratic spirit, under St. Paul's guidance. At the last resort he claims authority to declare the Gospel, and to excommunicate a scandalous moral offender, apparently even if the church will not do so for itself. But he uses all his efforts to carry the churches with him theologically, and to get all the members of the church to act together in excommunicating and in absolving.[4] He can write epistles to pastors, but almost all his correspondence is with churches. All

[1] 1 Thess. v. 19.

[2] Col. i. 28, cf. ver. 9; Phil. i. 9; Eph. i. 17 ff; 1 Cor. ii. 45.

[3] I do not say that a democracy might not be this. But if it were to believe that God had given it a divine law for its action and a divine revelation for its political guidance, it would cease to be a democracy in the ordinary sense, like the Puritan colonies in New England (see the history of *The Founding of New England*, by Truslow Adams). I mean by a democracy a society of men who believe that they have to find their way by consulting the general will and following it.

[4] So we should gather from 1 Cor. v., 2 Cor. ii. 8–11.

are to participate in the theology and in the discipline of the society; and he cultivates the representative spirit (see 1 Cor. xvi. 3–4, 2 Cor. viii. 19). And in the next generation this democratic spirit is seen in Clement's Epistle and downwards through Cyprian, though in a diminishing degree—preserved, however, in a measure in the right of the people to elect their bishops.[1]

An examination of St. John's Epistles would lead to very much the same conclusions as we have reached about St. Paul. He, too, views the Church as existing to maintain a once-for-all given standard of truth, which centres in the doctrine of the incarnation. There can be no toleration of any false teaching which contradicts this. "Let that abide in you which ye heard from the beginning. If that which ye heard from the beginning abide in you, ye also shall abide in the Son, and in the Father."[2] "Whosoever goeth onward and abideth not in the teaching of Christ, hath not God: he that abideth in the teaching, the same hath both the Father and the Son. If any man cometh unto you, and bringeth not the teaching, receive him not into your house, and give him no greeting: for he that giveth him greeting partaketh in his evil works."[3] The false teaching alluded to is apparently an early form of Gnosticism, preached by Cerinthus, which was a substantial denial of the real incarnation. What is enjoined by St. John is practical excommunication, which would no doubt have become formal. But St. John's ideal of authority, like St. Paul's, would have it encourage and guide, not suppress, active intelligence and spiritual independence. "Ye have an anointing from the Holy One, and ye know all things. . . . The anointing which ye received of him

[1] See Rackham's essay "Position of the Laity in the Early Church," in *Reform in the Church of England* (Murray).

[2] 1 John ii. 24. [3] 2 John 9.

abideth in you, and ye need not that any one teach you."[1]

Both St. John and St. Paul appear to have a robust confidence that the good man—the spiritual man—will come to a right conclusion. They do not seem to be vexed with our problem, that so many good and spiritual men, as we must judge them to be, come to what we must also judge to be the wrong conclusion.[2] They seem to assume that genuine goodness and acceptance of the truth even in this world will be found together. On the whole, we may suppose that, under our different circumstances, they would have said that good men who cannot believe, but find themselves bound to engage in active teaching of what contradicts the faith, must indeed pass out of the communion of the Church; but while in this sense the Church judges them, beyond this it must leave them to the judgement of God, who alone can make known the counsels of the heart, and who, we know, condemns only the proud will and the mind and works of darkness.

IV

When we pass out of the apostolic age into the age of the Fathers we find no change in the view of authority. The Church exists to exhibit a life and to maintain a tradition of doctrine on which the life depends. The tradition is what has been held from the beginning. The content of the tradition as given us by Origen and implied in Irenaeus is substantially the same. It is of obligation upon all Christians to accept it. "That alone is to be believed as truth which disagrees in nothing from the ecclesiastical and apostolical tradition"; but those who have the

[1] 1 John ii. 20, 27.

[2] See Dr. Pollock (Bishop of Norwich), *Good Men without Faith* (S.P.C.K.).

special gifts of wisdom and knowledge must seek to understand the reason of the things believed, the "how" and the "why."[1]

This tradition of course existed long before the canonization of the books of the New Testament; but as that canonization took place it seems to have been universally taken for granted that, while the tradition was needed to interpret the Scriptures, they, on the other hand, supplied the standard by which the doctrinal authority of the Church was limited, and by which its action was to be judged. The tradition was to be found in the Scriptures in its most authoritative form; and the principle of the Church of England, that "whatsoever is not read therein, nor may be proved thereby, is not to be required of any man, that it should be believed as an article of the faith, or be thought requisite or necessary to salvation," would, as far as we can judge, have commanded the cordial assent of the Fathers. Thus while in matters of discipline the Church could act freely, and give injunctions of binding force as circumstances required on its own authority, in matters of faith it could do nothing except declare and defend what had been held from the beginning. This is an exceedingly important principle, and it is the best safeguard against the tyranny of authority.

St. Athanasius states the matter very plainly in speaking about the Council of Nicaea, noting the difference in the formula used by the Council when settling the Paschal controversy and that used by them with regard to the question of faith. "With reference to Easter," he says, "such and such things were determined, and at such a date, for at that time it was determined that all should obey a certain rule; but with reference to the faith they wrote not 'such and such things were determined,' but 'thus the Catholic Church believes.' And they

[1] Origen, *de Princip.*, lib. i, Praef. 2, 3.

added immediately the statement of their faith, to show that their judgement was not new but apostolic, and that what they wrote was not any discovery of theirs, but was what the apostles taught." Elsewhere he insists that "in the Holy Scriptures alone is the instruction of religion announced—to which let no man add, from which let no man detract—which are sufficient in themselves for the enunciation of the truth." He also would have us recognize that a "point of view" is necessary in reading and interpreting Scripture, and this point of view should be the mind of the Church. But he would not have demurred to his contemporary, Cyril of Jerusalem, saying to his catechumens, "Do not believe me simply, unless you receive from Holy Scripture the proof of what I say"; "Keep that faith only which the Church is now giving you, and which is certificated out of the whole of Scripture." [1]

In a previous volume I have given reasons for thinking that the doctrinal definitions of the ecumenical councils were really justified by the necessities of defending the faith as St. Paul and

[1] Athan., *de Synodis* 5, *adv. Gentes* init., and *Fragm. Fest. Ep.* xxxix; Cyril, *Catech.*, iv, 17, 33, v, 12. I have given other quotations and references in *Roman Catholic Claims*, chaps. iii and iv (Longmans). Dr. Mason says: "I do not know of one article of belief which is asserted by the Fathers to be derived from tradition outside of the canon of Scripture." I have never seen even one passage in any of the Fathers which contradicts this. There is a passage in St. Basil, *de Spir. Sanct.*, cap. xxvii, § 66, which looks as if it were going to; but when he comes to specify the "dogmata" which are derived from unwritten tradition, they are all *customs* or ritual forms—signing the cross, turning to the east, ceremonies of baptism, the form of the Creed. And as to matters of faith he makes the usual statement in *de Fide*, c. 1. "It is a manifest falling from the faith, and a proof of arrogancy, either to reject any of those things that are written, or to bring in any of those things that are not written." There is a passage in St. Chrysostom's *Hom.* iv in 2 Thess. (on 2 Thess. ii. 2) in which he says tradition is enough without Scripture. But it is a very brief passage which demands elucidation. And without contradicting his usual and plainly expressed teaching, he could not mean to affirm this of truths of the faith.

St. John expounded it.[1] And something more will be said about this when we come to speak about the development of doctrine ; but we should notice that, at least in the beginning, the Church cannot be charged with any love of dogmatizing. They believed that their duty of maintaining the ground of faith forced them to frame these conciliar definitions. Knowing all that we know about the blessing which the dogmatic formulas have proved, we may be loath to call them " necessary evils " ; but that phrase does not misrepresent the mind of the fourth-century Church towards them. And the theologians accepted very gladly the limitation on the action of authority involved in the appeal to Scripture. Indeed it is most noticeable how little in days of very sharp controversy the Fathers refer to the then recent dogmatic decisions, as if they of themselves sufficed to settle the matter and no more need be said. Athanasius in particular in his voluminous writings about Arianism rarely mentions the action of the Council of Nicaea. All his argument is out of Scripture ; and the same may be said for most of the Fathers. Their canons of interpreting Scripture are not indeed always ours, and their arguments on particular texts we often cannot accept. But on the whole, I contend, they were profoundly right. The Arian, or the Apollinarian, or the " Nestorian," or the Monophysite Christ is certainly not the Christ of the New Testament ; and the Christ of the Nicene Creed is. And no one who recognizes how often the tendency of theological feeling and speculation inside the Church lay in a Monophysite direction, or at least in the direction of explaining away our Lord's real humanity, can fail to feel that the balancing and impartial action of the Councils, putting equal emphasis on the complete reality of both His Godhead and His manhood, suggests, in

[1] *Belief in Christ*, pp. 217–22.

spite of all the human infirmities which the history of the Councils shows in painful evidence, a real action of the Holy Spirit guiding the common mind of the Church.

The authority of the Church, then, was conceived of as a strictly limited authority; and as in the New Testament, it is an authority which seeks to stimulate and guide, not to drug or to suppress the judgement of the mass of churchmen. No doubt the victory of orthodoxy, as it came to be accepted, was due in great part to the insight of individual theologians and bishops, like St. Athanasius and St. Cyril and St. Leo. But the action of the mass of the bishops at least in the East was so vacillating and uncertain through long years of controversy, that it was truly remarked that the victory was won over the bishops by the steadfastness of the laity. And certainly the theologians and preachers of the fourth century did their best to make them understand the nature of the issue. They show the same robust faith as St. Paul and St. John in the capacity of the ordinary man for the understanding of his creed. Their popular sermons as well as their theological writings are one long appeal to reason and to Scripture, while even the mention of the authority of the dogmatic decisions is rare. Certainly they regard it as the function of authority to stimulate enquiry, and not suppress it.

One other point deserves notice. The man of an enquiring mind would have found in the early Church a very liberal temper of toleration. From time to time an overbold spirit backed by a strenuous will might promulgate some theory which was felt to be so destructive of the foundations of the Christian faith that the Church was called upon to condemn it as heretical. And certainly the opinions condemned as heresies were very capital heresies. But meanwhile the school of Alexandria in the third century was producing a type of theology very different in tone from that of the Africans ; and the difference of tone showed itself in opinions surprisingly different—for instance, about the destiny of the lost, or the meaning of the body of Christ in the eucharist. Later, Alexandria and Antioch and Africa and Rome nourished very distinctive types of doctrine among theologians who were pillars of orthodoxy, and differences of opinion are sometimes marked. We notice that Jerome and Augustine, of whom we should not have expected it, frankly approve such tolerance of differences. Thus they recall an occasion, very well known in history, when Rome, represented by Stephen, its bishop, affirmed the validity of baptism administered by heretics, while Africa, headed by Cyprian, with other churches, vehemently denied it ; but while Rome would have excommunicated those who held and acted upon the latter opinion, Cyprian and his friends declined to contemplate any such course. They demanded toleration—*salvo jure communionis diversa sentire.* And, though this involved on their side the acceptance as members of the Christian Church of persons who, in their theory, had never really been baptized, still Cyprian was ready to insist on mutual respect between rival traditions. And Jerome and Augustine recall all this " perseverantissima tolerantia " with emphatic commendation. " All these," writes Augustine, " Catholic unity embraces in her motherly breast, bearing each others' burdens in turn, and endeavouring to keep the unity of the Spirit in the bond of peace, until the Lord should reveal to one or the other of them, if in any point they think otherwise than as they should." [1] Thus I say the lover of freedom in the Church of the first four

[1] For Cyprian, see *Dict. of Christ. Biog.*, where quotations are collected. For Augustine, see *de Bapt.*, ii, 3–6. For Jerome, *adv. Lucif.*, 25. The matter is treated at rather greater length in *Roman Catholic Claims*, chap. viii, pp. 134 f.

centuries, though he would have found certain broad limits laid down, in passing beyond which he would pass out of the communion of the Church, would have been left with plenty of room to move within those limits and no prevailing desire to curtail his liberty.

No doubt there was another note heard from time to time which was destined to prevail especially in the West. Thus while Origen would find in the tradition a stimulus to free enquiry, Tertullian lays it down that belief in Christ and acceptance of the Gospel brings curiosity and enquiry to an end. "All the delay of seeking and finding thou hast terminated by believing."[1] The enquiring mind is apparently to be quenched. Belief should exclude enquiry. Two centuries later, when papal authority was rapidly developing, we find Innocent I, occupied with the case of Pelagius, speaking of the "secret treasury" (*arcana*) of divine truth, which apparently renders the Roman pontiff an oracle from which other bishops must receive decisions as certainly divine.[2] Here is a conception of a central shrine of divine truth which can act rapidly to determine controversies—in startling contrast to the notion of a diffused tradition which must be collected from all the churches; and can only laboriously find full expression by the cumbrous machinery of a General Council; and must then wait for the general reception of the Council before its title to ecumenical authority can be recognized; and must further be prepared to stand the challenge of an appeal to Scripture. Here is a contrast suggested, pregnant with very important consequences, and calculated to raise the question whether the authority provided by Christ

[1] *De Praescr.*, cc. 7–10.

[2] *Ep.* xxx, *ad Numid.*, *P.L.*, xx, 582 ff. In the Breviary, lesson vi for the festival of the Immaculate Conception, the dogma is said to have been proclaimed by Pius IX, "supremo suo et infallibili oraculo."

for His Church is a rapid and peremptory authority, a living voice of God, capable of perpetual disclosures and decisions, or the slow-moving authority of a diffused corporate witness to a voice once uttered, living indeed in power and application, but in substance final and never to be repeated. And, once more, half a century later, we find Leo the Great asserting that "the faith which is one and simple does not admit of variety"—the sort of utterance which represents a passion for uniformity, as thorough as possible. Such utterances, though they tend to different points, are alike one another in expressing a spirit which was to fashion an ideal of authority widely different from that which we have been considering. It is the Romanist and especially the Jesuit ideal. And we must proceed to consider it. On the other hand, we shall have also to take account of the ideal of authority which, by reaction from Rome, established itself as Protestant orthodoxy, showing itself sometimes in a form as autocratic and absolute as papalism, but grounding its authority on the Bible and the Bible only, and making Christianity the religion of the book. These developments will occupy us in the next three chapters. But we must pause, before going forward, to summarize the kind of conclusion about the nature of the authority of the Church which we have gathered from the New Testament and the records of the early centuries of the Church's life, especially under the influence of the Greek Fathers.

First, then, we found that the Church inherited from the prophets and from the Lord the sense that true religion is a life to be lived. The stress is on "the way"—the way of holiness and brotherhood. And there is nothing secret about it. It is to be lived in the eyes of men, and it is by the witness of the life that men are to be won for the truth. So the Lord had said, "Ye are the salt of the earth. . . .

Ye are the light of the world. A city set on a hill cannot be hid. . . . Let your light shine before men, that they may see your good works, and glorify your Father which is in heaven."

Dr. Brightman [1] has recently given us a singularly careful account of the instruction given to catechumens in the early centuries of the Church and of the moral discipline into which they were initiated. The required abstinence from idolatry, from bloodshedding, and from fornication closed to the Christian many professions, and when he was admitted to instruction he was not left in any doubt as to the meaning of 'the way.' And so long as professing the Christian name was a dangerous adventure, there is no doubt that our Lord's great words about the function of the Church were on the whole richly fulfilled. The salt did not lose its savour. As has been said already, the meaning of Church authority in doctrinal matters can never be understood till it is the life and not the doctrine which is put into the first place.

2. But the life is based upon a word or message of God; and the message declares not only the life which is to be lived, but also the reasons for living it. It is a message about God and His redemptive acts, and about the nature and destiny of man, and about the divine provision made for realizing the good life. And all this has come to men not as a conclusion of their own reasoning, but as a revelation from God—a divine self-disclosure; and of this authoritative message or word of God the Church is set in charge; and the convert won to the Church and desiring to live "the life which is life indeed" must accept the message in childlike faith, not as the word of men but as the word of God—on authority.

3. But authority is of many different kinds.

[1] See his essay on "Terms of Communion" in *The Early History of the Church and Ministry,*" pp. 320 ff.

There is the authority of the despot which seeks to subdue and to crush ; and there is the authority of a parent which seeks to quicken and to educate. And the authority of the Church should be of the latter kind. We took note how the infallible Master was exceedingly reserved in dogmatic teaching. He did indeed ask for whole-hearted self-devotion and faith in Himself and His word, and He could take for granted the faith of the Jew in the true God and in human destiny. But for the rest He plainly meant His disciples to learn for themselves from their experience of Him and to catch the truth from hints and parables. He certainly was not a teacher who thought that the best way for men was to have a plain statement of truth dictated to them on authority and a plain answer given to their questions.

Circumstances were changed after His death and resurrection and the coming of the Spirit. Thenceforth the Name of God has become the Name of the Father and of the Son and of the Holy Spirit ; and the incarnation of the Son and His sacrificial death and His glory and future coming, and the ministry of the Spirit in the Church, and the purpose of the sacraments—all this, as the background of " the word of life," constituted the Gospel which the Church was to deliver. It was the word of God ; and though, it may be, the only profession at first asked of the converts was the profession that " Jesus is Lord," yet in fact we find that St. Paul presupposes a full acquaintance with the Gospel in those he writes to. They had all been instructed in these articles of the faith. And St. Paul is fully conscious that this faith must be maintained, and at the last resort he is ready to say of anyone who would undermine it, " Let him be anathema " ; nevertheless, as we have seen, with St. Paul too the main stress is on the life to be lived, and on the faith which surrenders itself to God in Christ, and on reliance in the power and guidance of the Spirit. His conception of authority plainly disposes him to encourage liberty and to make light of differences which do not break the fellowship or undermine the faith. And he means belief to grow into understanding; and he seeks the co-operation of all the members of the Church in the fulfilment of a common vocation. He would have authority quicken and stimulate thought and liberate action; and he is afraid of "ordinances" as tending to legalism.

And we caught the note of the same spirit in the early Church, especially under the influence of the Greek Fathers. They conceive of the doctrinal authority of the Church as a restricted thing—restricted by Scripture. If it has to lay down dogmatic limits, they must be justified by the necessity for defending the central faith. And their Church was a broad Church which tolerated many differences of minor belief and varieties of practice. And intellectually life in the Church was a highly stimulating atmosphere in which enquiry was not quenched and there was plenty of room to move. So it was down at least to the fifth century. The Church says to the convert, You must accept the message as the word of God on faith; but your faith should grow into understanding. It will make you intellectually as well as morally free.

If this be the true method, it has two enemies. The first is the temper which treats all acceptance of truth on authority as degrading; and in particular appears to deprecate in religion the very idea of a divine word to be received in faith—a divine message such as can be expressed in true propositions and embodied in historic facts. It would apparently interpret intellectual liberty to mean that each man must start for himself to discover what he can about God and human destiny. No doubt the excessive dogmatism of the Church, especially at certain periods, has stimulated such a temper by reaction. But if Christianity is to mean anything at all resembling what it meant at the beginning and has meant in history, it must be rooted and grounded in the recognition of a word of God to be received in faith by all alike with the trustfulness of a child. Knowing what we know about the eccentricity of the human mind, we know that only the recognition of the authority of revelation could have generated a coherent Church.

And the principle of authority must be recognized as lying at the root of all stable human progress. Plato and Hegel may over-emphasize authority and underrate initiative. But they are great masters of education. They are surely right in recognizing that there is a heritage of truth, theoretical and practical, which each generation of children must begin by accepting in faith. Reverence, as Goethe was fond of pointing out, is the first quality requisite for learning. The power of mental initiative, the power of original contribution, which each individual has in him and which it is the function of education to liberate, is strengthened, not weakened, by reverent docility at the start. Hegel was right, I think, in saying to his youthful students that they would injure their capacity for original thinking by premature criticism. In the world of religion in our day it is both ludicrous and lamentable to see how men and women go utterly astray because they give themselves freely to the criticism of religion without any serious attempt to ascertain what, in its best form and as a coherent whole, that religion means. The first requisite is concentration of mind to receive and appreciate and use. The most fruitful criticism is based upon the sympathetic understanding which can only come from within the faith.

Nevertheless, the best evidence that the message of the Church is really the word of God lies in its being able to liberate and satisfy the reason which is God's original gift to man.

Thus the other enemy of true authority is that conception of it which identifies it with absolutism and faith with passive acceptance, which would find the essential mark of authority in its peremptoriness and declare that faith is the enemy and not the mother of free enquiry and criticism. And it is to this kind of authoritarianism that we must now turn our attention.

APPENDED NOTE (see p. 158)

THE TEACHING OF THE EPISTLES PRIMARILY MORAL

No one could doubt this in the case of the Epistles of Peter and James; nor in those of St. John, though he insists on the coherence of character and creed. We constantly are exhorted to strenuousness in defending the Creed by the words of St. Jude, " Exhorting you to contend earnestly for the faith once for all delivered to the saints "; but we have to notice that the contents of his epistle would lead us to believe that the internal foes whom he summons men to resist are enemies of Christian moral principle, rather than devisers of new doctrine. And I think it is true to say that St. Paul's strenuousness in maintaining doctrine is always conditioned very definitely by its bearing on the life of the Church, social and individual. There is very little speculative interest in theology to be found in St. Paul. He is quite content to recognize that intellectually we " know in part," " we see but in a mirror or a riddle "; but we know enough for the practical needs of the life to be lived. The life is the primary aim of the Gospel. To recognize this is not to depreciate dogma, but to appreciate it.

CHAPTER VI

AUTHORITY IN ROMAN THEORY

We have been looking attentively at the idea of authority as we find it in the Church of the early centuries, and especially in that part of it which spoke Greek; and we have noted especially two of its characteristics. First, that it is a strictly limited authority, limited especially by the appeal to Scripture—nothing, it appears, is to be promulgated either in substance contrary to or beyond " what is written." Secondly, that authority was not thought of as suppressing enquiry, but as encouraging it, even within the region of its own decisions. The appeal is constantly to the " open Bible " and to reason.

But no one can take a general survey of Church history without becoming conscious that a very much more unrestricted and peremptory conception of authority has become prevalent, particularly within the wide scope of the Roman communion, and still more particularly under the influence of the society which since the beginning of the Counter-Reformation has so largely moulded the Roman Church—the Society of Jesus. It is to this idea of authority that we must now pay attention.

Those who maintain this conception would not, I suppose, demur to our putting forward the life to be lived as the primary purpose of the dogmatic message, though in fact they have tended to present the life as a matter of individual conduct to be rewarded with salvation in another world, to an extent which seriously distorts the original Christian idea of " the life " and the " way " ; but they would contend that the more absolute the dogmatic law—the more completely it is placed aloft beyond criticism or discussion—the more easily and quickly can the individual devote himself to the practical saving of his soul. I do not want to forget this argument. I know how much it impresses many in our generation, wearied with constant discussions and contradictions in the world of contemporary religion. I remember how much one in the last generation whom many of us regarded with great veneration—Richard Holt Hutton, of *The Spectator*—used to feel it. He could not accept the Roman claim. Yet he used to press upon us Anglicans his sense that no type of religion was so successful as the Roman in providing a steadfast and tranquil background for the spiritual life. And we have read lately a good many lives of Frenchmen of intellectual distinction—Charles de Foucauld was only the last of many—who have passed almost at a bound from intellectual and moral licence to a totally uncritical acceptance of Roman authority in its extremest form, and therein found their peace.[1]

I

With this plea in mind, then, let us understand the idea. Briefly, it is that one who is outside the Church, and is yet conscious of its attraction, should exercise his free and critical judgement upon its claim until he is convinced of its divine mission, but that free enquiry is only legitimate up to the threshold of faith. The basis of faith once gained and the act of faith once made, reason, in the sense of the critical judgement, must, within the sphere of what is of faith, abdicate. You cannot criticize God's word without impiety! And while this

[1] I return to this plea for the spiritual value of absolutism below, pp. 225 ff.

abdication is required of any person converted from outside from the moment of his conversion,[1] one brought up in the faith should throughout maintain this critically passive attitude of mind. For the dogma of the Church entrusted to the hierarchy is God's word. The hierarchy is the *ecclesia docens.* And the attitude of the body of the faithful, the *ecclesia discens*, must be that of unquestioning acceptance. The famous rule of St. Ignatius of Loyola, the founder of the Jesuits, "To make sure of being right in all things, we ought always to hold by the principle that the white which I see I would believe to be black if the hierarchical Church were so to rule it"[2]—was seriously framed and must be taken seriously.

I hope and I suppose that there are many Roman Catholics who would not assent to this idea of faith as blindly submissive. Indeed, the principle of which I have quoted an expression from Father Woodlock is opposed to that of the great Schoolmen, as I shall seek to indicate. But it appears to be the prevalent principle in the Roman communion to-day. It is the same principle which lies behind the familiar Roman Catholic statement that all declared articles of faith present the same claim of certainty, and that "the infallibility of the Pope and the Godhead of Christ rest exactly on the same authority."[3] The same proposition would of course

[1] Cf. Fr. Woodlock, S.J., *Constantinople, Canterbury, and Rome*, p. 3 (Longmans): "The Catholic theory of the use of the reason in religion is this. A man uses his reason, his private judgement, to reach the Church as the mouthpiece of God's message. Once that is found, he uses his reason, not to criticize and reject, but to understand and assimilate what doctrinal authority proposes to him as God's truth."

[2] I have taken the translation from Father Rickaby's most useful edition of the *Spiritual Exercises*, p. 223 (Burns & Oates).

[3] I am glad to read the Rev. Father Al. Janssens' criticism of this statement, quoted in Viscount Halifax's *Further Considerations*, p. 58 (Mowbray). But it is certainly commonly made by Roman divines in England.

be maintained about the immaculate conception of Mary and the resurrection of our Lord. It means that the basis of faith is the absolute authority of the Church, irrespective of every appeal to the evidence of history or of tradition. I will cite a popular statement recently reported from a Roman Catholic mission in Birmingham as an instance of this claim of *absolute* authority:

> "The Roman Catholic Church claimed absolute exclusive truth; she dared to say that all the others were wrong. Did the Catholic or the Protestant Churches make the truth quite clear? The Protestant Churches obviously did not. . . . Three hundred millions, people of every nation, would affirm that the Catholic Church made the truth quite clear. They would say, 'Our Holy Mother, the Catholic Church, by the living voice of St. Peter and his successors, gifted with infallible utterance by Christ Himself, speaks clearly to each of us the absolute truth of God. That living voice never wavers, never quibbles, never hesitates. It cannot; for it is the voice of the God of Absolute Truth, speaking through His chosen instrument, the One, Holy, Catholic, and Apostolic Church.'" [1]

I quote this popular statement because it srtikes the sort of note with which we are made familiar in England.

Now, how do we stand in face of this claim that we must regard the teaching authority of the Church as peremptory and without appeal, and in face of the plea that this sort of authority best suits human nature? We have recognized to the full that the religion of Christ is for all men and not specially for learned men; and certainly the mass of men have neither the leisure nor the knowledge requisite for submitting

[1] A statement by the Rev. Owen Francis Dudley, "of the Roman Catholic Missionary Society," quoted from a Birmingham evening paper of November 5, 1923.

the teaching of the Church to critical and historical verification. If they too can pass from simply accepting the faith on authority to personal conviction, it must be in the main by a process of moral verification—verification in life and spiritual experience. But the gift of "wisdom" and the gift of "knowledge" are among the gifts of the Spirit of God, as well as the gift of "faith."[1] They constitute the vocation of the scholar—and that must be recognized in the Church, not for his own sake only, but for the sake of the whole body.

Surely nothing is more certain in history generally, and in Church history in particular, than that every tradition, entrusted to an authoritative body, tends, if left to itself, to deteriorate under the pressure of popular demands and for lack of self-criticism in the teaching body. So the authoritative teaching in Israel had deteriorated when our Lord came on earth. And as has been noted, there is no reason to believe that the Church of the New Covenant was exempted from this peril any more than the Church of the Old. It had no divine guarantee given to it which can be interpreted as meaning that it could neglect the means of self-enlightenment and still be secure against mistake.[2] What is needed is the free action within the body of the Church of the spirit of wisdom and the spirit of knowledge; and to secure that is the vocation of the scholar.

And the vocation of a scholar requires that he should think freely. It is mocking him to tell him to investigate and form judgements of truth, and at the same time to dictate to him what those judgements are to be. He must be free to go where the argument, duly weighed, leads him. It is all the better that he should be saturated from his childhood upwards in the Church tradition, or, if not that,

[1] 1 Cor. xii. 8, 9.

[2] See Appended Note A on the Infallibility of the Church, p. 205.

should at least have had time to learn by experience within the Church the meaning of its creed and worship and sacraments. It is only from within, or by a rare gift of sympathy from without, that the real meaning of any institution or tradition can be learned. The devout Catholic need be no more prejudiced, in the false sense, than the rationalist. But he must be prepared to receive light from every quarter, however hostile, and to follow the light. He must not "reason in fetters." The test of the truth of the tradition is that it can bear the whole light. If his thought leads him plainly and finally outside the Christian Creed, of course he must cease to hold the office of a Church teacher. Freedom for thinking has no connexion with freedom to violate one's engagements. He must no doubt take the risk of such an event. Anyway, the Church must sanction free enquiry—praying earnestly for its scholars that their faith fail not. If such freedom is refused inside the Church, it will assert itself outside; and that way lies revolution or schism.

In the days of the Fathers, from Origen to Augustine, the world of intellect was dominated in the main by a phase of Platonic philosophy. And into this world of philosophy the leaders of Christian thought advanced with bold freedom, and, on the whole, successfully established a synthesis between the tradition and the higher thought of their age. When in the dawn of the Renaissance[1] a revived Aristotelianism seemed so threatening to faith that there were those who, like the great St. Bernard,

[1] In the really dark age—which intervened between the age of the Fathers, when the spirit of Greek philosophy still lived on, and the intellectual renaissance of the twelfth and thirteenth centuries—there is a tendency, alien to what is to be found in the Fathers, to regard the intellect with something more than suspicion. Thus in the controversy with Berengar the belief in transubstantiation, not yet modified by the Schoolmen, is glorified for its irrationality. The more the faith violates the testimony of the senses, the more merit it has. See *Dissert.*, p. 260.

denounced the new logic as impious, nevertheless the liberty of reason asserted itself again, and a new synthesis established itself of which St. Thomas Aquinas was the master-builder.

There were differences between the positions maintained by different founders of scholasticism. St. Anselm, for example, following Scotus Erigena, seems to claim that everything that is believed on authority can be established on an independent basis by the reason. He gives this full interpretation to *Credo ut intelligam.* But St. Thomas is much more cautious.[1] He recognizes that reason cannot demonstrate (for example) the truth that God is the absolute Creator or the truth of Trinity in Unity; but reason can show the necessity for God's self-revelation, and recognize its reality; and while revelation must needs cover the ground of reason and transcend it, it must not contradict it; nay, more, reason should find within its own materials intimations, at least, of what is revealed. Thus revelation must satisfy reason.[2] There were then differences between the founders of scholasticism. But all were agreed upon the position that the dogma of the Church was not an obstruction to the free action of the reason, but a stimulus to it, and that revealed truth cannot be contrary to the conclusions of reason.

But neither the Fathers nor the Schoolmen had to face an intellectual world in which empirical science and historical criticism had become the dominant factors. The great St. Thomas, for example, in his treatment of his authorities is utterly uncritical. He appears to have no sense of what historical criticism

[1] See the admirable work of Dr. Philip Wicksteed, *Reactions between Dogma and Philosophy,* illustrated from the works of St. Thomas Aq., capp. i, ii (Williams & Norgate, 1920).

[2] See Appended Note, p. 334, on the Rationality of the Christian Belief in God.

means.[1] And to bring the faith to be at home in our modern intellectual world may be a harder task even than that set to Fathers and Schoolmen. Nevertheless, it is the task that is set us, if we believe the faith to be the truth. And there is no way to effect a new synthesis of faith and knowledge except by thought and examination which are both Christian and free. And this is for the sake of all. Not only is it the only way to avoid, or to recover from, a disastrous divorce between religion and knowledge; but it is also needed for the sake of the average man and woman. Half the attendants at our churches to-day are enfeebled in the spiritual life because they entertain a suspicion that what they hear from the pulpit is not true and will not bear sifting. Nothing will remove this pressing uneasiness except the widely spread conviction that the scholars of the Church are facing the light and the Church is eager to learn from them. We must refuse, then, any conception of faith such as would restrict or lay in fetters the free thought of its scholars.

There is also another consideration which it is important to have in view. Part of the teaching of the Roman Church is pronounced to be *de fide.* It is infallibly defined. Such, for example, are, I believe, the dogmas of the immaculate conception of Mary

[1] It is interesting to note that when a certain *catena* of passages from the Greek Fathers, intended to convince the Greeks that they ought to submit to Rome, came into the hands of Urban IV, he submitted it to St. Thomas Aquinas. Among the passages quoted many—supposed to be from St. Chrysostom, St. Cyril, etc.—were, as all now admit, forgeries. Now Thomas was acute enough in detecting certain theological inaccuracies in some of these passages, but he was quite without the spirit of historical criticism, which would have caused him, as it caused the scholars of the Renaissance, at once to detect that the supposed testimonies to the papal monarchy were glaring forgeries. So St. Thomas incorporated these forgeries into the structure of his defence of the papal claim, and they remained there to deceive students down to Sir Thomas More. See *The Pope and the Council,* by Janus, pp. 264 f., and Denny, *Papalism,* pp. 114 ff.

and the infallibility of the Pope, and transubstantiation. All these dogmas present peculiar and, as it seems to me, insuperable difficulties to the historical student. He is accustomed in the Creed to find facts of history propounded as articles of faith—the virginal conception, and death and resurrection and ascension of Christ. But in the New Testament these facts are very studiously and insistently presented as guaranteed by sufficient testimony of competent witnesses. This is apparent in the preface to St. Luke's Gospel, and the statement of requisites for the office of the Twelve (Acts i. 21, 22), and St. Paul's statement concerning the evidence of the appearances of the risen Christ. There is nothing propounded to be believed as a fact of history except on adequate testimony. And who, one asks, can resist the testimony to our Lord's resurrection, except under the influence of that sort of rationalism which refuses the miraculous *a priori*? But here in the doctrine of the immaculate conception of Mary there is propounded to be believed as a fact by the faithful, with exactly the same confidence as the resurrection of Christ, something which has no shadow of historical evidence, which was demonstrably not an element in the tradition of the Church from the beginning, which was repudiated when it came into notice by many of the greatest mediaeval saints and theologians, and which is only supported by the sort of logic which all historians know to be utterly untrustworthy, that is, *a priori* argument as to what must have happened or ought to have happened. We should indeed think and speak of the Blessed Virgin with a profound reverence and devotion; but to put the immaculate conception of Mary[1] side by side with the resurrection of Christ,

[1] The corporal assumption of Mary is, I believe, not "of faith" in the Roman communion, but it is celebrated as a "Double of the First Class," with the same liturgical honours as the commemorations of the birth and ascension of Christ.

as entitled to an identical faith as a fact, is to remove the act of faith altogether from its standing-ground in historical testimony.

The historical difficulty which attaches to the dogma of the infallibility of the Pope is well known. It appears to conflict with some certain facts of history; as, even more certainly, does the affirmation which accompanies it, that in asserting the dogma the Vatican Council was only "faithfully adhering to the tradition received from the first beginnings of the Christian faith."[1]

The dogma of transubstantiation is also involved not only in metaphysical but in historical difficulties, because it conflicts with an important current of Church tradition which affirmed the permanent reality of the bread and wine—a tradition not only important by the weight of the names which affirm it, but still more important because it is grounded on the same principle which prompted the Church's repeated insistence upon our Lord's real humanity, the principle that the supernatural does not destroy the natural substance or nature, but only elevates it to a higher plane; while, on the other hand, the dogma of transubstantiation is closely allied with a deeply monophysite tendency in the Church.[2]

I have cited these instances of *de fide* dogmas in the Roman Church as having implicit in them the claim that authority shall supersede history or do without it. But also it must be remembered that of the "authoritative" teaching of the Roman Church only a small part is strictly claimed as infallible. "A Catholic obedience is tried," says Father Rickaby,[3] "not by the supreme infallible decisions of papal and conciliar authority in matters of faith and morals: such high infallible utterances are rare . . . ; but obedience is tried by proceedings and declarations,

[1] See *Roman Catholic Claims*, chaps. v–vii.
[2] See *Dissertations*, iii. [3] *Op. cit.*, p. 229.

not infallible, yet authoritative." For example, Pope Leo XIII in 1893 issued an encyclical on "the study of Holy Scripture," addressed especially to ecclesiastics, in which the fullest and most extreme definition possible is given of the nature and scope of the inspiration of the writers of the books of the Bible. The efforts of Newman and others to show that the doctrine of inspiration might be given a more restricted sense, and be rendered compatible with the more certain conclusions of criticism, are utterly disregarded. In the most stringent sense God is declared to be the *author* of everything in the authentic text of the Bible, not only statements affecting faith and morals, but statements on every subject. To deny the infallibility or historical truth of any of its statements is to ascribe falsehood to God.[1] Now, this assertion of verbal inspiration in its most stringent sense as the doctrine of the Church, although the Pope is obviously intending to define the meaning of inspiration for the benefit of the teachers and students of the Church, and to exclude any other meaning, is, I suppose, not reckoned as infallible. There are signs that it is already being ignored. Perhaps in thirty years' time it will be as completely superseded as a much earlier pope's definition of the matter and form of ordination.[2] But the more we reflect on the matter, the more perilous do these not strictly infallible but authoritative utterances seem to be. There is a whole mass of theological utterances which the Roman Catholic student knows are not strictly the word of God—which may turn out not to be true—which yet he must not contradict, and which it is "temerarious" to doubt or at least call into question. The par-

[1] This amazing encyclical is quoted in *Roman Catholic Claims* (10th and later editions), chap. xi.

[2] Eugenius IV in 1439 in his *Decretum de Unione Armeniorum*. See *Roman Catholic Claims*, chap. ix, p. 149; and *The Church and the Ministry*, p. 79, n. 1.

ticular encyclical referred to had, it seems to us Anglicans, a disastrous effect on the study of Holy Scripture in the Roman Church. It still makes us feel that some eminent Roman Catholic critics and commentators are writing, not as they would if they were free to express their judgement, but as they dare. This attempt strictly to prohibit free thought among Church students of the Bible over a long period of time by the dogmatic action of authority, backed by its disciplinary resources, when all the time it is admitted that the prohibitory dogma may turn out to be mistaken, seems to us an amazing perversion of authority.

No one can survey the course of European thought since the Roman authority became the dominant factor in Western religion without seeing that it has been on many points, and not chiefly in virtue of decrees for which infallibility is claimed, the great misleader of Europe. It was so in the sanction given over long ages to the principle of persecution for heresy—persecution involving torture and death—which was flat contrary to the mind of the earlier Church, and is inexpressibly repugnant to the mind of Jesus. It was so in the claim implicit in the condemnation of Galileo, that the Church and the Bible have authority in matters of science, and that inductive reasoning from the observation of nature cannot be free when it appears to conflict with statements in the Bible. More recently, as just remarked, it has been so in its attitude towards historical criticism as applied to the Bible. In all these cases the authority of the Church, in Roman hands, did generate, and has kept alive on the vastest scale, a revolt of intellect and even more of properly Christian feeling, against the very idea of authority in religion; and we are bound to confess that, if the Roman idea of authority is the only idea, the revolt has been legitimate.

It is quite true that Protestant bodies have also sanctioned persecution. Anyone who reads the history candidly written of the founding of New England[1] will be obliged to recognize in the Puritan fathers a conception of ecclesiastical authority, and of the duty of persecuting heresy even to torture and death, which is as formidable as anything which can be laid to the charge of Rome. But it was short-lived, because it was incompatible with the whole spirit of the movement in which it occurred. Orthodox Protestantism again has from time to time sought to condemn and penalize free enquiry; but here also its own principles have forced it for very shame to repent. Its faults can never be on the side of over-emphasis on authority. And it must be admitted that by many centuries Rome led the way in these disastrous tendencies. And my point is that it is not only, or perhaps chiefly, by its pronouncements for which infallibility is claimed that Rome has been in certain respects the misleader of Europe, but by that far larger body of authoritative pronouncements which stifle criticism and resistance, but which after the lapse of time may turn out to have been confessedly mistaken.

II

The next point to be noticed in the Romanist conception of authority is that it appears in effect to give a new meaning to *tradition*. The "living voice" of the Church—which, of course, means the Church of the Roman obedience—represents what the tradition has come to be, and can express itself in an "irreformable" dogma, which may in words declare itself to have been received by tradition from the very beginnings of the Christian religion, but which

[1] This has been admirably done by James Truslow Adams in his *Founding of New England* ("Atlantic Monthly" Press, 1920).

in fact pays no real attention either to the silence of Scripture or to the actual facts about the tradition in its earlier stages.

As has been shown,[1] the Fathers did really regard the authority of the Church in matters of doctrine as *limited* by the appeal to Scripture. The appeal was to Scripture no doubt as interpreted by the Church tradition. But the function of the Church tradition was to interpret, not to add to, " what was written," and tradition meant the tradition as patent from the beginning. This ancient idea of Church authority was admirably explained in the little work of Vincent of Lerins written A.D. 434—*Adversus profanes omnium novitates haereticorum commonitorium* —which became the classic on the subject. Here the function of tradition is limited to interpreting Scripture, and it is not regarded as an additional source of doctrine; and a famous phrase defines authentic tradition to be what has been held in the Church " ubique," " semper," and " ab omnibus " —that is, in all parts of the Church, as opposed to any one particular Church; always, as opposed to only in recent ages; and by all, i.e. by the general body of the Church, as opposed to the private opinion of particular teachers. It is made quite plain by Vincent that the appeal to antiquity is an additional test, over and above the appeal to general consent.[2]

Now we shall have to discuss the reasonableness of combining the appeal to Scripture with the appeal to tradition, and also the reasonableness of erecting the Scriptures as a final standard of the doctrine of the Christian religion. This will be our business in a future chapter.[3] We shall also have to discuss the bearing of development on this theory of tradition immediately. All that I ask at present is that it

[1] See above, pp. 172–3.

[2] This is acknowledged by Cardinal Franzelin to be Vincent's meaning but is by him repudiated. See *Roman Catholic Claims*, chap. iii, p. 58.

[3] Chap. viii.

should be recognized what a vast difference there is between a theory of the Church which makes it a continuous and living witness to a once-spoken voice —a "faith once for all delivered"—and one which makes it, in effect, a continuous organ of divine revelation. If the former theory is the truth, the authority of the Church is a very restricted authority. For instance, it cannot make the immaculate conception of Mary an article of faith—because no one can reasonably claim for it ancient tradition or scriptural sanction. Or again, it cannot get to know, or become authorized to require of the faithful, more concerning purgatory than the ancient Church knew or than is to be found in Scripture.

Plainly in St. Augustine's day there was no tradition about a purgatory in the intermediate state for the imperfect. St. Augustine tended strongly to believe it, as I suppose we almost all of us must do, on grounds of reason. But it has no real grounds in Scripture,[1] which is, in fact, totally silent on the subject. St. Augustine finally can only say in his latest work, "I will not dispute it; for it may perhaps be true."[2] Three centuries later the authority of St. Gregory's *Dialogues*, full of tremendous ghost stories, gives the doctrine unlimited vogue. Gregory quite admits that his vivid teaching is dependent on the new information contained in the visions he records.[3] The approaching end of the world, he

[1] The text so often quoted, 1 Cor. iii. 15, has nothing to do with it. It concerns not the purging of character but the testing of work, and that by the fire of the last day.

[2] *De Civ.*, xxi, 26. Dr. A. J. Mason in his *Purgatory* (Longmans) has given the best account of the development of the doctrine.

[3] See Mason, *op. cit.*, p. 43. The passage of chief importance is in St. Gregory's *Dialogi*, iv, 39–40. Peter, Gregory's submissive disciple, asks why in these last times so many things about souls are becoming clear which were unknown before, "so that by manifest revelations and disclosures the world to come appears to invade us and open itself to us"; and Gregory replies it is like the dawning light before the sun rises—the clouds of this disappearing world are shot through with rays of the light that is to be.

thinks, has been the occasion of these enlightening visions. We have thus been allowed to know more than our fathers. But the ancient Church would not admit any new revelation as an addition to the word of God.[1] What an immense difference it would have made if, instead of using the doctrine of purgatory as one of the keystones of its system, with results so disastrous in many ways, the Church had maintained its ancient reticence! It could not deny that there might—there even must be—a purgatory. But it had no authority to proclaim it as part of its message, and still less any authority over it. There was no original tradition of a purgatory and nothing about it in the word of God.

I say, then, that no one can dispute the importance of the ancient rule of faith in restricting the authority of the Church and keeping the conscience of men free from additional burdens. There is something infallible[2] in the Church, which is the original Gospel, proclaimed by the apostles, and recorded in the New Testament. The Church is endowed with the Spirit of truth in order to realize, to propagate, and to defend this faith and to explicate its meaning. But it cannot add to it. Where Scripture gives no information (for "we know in part and we prophesy in part" only), the Church must be content to remain silent till the day dawns of greater light. Meanwhile men of discernment may enquire and speculate and suggest pious opinions. But the Church can make no new article of faith. In that category, as Vincent constantly insists in various phrases, what is really new is certainly false.[3]

[1] This is still the official position of the Roman Church, though it is manifestly violated in practice.

[2] Appended Note A, p. 205, on the Infallibility of the Church.

[3] No one interested in the subject ought to be content without reading Vincent of Lerins's luminous little book. No doubt, though he does not mention the name of the great Augustine, he has him in his mind, alongside of Origen and Tertullian whom he does name, as an instance of one who had not only done brilliant

The history of the alteration by the Church of the West of its ancient rule of faith is fairly plain. The first five centuries were days of general enlightenment and there were a multitude of Church teachers and an intelligent public. By the beginning of the seventh century things had changed. In the West at least Gregory the Great stood almost alone. As we have seen, in respect to the after-world he did not hold to the ancient rule. He admitted new teaching based on fresh disclosures. And his word became law for the dark ages. When we reach the period of the controversy concerning Berengar and transubstantiation (eleventh century), the distinction between the authority of Scripture and every other kind of authority appears to have vanished.[1] Neither Berengar nor his adversaries appear to be conscious of it. The appeal is to authorities of various kinds, and they are all called "authentic scriptures." Two centuries later, in St. Thomas Aquinas, what the modern student finds most baffling is the total absence of any criticism of his authorities. His argument in particular cases manifestly depends not only on the subtlety of his reasoning, which is seldom at fault, but on the relative value of the different authorities to which he defers. And of these we find no reasoned estimate. Meanwhile the actual teaching of the Church had reached such a point that it must make its appeal to an "unwritten tradition," additional to Scripture, if it were to be justified. Practically, though perhaps not theoretically, St. Thomas *adds* tradition to Scripture, as a source of doctrine, and tradition, as I have said, treated quite uncritically. At the fourth session of the Council of Trent (1546) the written books of Scripture and the

service to the Church, but had also "tried" it by promulgating ideas (the conception of absolute predestination, etc.) which were neither according to antiquity nor consent, but which enthusiastic disciples would fasten upon the Church as obligatory doctrine.

[1] See *Dissert.*, p. 250

"unwritten" traditions, whether received by the apostles from the mouth of Christ Himself, or dictated to them by the Holy Spirit, were formally put upon the same level of authority, in respect of matters of faith as well as of discipline, with the books of Scripture.[1] This was a serious alteration of the ancient rule. But it makes little difference in fact if tradition is interpreted, as Vincent insists that it must, in the sense that nothing belongs to tradition which cannot be shown to have been held in the Church from the beginning and universally. Still, in the Creed of Pope Pius IV, who brought the Council of Trent to a conclusion, the Scriptures are to be interpreted not "otherwise than according to [*juxta*] the unanimous consent of the Fathers."[2] Döllinger pleaded his oath to this Creed as preventing him from assenting to the Vatican decree concerning the infallibility of the Pope. But in the decrees of the Vatican Council there is a notable difference from the Creed of Pope Pius. There it is forbidden to interpret Scripture "*contrary to* the unanimous consent of the Fathers."[3] There may, apparently, be additions to their unanimous teaching, if they do not amount to contradictions. Cardinal Franzelin, also, as we have just seen, rejects the restraint which Vincent would impose on dogmatic novelties. And, in fact, without the abandonment of the restrictions of Vincent certain Roman dogmas are plainly disqualified. But here we touch the question of the meaning of "development," which will be the subject of the next chapter.

III

The third point to notice in the Romanist conception of authority is that it involves centraliza-

[1] Denzinger, *Enchiridion*, § lxxxi.
[2] *Op. cit.*, lxxxii. [3] *Op. cit.*, lxxxix.

tion.[1] In the early conception of authority there is no centralization. Cyprian seems at one moment of his life to proclaim an unrestricted independence among bishops, though he can hardly have meant this in its full sense. Augustine corrects this exaggerated estimate by bringing the individual bishop under the authority of the Council of Bishops, and finally of the General Council. But the idea of the General Council was that its predominant authoritativeness depended upon the fact that in it all the streams of tradition in all the different churches of the world were represented, and could check one another.[2] Thus its decision represented the consentient witness of all parts of the Christian world. And again the conclusion reached was dependent for its final authority upon the acceptance of the conciliar decision by the churches, when the bishops had returned to their sees and promulgated it. Thus the conception of the General Council suggests no

[1] It involves centralization in a double sense—in the sense argued in the text, and in the sense that within the Roman Church the authority is (I believe) restricted to the *ecclesia docens.* In the New Testament the Church officers have a special function as teachers, but the Church as a whole is felt to be "the pillar and ground of the truth." The whole Church is appealed to in moments of controversy. This tradition is maintained in the Church of the Fathers. And still the Eastern Orthodox Church maintains it, repudiating the Roman distinction between the *ecclesia docens* and the *ecclesia discens.* The hierarchy in the Roman Church, which is the *ecclesia docens,* "consists of the Sovereign Pontiff, who is assisted by the Sacred College of Cardinals, and by several sacred congregations . . . ; of the patriarchs, archbishops, and bishops; of the apostolic delegates, vicars, and prefects; and of certain abbots and prelates." The ordinary parish priest does not, I believe, belong to it.

[2] It is noteworthy that when Irenaeus assigns a special importance to the Roman Church in maintaining the tradition, it is because its pre-eminence brought Christian men from all parts of the world to it; so that tradition there was not merely local but ecumenical, because the tradition was there maintained by men from all parts. This is the undoubted meaning of the famous phrase (Iren., c. *Haer.*, iii, 3). See references in *Roman Catholic Claims*, pp. 97–8. Rome after the fifth century quite lost this distinction and became for many centuries strangely isolated.

centralized authority, but, on the contrary, a common tradition or authority universally diffused, and needing to be laboriously collected. But the Roman mind demanded something more easily effective—a central authority at Rome and, as it soon appeared, a spiritual monarchy. In the developed papacy it is regularly assumed that monarchy is the form of government most to be desired, as in temporal things so in spiritual. No doubt this follows from a certain conception of effectiveness. But it is bought at a great price, and it has inflicted on Christendom deplorable losses. First, in that it has tended to narrowness. It has emphasized the virtue of obedience at the expense of liberty and diversity and reverence for truth—qualities for which the earlier and more really catholic idea of authority allowed ample scope. This has been especially apparent since the Counter-Reformation, and since the influence of the Jesuits became dominant, alike in respect of doctrine and of discipline. Secondly, it has involved violence to history and has tended to schism. The Papal Monarchy makes claims on history which history fairly interpreted wholly refuses to verify. The Greek-speaking Church, holding fast to an earlier conception of authority, has consistently, in its official utterances, and in the opinion of almost all its theologians, repudiated the papal claim, and on wholly valid grounds.[1] The more and more insistent pressure of those claims on the part of Rome meant schism in the long run.

And lastly, what is the most serious point of all, the facts of history being what they are, the maintenance of the Roman claim has involved a constant perversion of truth. This is an awful charge. But it has been pressed home by two of the most learned of modern historians who were themselves shining

[1] Appended Note B, "The Constant Repudiation by the East of the Roman Claim," p. 207.

lights of the Roman Church—Von Döllinger and Acton. The one was excommunicated, the other lived and died in the communion of Rome. But he did not mince his words in charging with treason to the truth the maintainers of the later Roman claim. Certainly as one reads the record of forged documents and misquotations which have been used to support the Papal claim, it seems an inevitable conclusion that an assertion of authority which has needed so much falsehood to support it in the past, and still needs so much distortion of fact in its histories, cannot be wholly of God.[1]

But as I write such words there rises before me the vision of the glories and sanctities of the Roman Church, as conspicuous in modern as in ancient days. Certainly God is with them and His Spirit is powerful among them. But the Roman Church claims to be the whole Church. Whereas it seems to me to be written on the face of history that, for all its glory and strength and beauty, it is a one-sided development. It is not the whole. As to the combination in one communion of so much excellence with so much defect, and of so much truth with so much treason to truth, I shall have something to say at a later stage.[2]

[1] I think Denny's *Papalism* (Rivington) is fairly unanswerable. It suffers through following the lines of the encyclical of Leo XIII, *Salis Cognitum,* which is not widely read to-day. But this enables the author to cover the whole ground of debate. Also following the encyclical, he says little about the theory of development. He assumes the Roman theory to be—what officially it is—that the doctrine of the Vatican Council has always been in substance the doctrine of the Church. Though he occasionally shows an unwillingness to admit points in the Roman case which he had better have admitted, his case on the whole is (as I have said) fairly unanswerable. Our other strongest book is Father Puller's *Primitive Saints and the See of Rome* (Longmans).

[2] See below, p. 357.

APPENDED NOTE A (see p. 199)

THE INFALLIBILITY OF THE CHURCH

There is something deep in human nature which calls for an infallible refuge. It has been found in conscience, and in Scripture, and in the Church, and in the Pope. But as soon as you begin to cross-question the authority of these diverse seats of infallibility, in each case, though in various degrees, you find a grave necessity for discrimination. The suggested authority is infallible only when it speaks under such and such conditions. And the difficulty is to distinguish when these conditions are fulfilled. Conscience may, and sometimes does, simply convey the voice of God to the soul. But it may be perverted by ignorance or invincible prejudice or social tradition or individual wilfulness, so as to convey a guidance which is very far from being divine. Scripture, again, is the record of a real word of God in the different stages of its delivery, and the Word of God is infallible. Here is something which in its main lines is clearly distinguishable. But Scripture contains much that is imperfect in its earlier stages, for the divine education of mankind was gradual, and what was right for ancient Israel would not be right for us. Also the record of the divine message is given in a literature which contains historical records of very different historical values and statements of a quasi-scientific character which are not according to the facts as we know them. The word of God is infallible, but you cannot call the books which convey it to us infallible without disaster.

Again, the function of the Church is to convey the message of God which is infallible, and it has authority to interpret it and proclaim it as true. There are certain occasions—the Ecumenical Councils—when the Church has squarely faced a question definitely raised, and has definitely answered it after full consideration, and in a representative assembly, and the answer has been accepted so widely and continuously that you may truly say, This is the voice of the Catholic Church; this you can rely upon with the same confidence which inspired the first church at Jerusalem to say, "It seemed good to the Holy Ghost and to us." And in spite of the disagreeable moral impression which some of the General Councils leave upon our minds, I believe the claim to be justified.

And we ought to feel the same sort of reliance upon the diffused witness of the Church in proportion as it is really unanimous—ubique, semper, ab omnibus—and can make a legitimate appeal to Holy Scripture.

But what average human nature is apt to want is a much more general infallibility. Yet in fact "the voice of the Church," even before the Church was divided, has been through its ordinary mouthpieces very far from infallible. Not even the warmest defender of the infallibility of the Church or of the Pope can fail to recognize such serious limitations to the infallibility in which he desires to believe as to deprive it largely of its practical value. The fact is that when men cry out for an infallible voice they are generally crying out for something which, in the large sense in which they want it, it does not appear to be the will of God we should have. There is a word of God which is utterly trustworthy of which the Church is the carrier; and it has divinely given authority to teach it and to interpret it; and its great central utterances where it speaks with fullest unanimity we can rely upon with a wholehearted confidence. But in view of the facts of history we had better be careful in talking about the infallibility of the Church. Christ is the truth, and the Holy Spirit is the Spirit of Jesus and the Spirit of truth, and infallible. And because He is in the Church there is something there infallible.[1] But indefectibility and God-given authority are, in general, better words to use concerning the Church.

[1] St. Thomas tells us that to say "I believe in the Church" is permissible only because "our faith is referred to the Holy Spirit who sanctifies the Church, so that the sense is 'I believe in the Holy Spirit who sanctifies the Church.' But it is better, and in accordance with the more usual practice, to omit the word 'in' and say only 'I believe [that] the Holy Catholic Church [exists],' Credo sanctam ecclesiam Catholicam." So also Rufinus and Augustine. In fact, however, the Eastern Creeds, including the "Nicene" and some Western Creeds, certainly contain the εἰς or "in" before the mention of the Church. And where the preposition was not repeated, it was commonly understood. See *Church and Ministry*, p. 14, n. 2.

APPENDED NOTE B (see p. 203)

THE CONSTANT REPUDIATION BY THE EAST OF THE ROMAN CLAIM

It appears in history that the Greek-speaking Church never regarded it as part of the faith that it had received that the Bishop of Rome has *by divine right* any special position in the Church. We Anglicans have always appealed, in vindication of this statement, specially to the formal utterances of Eastern Councils reckoned as ecumenical—the third canon of Constantinople and the twenty-eighth of Chalcedon. (See *Roman Catholic Claims*, p. 102.) Romans reply that the latter—the most explicit—canon was not accepted by Rome and that the Easterns must therefore have admitted that it was not valid. But this is not the case. Whatever polite and conciliatory language they thought it wise to use to the powerful pontiff at Rome, the canon remained in their eyes valid, and was explicitly reaffirmed in the Council at the Trullo (can. xxxvi). Cf. Duchesne, *Origines du Culte chrétien*, p. 24: "Leur voix" (i.e. Leo's voice and his successors') "fut peu écoutée: on leur accorda sans doute des satisfactions, mais de pure cérémonie."

Certainly Eastern theologians recognize a leadership of Peter among the apostles, as we all do. Chrysostom is quoted as going beyond this; but on investigation [1] it seems to be doubtful whether he recognizes any authority in Peter peculiar to him; and of course Antioch, where Chrysostom was teaching, was, like Rome, a "see of Peter," and may have loved to recognize his primacy in a somewhat fuller sense than other churches. What is quite certain is that neither Chrysostom nor the other Eastern doctors recognized the persistence of the Petrine privilege (whatever it was) in the Roman bishops. When St. Chrysostom, for instance, speaks of our Lord as having intrusted His sheep "to Peter and those who came after him" (*de Sacerdot.*, ii, cap. i, § 88), it is of all the bishops he is plainly speaking.

[1] See Denny's *Papalism*, pp. 86 ff.

CHAPTER VII

THE TESTS OF LEGITIMATE DEVELOPMENT

THOSE who assent to the course of thought pursued in this volume find themselves maintaining an idea of the authority of the Church which is both conservative and moderate. It is conservative because it postulates not only that the Christ is the final word of God's self-revelation to men, but also that the apostolic preaching, which was the source of the Church tradition, gave the true and final interpretation of the person of Christ and of the mission of the Spirit, and that their preaching finds its adequate record in the books of the New Testament. It is a moderate view of the authority of the Church because, while it would bid us hold that it was the duty of the Church to propagate, defend, and interpret the teaching of the New Testament, it would deny that it had authority to add to it, or at any rate to claim acceptance as part of the faith for anything either contrary to or over and above "what had been written." In the next chapter the question of the legitimacy and reasonableness of this claim for Scripture will come up for discussion. But we have also found that the greatest of the Christian Churches —the Roman communion—in a measure in theory and much more completely in fact repudiates this moderate canon of Church authority. It adds tradition to Scripture as an equal source of knowledge about the contents of the revelation, and in effect claims that "tradition" means what at any period the Roman Church has come to hold, whatever the records of the past may say.

It is to account for the difference between the present teaching of the Roman Church and the original tradition that appeal has been made to the idea of development. The present Roman tradition, it is contended, represents not simply the original tradition, but the proper development of the original tradition. The principle had been appealed to in one sense by the famous Jesuit Petau, or Petavius, the antagonist of Bishop Bull in the seventeenth century; and in a rather different sense by Möhler in his *Symbolik*, published in 1832. But for England and America the idea gained a quite new importance by the publication in 1845 [1] of Newman's brilliant essay on *The Development of Christian Doctrine*. Newman in this essay finds in the idea of development the instrument for bridging over for his own mind and conscience the interval between the present doctrine of the Roman Church and that of the early Church, in the study of which he had so long been immersed.[2] And he gives the idea an extension which sounds, as one first reads it, startlingly 'modern,' or even 'modernist.' "Christianity," he said, "though represented in prophecy as a king-

[1] Fourteen years before Charles Darwin published his *Origin of Species by means of Natural Selection*. The controversy about Newman's book is remarkable as showing what ideas about development were *not* current when he wrote: see especially Mozley's *Theory of Development*, written in reply to Newman, pp. 3 ff. (Rivington, first published 1847).

[2] Cf. Acton's *Correspondence* (ed. Figgis and Laurence, 1917), i, p. 77. Acton is accounting for the suspicion of Newman entertained at Rome, and he writes: "J'arrive à croire qu'on le soupçonnait à cause du Développement qui était, en effet, une révolution, et qui lui donnait un peu l'air d'un personnage qui exigeait, pour le satisfaire, une théorie imaginée exprès pour lui et qui justifiait sa première manière, ses attaques, et la lenteur de sa conversion, jusqu'à ce qu'il l'eût découverte. Car en Angleterre comme en Amérique, elle était toute nouvelle, et on sentait qu'elle renversait l'ancienne défensive Catholique en faisant droit à ses adversaires."

dom, came into the world as an idea rather than an institution, and has had to wrap itself in clothing, and fit itself with armour of its own providing, and form the instruments and methods for its own prosperity and welfare."[1] The amount of change involved in development was illustrated in some startling arguments—as when it was suggested that one effect of the Arian controversy was that "it discovered a new sphere, if we may so speak, in the realms of light, to which the Church had not yet assigned its inhabitant." This "new sphere" was the position which Arianism had imagined for the Son—that of a creature, but a creature invested with divine attributes. This had been adjudged by the Church to be a sphere too low for the Son. But it was left vacant, and in course of time Mary the Mother could be found to fill it. "I am not," wrote Newman, "stating conclusions which were drawn out in the controversy, but premises which were laid broad and deep. It was then . . . determined that to exalt a creature was no recognition of its divinity." Indeed the conclusion suggested was not drawn out in the controversy! for all the Fathers had argued that the Arian Christ, as a being who was a creature and yet was to be worshipped, involved an idolatrous and, for Christians, for ever impossible conception.

Of course Newman's whole argument for development was made to depend upon the existence of an infallible authority to preside over and judge of developments. Nevertheless, the argument was startling enough. It stirred against itself not only Anglican controversialists,[2] but indignant Romans,[3] scandalized at what seemed the abandonment of

[1] p. 116. See also the passage quoted in Oliver Quick's *Liberalism, Modernism, and Tradition*, pp. 27 ff.

[2] The ablest answer, brilliant as the essay itself, was J. B. Mozley's already alluded to.

[3] See Mozley, *op. cit.*, pp. 215 ff.

the whole tradition of Roman apology. It served its primary purpose in building a bridge for the author himself with many others to pass into the Roman communion. But in later years he would appear to have retreated from his first position, and he used language which reaffirms the traditional view:

> "First of all, and in as few words as possible, and *ex abundanti cautela*, every Catholic holds that the Christian dogmas were in the Church from the time of the apostles; that they were ever in their substance what they are now; that they existed before the formulas were publicly adopted, in which as time went on they were defined and recorded."[1]

I

It was the extremer doctrine of the essay which caught the attention of the world and fascinated the imagination of many, and we will return upon the idea of development, doctrinal and general, in its larger sense. But first let us take the idea stated in the last quotation from Newman, which practically represents the old view of tradition, and which is still the official language of the Roman Church; and we will seek to answer two questions: (1) does it really cover the action of the Church of the first centuries in formulating the Creeds and the decisions of the Ecumenical Councils? and (2) does it cover the later action of the Church of Rome?

(1) The answer to the first question is with a certain qualification in the affirmative. In the earliest period of the Church, before St. Paul's conversion, it does not appear as if the Church had any other thought in its mind except that of the divine glory of the exalted

[1] *Tracts Theol. and Eccl.*, p. 287. "After sixteen years," wrote Lord Acton in 1890, "spent in the Church of Rome, Newman was inclined to guard and narrow his theory of development."

Christ, and the power of the Divine Spirit bestowed upon them. It does not appear to have yet asked itself theological questions about Christ or about the Spirit. When then I affirm Newman's later words, I must lay stress upon the phrase "from the time of the apostles" as explaining what is meant by "ever." I mean that the doctrine of St. Paul and St. John is really in substance the doctrine of the Nicene Creed, neither more nor less, and really the only doctrine which interprets the Christ of the Gospels. And if the Church was really set in the world to maintain the teaching of the New Testament about His divine sonship and His incarnation and His indisputably real manhood, it had no choice but to condemn the theories of His person which it did in fact condemn; and we know no better formulas to protect the essential truth than the words the Church selected to be used.[1] Thus I think the claim of the Fathers of the Councils that they were simply protecting the apostolic teaching is a true claim; and though early apologists and theologians had, as was to be expected, in their first attempts to explain their beliefs, used language such as was repudiated in later days, yet the tradition, as Origen stated, had always really ascribed to Christ both Godhead and manhood.

When we pass from the doctrine of the Incarnation to that of the Trinity, we are still entitled to maintain that in the New Testament the name of the one God had already become the threefold name of the Father and the Son and the Holy Spirit, each personal, distinct, and co-inherent; and in spite of the ambiguity of such writers as Hermas, Justin Martyr, and even Irenaeus about the Holy Spirit, there was always behind them the tradition of the threefold

[1] See Appended Note on Dr. Mackintosh's criticisms of the phraseology of the Councils, p. 228. On development within the New Testament, see a criticism of Dr. McNeile, p. 278.

name of God, as it appears in St. Matt. xxviii. 19,[1] and in Clement's formula for the "living God" ("As God liveth, and the Lord Jesus Christ liveth, and the Holy Spirit"), and in Origen's statement of the tradition that "the Holy Ghost is associated in honour and dignity with the Father and the Son." It is true, then, that the definition of the Trinity did only give distinctness and explicitness to the conception already implicit in the apostolic teaching.[2]

(2) On the other hand, there was demonstrably nothing implicit in that tradition to the effect that the primacy of Peter among the apostles was inherited by divine right by the Bishop of Rome—still less that he was endowed with monarchical authority or infallibility. Such a doctrine was there neither in terms nor "in substance."[3] The Greek-speaking

[1] Which, whether it be an authentic word of Christ or no, certainly represents the Trinitarian belief of the Church to which the Palestinian editor of the First Gospel belonged, not much after the destruction of Jerusalem.

[2] The decree of the second Council of Nicaea, which is claimed as ecumenical, rests on a different basis, as it concerns a practice (the veneration of images) rather than a doctrine. See below, p. 291.

[3] I have already (p. 186) referred to Fr. Janssens' criticism of a statement of Fr. Woodlock's. It contains a very interesting distinction between the "fundamental" doctrines of the Christian faith (meaning, I suppose, the doctrines of the Deity of Christ and the Incarnation and the Holy Trinity, and perhaps the doctrines of the sacraments in general and the ministry and the resurrection —but he does not specify what doctrines are included in the term) which "do not admit of real development" and others, such as the infallibility of the Pope, which do. Of the fundamental dogma of the deity of Christ, he says: "It has always been explicitly held. There was no development in the doctrine, but only in its terminology." And of fundamentals in general: "Quod non fuit ab initio doctum et universaliter creditum non pertinet ad Christianae fidei fundamenta." But of the infallibility of the Pope (a non-fundamental doctrine, therefore) he writes: "It has admitted of a true development, a real doctrinal progress. It has been held but implicitly in the first three centuries and has been doubted afterwards, even until the time of the Vatican Council." I should venture to criticize this statement. I should have thought that of the doctrine of the Holy Trinity it was true to say that it was held only implicitly in the apostolic or sub-apostolic times and became explicit. But of the infallibility that it was neither explicitly nor implicitly held in the early centuries.

Church neither recognized this as tradition nor ever came to acknowledge it as a legitimate claim. Nor does Scripture suggest it. This is as certain as history can make it. So, again, there was no tradition about a purgatory in the intermediate state and really nothing in Scripture about it. Again, though the Church always believed that the bread and wine in the eucharist became the body and blood of Christ in some real sense, there was nothing in Scripture or tradition to suggest that the substance of bread and wine ceased to exist by the consecration of the elements, and on the other hand, there was a strong tradition in the contrary sense. Finally, there was nothing even remotely suggesting that Mary was immaculately conceived. Accordingly it is a certain conclusion that, if all that the Church has the right to do is to make explicit in language what has always been substantially present in the tradition from the days of the apostles, the Roman dogma concerning transubstantiation, and the dogma affirming purgatory under anathema, and the dogma of the Immaculate Conception, and the dogma concerning the Bishop of Rome, are as dogmas certainly illegitimate.

II

It is the feeling that the justification of the Roman dogmas needs something more than the traditional formula which has made Newman's earlier and much freer conception of development very popular among those who are looking Romewards and among some Roman Catholic exponents of doctrine. But also, and much more widely, the general prevalence of the idea of development has reinforced Newman's conception, often in a sense quite antagonistic to his own. German writers of *Dogmengeschichte* and French modernists have accepted it as a matter of course. Also it is quite plain that the principle of development must be applied not only to the doctrines of the Church but to its institutions and methods as a whole. So we will turn back to the freer conception of development as Newman first suggested it, in order to see if he can help us, or we can help ourselves, towards some adequate conception of development, both in Church doctrine and more generally in the Church as an institution; and also whether we can discover the test or tests which would seem to distinguish legitimate from illegitimate developments. And we will take this latter point first.

For Newman was not content simply to accept the infallibility of the defining authority as rendering all further argument unnecessary. He seeks to establish tests by which to discriminate legitimate "development" from "corruption." They are the "preservation of the type or idea," "continuity of principle," "power of assimilation," "early anticipation," "logical sequence," "preservative addition," "chronic continuance." Now one of the most effective points in Mozley's reply to Newman is that he calls our attention to the slight consideration paid by Newman to one of the most characteristic features in developments all the world over, by which institutions may radically change their character in the course of time for good and all, viz. one-sided exaggeration of some tendency or feature which was always present in the system, but which had been balanced originally by other tendencies or features which in course of time were suppressed or ceased to act. So it was that the Roman State passed from being a republic to being an autocratic monarchy. Similarly no one would question that *in the West* the development of the Papacy as a doctrine and as an institution was a real development, which exhibited unmistakable continuity of principle since the days of Damasus, and power of assimilation, and which had early anticipations going back to the second century, and which was in logical sequence; and could claim that its "addition" to the original idea of Christianity was "preservative" of the idea as entertained at Rome, and that it showed, step after step, "chronic continuance." Newman triumphantly asks where in the Roman development you can find a point at which it breaks with the past either as doctrine or as institution. Very likely nowhere. Neither can you in the process by which historical institutions or ideas have generally developed. There are, of course, revolutions and chasms in history. But they are apt to lead to reactions. The most permanent transformations are apt to come gradually. And the result of the actual development may prove to be a one-sided accentuation of some feature or idea at the expense of others, which again in total result may be deterioration, not progress. Without any manifest break or violent change the last state of an institution or doctrine may become worse than the first simply in virtue of this one-sidedness of development, seriously altering and corrupting the original "type." Nothing, in fact, would seem to be more indisputable than that the Roman development of Christianity was a one-sided exaggeration, congenial to the old imperial spirit of Rome, of the element of regimental and official authority in the Church; and that it was accomplished by the gradual repudiation and supersession of all the restraints upon the action of authority which the ideas and institutions of the early Church supplied. Such restraints were the requirement laid on dogmatic authority to justify itself by the appeal to Scripture; and the assertion of the fundamental identity of the episcopal authority in all bishops; and the consequent subordination of all individual bishops or provinces of bishops to the General Council; and the refusal of the idea of physical force or state compulsion as an instrument in propagating the truth; and the recognition of the democratic element in Church government; and the freedom of appeal to Scripture and reason on the part of all Christians. All these were unmistakably principles of the early Church which in the Roman system were gradually superseded and denied, and in effect dropped out. So authority developed towards autocracy.

It is also evident that during the dark age which followed the break-up of the Western Empire, and the Middle Ages in which society reconstituted itself, the Church maintained its hold on the people by large concessions to popular appetites in religion, with little or no regard to scriptural sanction. Purgatory was a popular doctrine, softening the terror of hell; again, it was popular to soften the terror of purgatory by extending into the unseen world the Church's power of remitting penalties or granting indulgences, and for this purpose the doctrine of the treasury of merits which the Church could dispense was established. Again, there was a popular demand for intercessors, powerful in heaven and more lenient than the awful judge Jesus Christ could be believed to be, and it was allowed to prevail. To all these popular appetites the Church showed itself charitable indeed. But the result would have astonished the Fathers of the Church; and the type of religion which came to prevail could not be called scriptural.

The time came when the Roman Church was full of glaring scandals; and the Reformation became a revolution which deprived the Church of the Roman obedience of many of its fairest provinces. Arrested under the blow, the Roman Church reformed and recovered itself in what is called the Counter-Reformation. It reformed itself in respect of many of those moral scandals which had chiefly provoked the revolution. But the Counter-Reformation in its results intensified dogmatic autocracy and regimentation, and left the springs of popular superstition as open as ever. On the whole, it is impossible not to judge the Roman Church, with all its wonderful powers and spiritual glories, to be a one-sided development of the Christianity of the New Testament and the early Church, in which multitudes of men and women and those of the best, who would have been surely amongst the most whole-hearted of the disciples of Jesus, can find no home. In regard to them the very things in which the Roman Church glories as the instruments of its effectiveness have been really its hindrances.

There are a great many people in every age or country, and in some ages and countries the great majority, who are prepared readily enough to accept their religion absolutely on authority, without enquiry and without any obvious horror of superstition, if only the authority will give them a fair guarantee of salvation in the world to come and of consolation in the troubles of this life—and, it must be added, in the case of the majority, without making any very exacting moral demand. But there are some in every age, and in our generation and country they are the majority of good religious people, who are quite incapable of this sort of blind submission, without what would seem to them an act of treason against the light. They are people who, in the spirit of the Reformation, will accept nothing but what can be shown them to be really the teaching of the New Testament—and there is still a great, though mostly inarticulate, multitude of such people ; or they are honest students who must "test all things" with all the powers of their mind and by the freest enquiry they can give ; or they are people to whom dogmas are not attractive, but who are aflame for the building of the Kingdom of God, and whom the spectacle of injustice and needless suffering in human life stirs as with the call of a trumpet ; or they are ordinary sensible Englishmen with a horror of superstition. To multitudes of such men and women the Roman Church, as it stands, is utterly remote and impossible; yet, with the best of them, we feel, as I have said, that they would have been among the most ready disciples of our Lord and of the apostles, and they would have been at home in the primitive Church, carried along by its moral enthusiasm and the spirit of brotherhood.

This one-sidedness or narrowness in some directions is no argument against the Roman Church as a great and glorious part of the Church Catholic. For every part of the Church has its lamentably manifest limitations. But it is a very strong reason for refusing to recognize the Roman Church as the whole Church. For surely it is self-evident that if the love and the claim of God are perfectly disclosed in our Lord, the Church which is His body must be—exclusive indeed where He would have been exclusive, but inclusive where He would have been inclusive. It cannot be intended that it should be narrowed as it comes down the ages, or present obstacles where there were originally none. All parts of the Church alike have in fact created needless and formidable obstacles and scandals for good souls, whether by toleration of abuses or in other ways. But they can repent and reform themselves. The Roman Church of the Counter-Reformation did gallantly set itself to reform certain moral abuses in its system which scandalized the conscience of men before the Reformation, and played a large part in provoking the protest which produced schism. But the Roman Church appears to have worked the intellectual obstacles into its dogmatic system; they have been made "irreformable"; and it has thus made itself incapable of "receiving" some of those whom Christ would certainly have received. It is a one-sided development which has made itself exclusive.

III

Without further reference to Newman's essay, let us go back upon this postulate—that any development in the doctrine or practice of the Church which narrows it, so that it is no longer a home for men of goodwill who in its earlier days would readily have found a home in it, is thereby marked as a spurious development.

It is remarkable that in the discussion of " development " in connexion with the Catholic religion two mistakes have been commonly made. It has been assumed that development is the same thing as progress—a mistake to which the early enthusiasts for development in all departments were very prone. But we know it is a profound mistake. Every institution develops ; but the development—whether by intensification or by assimilation—may be for the worse and not for the better ; or in some respects for the better and in others for the worse, as appears to have been the case with the Roman Church. But also another mistake has been made. Attention has been almost concentrated on the development of doctrine. Now of course in any Christian Church the doctrine it teaches is an important part of the whole spiritual structure ; but by the development of the Church we ought to mean something much wider and deeper than the intensification and amplification of doctrines by a sort of logical process. The Church was set in the world to develop, not mainly by amplification of doctrines, nor by the increasing provision of plain answers to plain questions, which perhaps ought never to have been asked or answered, but by demonstrating its power to become the truly catholic home of all races and kinds of men. All sorts of human faculties and dispositions and personal needs are capable of being enriched and sanctified and met and harmonized by the Holy Spirit. And it is only by such gradual penetration of the darkness by the light that the treasures of wisdom and knowledge which lie hid in Christ—who is the light of the whole world and not merely of a section of it—can be progressively appropriated, and Christ Himself brought to fulfilment in His manifestation on earth.

This expansive function the Church Catholic was to fulfil, not primarily as a teacher of doctrine, but by the exhibition of a life—the corporate life of a community—which by its moral attractiveness and power was to impress and win men and convert them to the acceptance of its message. And it is fairly obvious that if the Church is to fulfil this function effectively, while there must be something which must be called essential catholicity—something which alone entitles any society to be reckoned a part of the Catholic Church of Christ, and which it must always assert and maintain—the Church needs also to have as free a power of adjustment and mobility as is consistent with real continuity. It went out into a world which proved to be a very changing world. There was first the world of the Greco-Roman Empire, and in this the Greek-speaking Church, with all its faults, showed its power and won its glory. Then, to take account only of the West, there was the world dominated by the barbarian invaders—the dark age—and the renascent world of mediaeval feudalism. Then was the glory of the Roman Church with its Benedictine monasticism and its papal authority. Something of Christ had been really manifested in the world order. There succeeded the period of the modern nations, armed against one another in successive rivalries; and the world of modern industrialism, almost cynically repudiating the control of Christian principles; and the world of inductive science and criticism claiming absolute emancipation from ecclesiastical authority; and the world of modern individualism with its startling contrasts of wealth and destitution. No one can say that in this new world of many aspects Christ has been manifested in His Church. On the whole, the Church has devoted itself to private soul-saving and works of mercy, which are parts, but not the whole of its work. In the international world its voice has hardly made itself heard effectively as a moral authority at all. The attempt in the fifteenth century to resuscitate the General Council as a supernational authority, and as supreme over the central papacy, proved a failure; and its failure was in great part the cause of the protest which rent the fabric of the Western Church. And Erasmus' *Complaint of Peace* remained unattended to. Again, the failure of the Church to make intelligible and effective the principle of brotherhood in modern industrialism is conspicuous. It has seemed to have no courage for the fray. Its most decisive action was a negative one—its abandonment of the antiquated prohibition of usury, the place of which ought to have been taken by some positive assertion of moral principle. Face to face with the claim of science it took a disastrous line towards Galileo, asserting that a conclusion of science could not be right because the Bible said otherwise—as if it were a function of the Bible to control science on its own field; and, in the same field, the like mistakes have been frequently made. Thoughtful people have been asking whether Christianity has failed; and more thoughtful people have been replying that it is *we* who have failed to apply the Christianity of Christ. But if we go to the root of the matter, we find it has been that the Church—in all its forms—has lacked mobility.

A religion claiming to be permanent and universal, and appealing to the permanent and universal elements and needs in man, but at the same time set in a changing world, presents a special problem. For in each more or less settled age and civilization the permanent religion becomes incrusted with impermanent intellectual assumptions and social institutions from which, when the turn of the wheel comes, and the ideas and institutions are seen to be changing, it can only be disentangled with immense friction and difficulty. And in each new age the prophets of the renascence are intoxicated with the new learning and lamentably unconscious how much they need the old. To turn the hearts of the fathers to the children and the hearts of the children to their fathers is a hard task. It needs a deep wisdom to teach the Church to bring forth out of her treasures things new and old. But it is evident that to deal with such a situation the Church must ask for the maximum of positive mobility that is compatible with real continuity; and that in this relatively mobile self-adjustment lies the principle of true development—not in the accumulation of dogmas.

But if this has been apparent in Europe, it has been even more apparent in the efforts of the Church since the sixteenth century to convert the heathen world. The efforts of early Jesuit missionaries to accommodate Christianity to the Eastern atmosphere were not, I suppose, fortunate, and they were perhaps justly condemned by the Roman authorities. But they showed a true instinct. And if to-day we contemplate the world of missions in the East, there is one lamentation everywhere heard—that we dragged our Western developments and Western controversies and Western ritual and Western ideas of organization and efficiency into an alien atmosphere. These things do not belong to essential Catholicism. We should have sought to start again much further back. We have lacked mobility.

What essential Catholicism is in respect of doctrine and in respect of order is a question which, in part, an attempt has been made to answer in these volumes and to which we shall shortly return; but can we not agree that in any case it falls far short of that highly Western complex of organization, dogma, ceremony, and controversy which we sought to impart to the East and to acclimatize there? It would have been much wiser to convey a simpler message and leave it to fructify and develop on Eastern soil as an indigenous growth. We have shown a lack of mobility.

And may we not assert the general proposition that, while some things are essentials of Catholic Christianity, the smaller the requirements to be carried over from one epoch to another and one race to another, the better? May we not assent to the proposition of Erasmus, "Let the essentials of the faith be limited to the fewest articles possible"? [1]

And if this is so, is there any technical test of the legitimacy of a doctrinal development so important as the requirement that what it asserts shall be really found implicit at least in Scripture—specially of course in the New Testament? This test recognizes the danger of extending the dogmatic requirement, and the necessity of its restriction, as the very condition of Catholic breadth; and it provides the effective safeguard against the peril. We cannot readily conceive that the requirements which our Lord makes on men in these later ages through His Church should be substantially different in emphasis or stricter than His earlier requirements, or His appeal become narrower in its range as the ages pass. Surely all those whom Christ would have welcomed ought to be welcomed now; those whom Christ would have refused, as they were, ought to be refused now. And to embody this principle negatively and positively, nothing is so serviceable as to reiterate

[1] "Quae pertinent ad fidem, quam paucissimis articulis absolvantur." See *Erasmus the Reformer,* by Mr. Elliott Binns (Methuen, 1923).

and insist upon the primitive principle that no doctrine can be made into a dogmatic requirement of the Church, except what is really found implicitly at least in the New Testament—with its positive accompaniment that the Scriptures must be an open book for all the faithful, and the teaching of the Church, public and private, must be so permeated with Scripture, that what is unscriptural in spirit shall pass into instinctive reprobation. The Church ought to embark upon every new age or new region in "the power of the Spirit," expecting to find there much that is properly human and needs to be encouraged, and much that is properly inhuman and false and wicked and needs to be reproved. And the touchstone of fidelity to the Spirit, the touchstone for true discrimination, is—boldly be it said—in the New Testament and nowhere else.

I have been seeking in these last chapters to present two contrasted types of authority—the Roman and the ancient—and to show reasons for preferring the latter. Now I must go on to contrast the ancient Catholic ideal with that of orthodox Protestantism, which, asserting the authority of "the Bible and the Bible only," would ignore the authority of tradition in the Church. After that I must endeavour to work out the old ideal in its modern application. But before the present subject is left behind, I want to go back upon the plea, which is so often appealingly made on behalf of Rome, that its peremptory idea of authority, backed by its effective regimental discipline, is what is best for the needs of the plain man. We of the Church of England often hear the complaint that, in our day of mental confusion and conflicting voices, and with our certainly scandalous lack of discipline, there is no certainty to be found by anxious souls except in the Church of Rome.

Whatever limited *apologia* can be made for the

Church of England shall be made later. Here I am only concerned with the plea that the particular kind of authority which is represented in the Church of Rome is what the ordinary good man needs to lift him out of the strife of tongues. But there are so many kinds of " plain men " and their requirements are so different. One of those most commonly met since the war is the man who is altogether 'offended' because God did not stop the war, or more largely, because a world, which is in so many ways godless and repulsive to our moral sense, is allowed to continue triumphant, as it seems, over the Kingdom of Heaven, or perhaps because in his own case God has seemed so cruel and unjust. Such men cannot bear the trial of Job, or believe in a " God who hideth himself," or " endure as seeing him who is invisible." So they reject, or bitterly criticize, the Christian faith as a whole.

Then there are others, and they also are a large crowd, whose complaint is not of the faith in its fundamentals, but of the Church because it is so untrue to Christ. Why has it not spoken up for justice? Why does it cringe to wealth? Why has it not protested with a unanimous voice against this or that plain outrage upon brotherhood? There is no satisfactory answer to these questions; for the answer that, throughout the Church, the purpose for which it is in the world has been in part forgotten or the sense of it distorted, and that we have to strive to restore in the Church the fuller sense of its vocation, is not satisfactory either to indignant complainants or to anyone to whom the honour of the Church is dear. Nevertheless we must refuse to lose the vision of the Church, as it stands in the purpose of Christ, even though in actual fact the divine image in her is sadly dimmed, and the divine life, as St. Augustine says, frost-bound. Here, too, we must endure as " seeing him who is invisible." The trial of our endurance comes in different ways to different people—through personal trials, or through the silences of God in the great world, or through the faults of the Church everywhere. But to none of these types of distressed souls does the Roman Church make any special appeal.

No doubt the Roman Church does make a special appeal to the particular disposition which craves simply the authoritative voice, and wants, in passive acceptance, to get rid of all personal responsibility for the truth. But I fancy this kind of spirit would have found our Lord a great trial when He was on earth, showing such reserve in providing plain answers to plain questions and leaving His would-be disciples so much to do for themselves. I fancy it would have found more satisfaction with the dogmatic Pharisee. Certainly in the early centuries of the Church in the East such a spirit would have found approximately the same trials as it does among ourselves to-day; for the theological confusion was appalling, and the decisions of bishops in council were bewildering in their contradictions; and indeed the bishops seemed to have lost all steadfastness, and to bend before the contrary winds of imperial tempers; and there were rival bishops in a number of sees; and an insufferable strife of tongues. No one who wished to say bitter things of the Church of England could find more bitter things than St. Basil and St. Hilary said truly of the Church of their time.[1] And they had no idea of any "way out" by centralizing authority and making it absolute. In fact, as historians have perceived, the "way out" was found in the main through the faithfulness of the laity, who persisted, on the whole, in holding fast both to the Godhead of Christ and to His manhood, though their vision also was distorted by the partisan loyalties of rival cities.

[1] See for quotations *Roman Catholic Claims*, Appended Note, iii, p. 212.

Nevertheless the Church did emerge and the Catholic faith did subsist. And in our time plain men have no right to complain if a like trial befalls them.

The great leaders of the Eastern Church of old have been reckoned ever since their age as the Doctors of the Church; and through their days of wild confusion they argued from Scripture, and pointed to tradition, and appealed to reason, and encouraged to steadfastness; and never showed any disposition to seek a remedy in the claim of spiritual monarchy which was already beginning to make itself heard from Rome. We cannot choose for ourselves the particular form in which the trial of our faith is to make us perfect. It is a stern discipline for most of us to learn to "test all things and hold fast that which is good" and to become "in understanding grown-up men" and "spiritual men judging all things and themselves judged of none"; but this is the apostolic ideal for the common Christian to aim at. After all, the fundamental faith of the Church and the New Testament is fairly plain; and rooted and grounded in that, we can devote ourselves to living the life with courage and self-sacrifice, although there may remain many not unimportant questions, to find the answer to which we remain at a loss.

APPENDED NOTE (see p. 212)

DR. MACKINTOSH'S CRITICISM OF CHALCEDON

My excuse for returning at some length to the subject of the Chalcedonian formula is that when I wrote *Belief in Christ* I had not read Dr. H. R. Mackintosh's work on *The Doctrine of the Person of Jesus Christ*,[1] and while this book is a masterly vindication of what is in the main the traditional doctrine of Christ's person, the doctrine of the Nicene

[1] In the "Internat. Theol. Library," reff. to 3rd edition.

Creed, he finally pronounces the terms of the Chalcedonian formula to be unacceptable to the modern mind, and suggests the line on which they should be remodelled. His theological standing gives so much weight to his criticism that I am bound both to state it and to examine it.

The formula of Chalcedon is in part a summary of the decisions of the previous Councils, which came to be reckoned as ecumenical, of which the first was Nicaea. With regard to the Nicene decision, then, we find Dr. Mackintosh speaking with contempt of the Arian Christology which it condemned. He identifies himself with the statement that it is " dogmatically the most worthless of all the Christologies to be met with in history " (p. 178).

And neither on the ground of this particular controversy, nor anywhere else, will he tolerate any criticism of the action of the Councils, or of the writings of the theologians, on the pragmatist ground that " metaphysical explanations " or attempts at a " philosophical theory " of Christ's person are essentially futile. " No escape then is possible, in this field [i.e. the field of Christ's person] or any other, from the obligation to think things out persistently to the end " (p. 304). And further he gives a modified approval to the term *Homoousios*. " With the New Testament in our hands it is impossible not to acquiesce in his [Athanasius'] main conclusion. Even the word 'consubstantial,' so fiercely assailed both then and now, is but the assertion of the real deity of Christ in terms of the philosophy by which it had been denied " (p. 188).[1]

It was the right word, he means, for those times, but not for ours. For he suggests repeatedly that we have left behind the philosophy which speaks in

[1] Cf. " Not less for us to-day faith in God means faith in Jesus. In this naive and experimental sense it is not too much to say that the Godhead of Jesus is *de fide* for the Christian mind " (p. 288).

terms of "substance." This is so important an argument, and, I believe, so mistaken, that I must quote several of Dr. Mackintosh's statements of it. After speaking of Greek sacramentalism as implying a "quasi-physical change in our essential manhood," he remarks (p. 323) that by such a conception "we are naturally led to define Christ's person in terms of substance, not spirit. For reasons which are both religious and psychological or philosophical, this is out of touch with the modern mind. But we are in accord with these great thinkers in the fundamental conviction which inspired them." Again (p. 334): "Substance was simply the category by which earlier thinkers strove to affirm the highest conceivable degree of reality; it was indeed their loftiest notion of God Himself. . . . But we have put aside the category substance, and construe the facts freshly in terms of personality. On the accepted principle of modern philosophy that there are degrees of reality, a personal union ought to be regarded as infinitely more real than a substantial one." Again (p. 416): "Others have insisted that behind the will and thought of Jesus stood a divine substance or nature, of which will and thought are but attributes, and which is somehow real apart from them. This, however, . . . has no meaning except on the assumption that substance as a category is higher than subject or intelligent conscious will—a view against which the history of philosophy since Kant has been one long and continuous protest. If we have learnt anything from the modern criticism of categories, it surely is that no category can be higher than personality or self-consciousness. For us then the proper inference is that the essential and noumenal divinity of Christ the Son ought to be formulated in conceptions other than substance or nature and the like, which really oppose the metaphysical aspect of Sonship to the ethical." Finally (p. 421), he speaks of the orthodox as "placing the reality of God not in His will and character but in an inscrutable and unethical substance."

Now, I am far from denying that this unethical conception of substance is one into which Greek philosophy was liable to fall and which is to be found among Greek theologians. You feel this tendency in the thought of Apollinarius and St. Cyril of Alexandria and in the Monophysites and in John Damascene and in later Greek mystics like Nicholas Cabasilas. The Antiochenes, on the other hand, orthodox and unorthodox alike, were the freest from it, and the Cappadocians, I suppose, on the whole. But anyway, let Dr. Mackintosh repudiate with all his force any such conception of God as is open to this charge of being unethical. Let us cling to the three great definitions or metaphors, "God is light," "God is love," "God is spirit." But I think it can be shown that Dr. Mackintosh's crusade against the category of substance is a disastrous crusade which must be abandoned.

And, first, the Fathers used it simply to express "real being." To say that God is the supreme substance and Christ is of one substance with the Father means simply that God is the supreme reality, and that we say Christ is God in the sense that He belongs essentially to this eternally real being and not to that different kind of dependent being which belongs to creatures. But all kinds of creatures have real, though dependent, being. They are "substances" of different kinds, and in the process of the fourth and fifth centuries it was found so important to distinguish one particular kind of substance, viz. personality, from all others, that an old term, hitherto used indistinguishably from *substantia*, viz. *hypostasis*, was endowed with this special meaning "person," and henceforth *hypostasis* is a name for a special kind of *substance*. But it is really absurd to suggest that the theology of the Councils admits of "substance" being put into opposition to "person," or that "substantial" can be opposed to "ethical." Person was a subdivision of substance, having more content—according to Boethius's famous definition of person, "naturae rationalis individua substantia." This definition was only the summary expression of the terminology on which the Church had settled down.[1]

It is very easy to exaggerate the extent to which the Fathers of the Councils were acting *philosophically*. They simply wanted to say that Christ is really and fully God and really and completely man. The relation of the Father and the Son is different from the relation of one human being to another. Nevertheless there exist two kinds of reality—God and mankind; and the Fathers were content to say that Christ was consubstantial with God the Father as eternal Son and consubstantial with us men in the manhood which He assumed. They only used the best word they could find to describe the real being both of God and of man.

And as to the philosophical crusade against substance, Dr. Mackintosh must really be careful before he joins it. For it certainly imperils his fundamental position—I think I should say it undermines it. The authors of the crusade are pantheists like Spinoza, or are of the Hegelian school. They will acknowledge no substance but one, the Absolute.[2] That alone has reality. All so-called lower "substances" are more or less unreal. And the one thing that is "substantially real"—the Absolute—must somehow contain in itself all the variety of the universe. Thus the absolute cannot be personal, nor have a

[1] On the history of the meanings assigned to οὐσία, substantia, ὑπόστασις, persona, etc., see Professor Clement Webb, *God and Personality*, lecture ii.

[2] Or decline the idea of substance altogether.

determinate will and character. And the unreality of material objects is shared by all personalities. Personality no more than material existence will bear examination. It is not real. And the whole idea of a personal God, the Creator of real things and persons, distinct from Himself, although dependent on Himself, is gone. This is the philosophy which, by the intolerable chaos which it produces in the minds of men, has stung its opponents into sarcasm from Mansel to Lord Balfour.[1] But I will appeal to one who would by no means wish to be regarded as an opponent of Hegelianism, Mr. C. J. Shebbeare, and ask Dr. Mackintosh to read an article of his in *Mind*,[2] in which he makes an urgent appeal to philosophers on behalf of the idea of substance in the sense of real thing. It is, in fact, necessary to retain the idea and the word, if there is not to be a hopeless conflict between philosophy and common sense—the kind of conflict in which philosophy always at last becomes negligible. Philosophy must interpret common sense, not contradict it. Also it is of paramount necessity for Christianity, which believes in God as the creator of persons and things which are real, to insist on retaining the category of substance or "real thing." Thus if it be necessary for the Church to affirm (as Dr. Mackintosh admits) that in worshipping the Son and the Spirit it does so only because they are really God—integral to the divine being—I do not know how that could be better affirmed than by the phrase *consubstantial*, all the more that now that phrase has behind it the tradition and reverence of 1,600 years, and no one could make any effective attempt to dislodge it without stirring the most determined resistance and producing a new and profound schism. Rather let us proclaim to all the winds of heaven that by "substance" the Church means no more and no less than

[1] See *Belief in God*, p. 222. [2] Vol. xxxii, N.S., No. 127.

"real thing," so that when we speak of the Son and of the Spirit as "of one substance" with the Father, we mean that they belong to that one real being which we call God; and when we speak of Christ as of one substance with us, we mean that He took the real being of man, and is that real thing, in all respects, that a man is. Do not let us be hyper-critical.

Passing now from Nicaea to Constantinople, we find of course that Dr. Mackintosh is thoroughly in accord with the rejection of the theory of Apollinarius, and of any theory that would maim or render unreal the manhood of Christ. But I do not think he is sufficiently impressed with the evidences of a divine guidance of the Church, leading it through all the period of the Councils to resist so firmly the decidedly Monophysite tendency of Alexandria, and to stand so jealously for the full reality, physical and spiritual, of the manhood of Christ.[1] Surely he should recognize that it was specially for the spiritual, and therefore ethical, reality of the humanity of Christ that they had to contend. Apollinarianism and Monophysitism were content enough to leave to Him a kind of quasi-human physical nature penetrated with the divine. What the Church demanded was the recognition that the true manhood of Christ, as indeed the true manhood of all of us, lies especially

[1] Luther is quoted (p. 232) as insisting "that the Scriptures begin very gently and lead us on to Christ as to a man, and then to one who is Lord over all creatures, and after that to one who is God." This is no doubt the method suggested by the Synoptic Gospels and the Acts. Dr. Mackintosh puts it in contrast to the method of the Scholastics and many of the Fathers. But Luther's idea is also St. Chrysostom's. "Why," he asks, "does St. Paul (Rom. i. 3–4) not begin from the higher side? [i.e. why does he speak first of the human nature of Christ?] Because Matthew, also Luke and Mark, begin from the lower. One who would lead others upwards must begin from below. And this was in fact the divine method. First they saw Him [Christ] as man on the earth, and then perceived Him to be God." And other references could be given to the same effect.

in its spirit, reason, and will. And though the second Council devised no new term, as far as we know, it made it necessary to fix a term to describe "all that properly belongs to manhood." And is there any better term to use for this purpose than "nature"? St. Paul had used "form" in practically this sense, and Chrysostom identifies the two words. But "the form of God" might have had a really materialistic meaning. Surely "nature" was better; and surely if we believe, in accordance with the fundamental requirements of common sense, that real objects exist in groups, distinguished by identity of qualities, we must speak of them as having the same nature.

This was the outcome of the second Council—to affirm of Christ the nature of man in all its spiritual and ethical completeness and to repudiate anything which denied this completeness.

The Church at this period exhibited no love of dogmatizing. But it was driven to it by the necessity for guarding the foundations of its religion. Arius and Macedonius and Apollinarius really imposed upon it this necessity. It would have been disastrous if the idea of Christ as a demigod, or of His humanity as a truncated humanity, had been tolerated, or if the Spirit had been regarded as a creature. So again it became really necessary to resist the tendencies of the Antiochene school, when they came to a head in the doctrine called Nestorian. Whatever may be said about Nestorius, Nestorianism was a reality. And we have Dr. Mackintosh with us in repudiating any conception which denies the eternal existence of the person of the Son, who, at a certain moment in time, became man.[1] The infant

[1] See p. 450. "In the N.T. the very signature of Christianity is the faith that the Divine Son passed from glory to humiliation"; and p. 453, "In a verse like 'though he was rich, yet for your sakes he became poor,' there is surely little or no significance unless the pre-existent One is a 'person,' a 'self,' in the usual connotation."

child of Mary who grew to be the man Christ Jesus was from the beginning of His human existence the divine person who "impoverished himself" to become like us and to be born of a woman. There is no doubt that this is the doctrine of St. Paul and St. John, and of the Nicene Creed. It is only this that the formula of Ephesus was set to protect. Let it be admitted that there were perils in Cyril's theology, as in fact soon appeared. Let us grant to the full that the Incarnation involved such self-limitation of the eternal Son as admitted of His becoming the subject of real human growth, not in body only but in mind; but it was the same "person," who eternally was as Son with the Father, who, thus pre-existing in the "form" of God, emptied Himself in taking the "form" of man.[1]

Then finally it became necessary at Chalcedon to complete the work of the second Council and to repudiate any theory which suggested that the manhood was so absorbed into the Godhead as to cease to be real.[2] Of course those who made the suggestion had no doubt as to the real Godhead of Jesus. Nor had the Fathers of Chalcedon. He had the "form" or nature of God. That belonged to Him essentially. But He took the created nature of man. So in the unity of one

[1] I do not think Dr. Mackintosh is justified in saying roundly that St. Paul in Phil. ii. "describes our Lord as having abandoned the one mode of being (the divine 'form') for the other (the human 'form')." St. Paul is certainly not a precise logician in his use of terms. He speaks of Christ as "pre-existing in the form of God" and apparently as having the prerogatives which are described as τὸ εἶναι ἴσα θεῷ, and then as having "emptied Himself" in taking the human "form." But he does not say precisely of what He emptied Himself. He did so so far as was necessary for really becoming man—that is all we can ascribe to St. Paul. He certainly did not cease to be Son of God. And he speaks of the cosmic functions of the Son (Col. i. 17, 18, and 1 Cor. viii. 6) as if they were perpetual.

[2] And again later in the sixth Council to affirm that in the abiding nature of man as it exists in Christ are included the human will and the whole human activity.

person there are two natures. That was the phraseology determined at Chalcedon. Dr. Mackintosh does not demur to the unity of the person, or to the affirmation of the full and permanent human nature. But he demurs to the affirmation of two natures in Christ. Not, indeed, that his language always points this way. "We cannot," he writes, "eliminate the duality. As it has been expressed: 'In several passages [of the Fourth Gospel] the contrast is expressly marked between the present revelation of Jesus as Son of man and the true glory of His divine nature. . . . The significance of the name [Son of God] in all these verses lies in the suggestion that the human nature of Christ was united with a higher nature which was present in it even now, and would at last become fully manifest.' This note of contrast seems never to fail."[1] Here Dr. Mackintosh approves of a quotation which affirms the two natures in Christ. So again he speaks of "the union of Godhead and manhood in His person."[2] And he writes with a certain cordiality of Chalcedon. "A clearly felt soteriological interest is behind the careful phrases, and enables us to interpret the whole as a combination of the vital elements which faith has always insisted on combining in its view of Christ the Saviour. Thus the reality and integrity of each nature, of Godhead and of manhood, is upheld: the incarnation has not issued in a being that is somehow neither divine nor human or either exclusively. . . . Thus the decisions of Chalcedon may reasonably be viewed as a great utterance of faith, aware of the wrong turnings that theory may take so easily. They have been well compared to buoys anchored along a difficult estuary, on the right and left, to guide the ship of truth. With the religion of the Creed accordingly we have no quarrel."[3]

[1] p. 109. [2] p. 428. [3] p. 213.

That, one might have hoped, was enough. But Dr. Mackintosh cannot away with the phrase "the two natures." It involves the idea of "two consciousnesses and two wills. The New Testament indicates nothing of the kind, nor indeed is it congruous with an intelligible psychology."[1] "To return thus to a theoretic duality of mental life in our Lord, against which all modern Christology has been a protest, is surely to sin against light."[2] And he speaks of breaking up Christ's single person into two unrelated halves,[3] and he complains that "nature is not an ethical word at all,"[4] and he objects to the idea of an "impersonal manhood."

Now, let it be granted that the phrase an "impersonal manhood" is a very unfortunate one. It does not occur in the definition of Chalcedon. What it means is that there was no *independent* seat of personality in the manhood of Jesus, but that it found its personality in being taken by the Son.[5] That, I think, Dr. Mackintosh must admit. Christ throughout was the Son who is God. "It is very God Himself"[6] which constitutes Jesus our Redeemer. And Jesus is not two persons. Human nature, we recognize, is so akin to God that the Son can take human nature and become the real *ego* of the man, the real subject of all its affections and actions. Thus the man Christ is supremely and emphatically personal; and Scripture calls Him not only man but *a* man,[7] and postulates for Jesus, whom we believe to be the Son incarnate, a proper human development, spiritual and mental as well

[1] p. 470. [2] p. 482. [3] p. 492.

[4] p. 214: surely it is when applied to God and to man.

[5] This is what Leontius of Byzantium means by his phrase *enhypostasia*, which became through John of Damascus the orthodox phrase—"enhypostasia," not "anhypostasia."

[6] p. 411.

[7] Acts ii. 22: "Jesus of Nazareth, a man (ἄνδρα) designated of God," etc.

as physical. Also the Gospels certainly do not present us with the picture of a Christ with two juxta-posited natures, divine and human, acting now in one and now in another. That idea was customary in the theology of the fifth century, but it did not enter into the definition of the Council.

We must view the definition of the Council as what its origin shows it to have been (and Dr. Mackintosh recognizes it as having been), the outcome of negations —the necessary negations of ideas about Christ which would have been destructive to the Christian religion. The result of these negations is a positive framework within which the truth of Christian thought must lie. To quote the simile which rightly pleased Dr. Mackintosh, it marks out the right channel by warning Christians off perilous shoals and currents. But for the positive conception we go to the Gospels, and there we find a positive conception for which the dogmatic boundaries leave room, but which the theology of the period did not generally suggest—a positive picture which requires us to think of the eternal Son of God, within the scope and period of His mortal life, as living and acting under the limitations of a real humanity and from the human point of view. About that I have perhaps said enough in the second volume of this series and elsewhere. Certainly in this respect I find myself in sympathy with Dr. Mackintosh. But that picture in the Gospels requires, so it seems to me, the recognition, in the background, of the two natures and the two wills. Here is a human will obedient to the Father. But only a human will? No; if so, there would have been no redemption. It was "in eternal spirit" that Jesus offered Himself to the Father. The person who willed and the will of self-oblation by which He lived and died were more than human, or they would not have been redemptive. The dogma of the Council had for its object to guard the reality of the human will; but it took the underlying reality of the divine will for granted.

And the consciousness of Jesus, is it merely human? No; there is another element in it. A superhuman and divine consciousness shines out of the human organ, the consciousness which qualifies Him to say, "No man knoweth the Father save the Son," etc., and to speak with the inherent authority of God. True it is we cannot realize as from within the experience of Jesus in willing and knowing. We must be largely agnostic. We cannot form a psychology out of one example which we can only very imperfectly understand. But of one thing we can be sure. Here are fundamentally two natures, a divine and a human—two wills or consciousnesses, a divine and a human; and these "natures" are diverse: only by a supreme act of the divine sympathy the divine has so emptied itself of divine prerogatives as to be able to live and act in and through a human nature and human faculties.[1]

So there is, I feel convinced, no necessity why we should discard the venerable terminology of the Councils—if I add, "until we have a better," I should not be speaking in entire sincerity, for I do not believe the better will be forthcoming. And I am the more inclined thus to feel, because when Dr. Mackintosh advances from criticism to reconstruction, I do not think he is successful. I have not rarely found myself cross-questioned by an undoubted believer in our Lord who was at the same time

[1] Not long ago at a meeting on behalf of reunion among Christians a well-known theologian of the Free Churches was heard to exclaim that "Schleiermacher had proved that a union of two natures in one person was an impossibility"; but we have much less confidence to-day in *a priori* logic than either the Greek Fathers had or the Schoolmen or the German philosophers of a generation or two back. The fact is that neither human nature by itself nor divine nature by itself can account for the Christ of history. And we all know that Schleiermacher's idea of God was much more akin to Spinoza's than to St. Paul's.

sincerely puzzled as to what he or she should think about His person. And again and again I have found the definitions of the Councils, considered rightly as primarily negative, of the greatest help. And I have found the puzzled mind thereby—not satisfied, as if it could know all about an impenetrable mystery, but set at rest and made thankful, and able to read the Gospels with a fuller apprehension.

But I could not get this help from Dr. Mackintosh's suggested terminology. The essence of personality, he insists, is will. "Whether it be in God or man, it [the will] is the last home of essential being." It is enough therefore that Christ should be one with God *in will* (pp. 113 f.). And this is what the Gospels disclose. The will of the Man (Jesus Christ) is identical with the will of God (p. 304). And to affirm this is to affirm "in ethical terms, the highest terms available, . . . His ontological unity with God, in a sense generically different from that which is predicable of man as man." Now, what we read of in the Gospels is the human will of Jesus moving in perfect unity with the will of the Father. Surely the Council was right in affirming so strenuously that He had a human will. But is this all ? Is all we have to think of the human will of Jesus and the will of the Father ? Dr. Mackintosh cannot, does not, mean this. The human faculty of willing in Jesus came into existence when He became man. But there was another will-power, older than the human being of Christ, the divine will of the eternal Son—the will of Him who, not yet incarnate, emptied Himself, impoverished Himself, to be made man, and to "learn obedience" under conditions of human nature. True, this will of the eternal Son, when incarnate, acts under conditions of the humanity, and therefore of the human will-power which He had assumed. But the will of Jesus is still the will of the eternal Son, though acting in and through a human will. Again, the consciousness of Jesus in His human life is the consciousness of the Man; but behind it is an older consciousness—that of the eternal Son who has temporarily condescended to act under conditions of a human mind. And I cannot gain or keep a true thought of Jesus Christ unless I have always in mind that the willing and knowing and acting of the Man was not merely human, but had for its substratum the willing and knowing and acting of the eternal Son. I cannot get away from the necessity for recognizing that fundamentally there are here two wills, two consciousnesses, two natures, though the greater will and consciousness and nature are acting under the conditions of the lesser, within the sphere of the incarnate and mortal life.

To sum up: 1. It was necessary for the Church to repudiate the teaching of certain heresiarchs, if it was to retain the substance of its gospel; and the primary aim of the conciliar definitions is to say "no" to these fundamental errors.

2. But in repudiating these errors the Church built up a certain framework of thought within which the current of men's thoughts and feelings about Christ and the Holy Spirit should move. This framework cannot be bettered—that is to say, we cannot dispense with the ideas of "substance," "nature," and "person," or deny that in Christ we worship one person who, as incarnate, has fundamentally two natures.

3. But for our positive conception of Christ we are constantly to go back upon the Gospels; and the theology of the period of the Councils (as distinct from the dogmatic definitions) has, like the theological thinking of every period, its characteristic defects. The study of the Gospels forces us to recognize that in the Incarnate we have not two, simply juxtaposited, natures and wills and consciousnesses; but

that the Divine Son during the period of His mortal life so fully accepted the limitations of humanity as to act under the conditions of human willing and knowing. Still fundamentally we are also forced to recognize that what is presented to us is not only humanity and human energy, but there is also the divine energy, "eternal spirit," living and acting under the human conditions.

I cannot leave the consideration of Dr. Mackintosh's great work without again expressing my admiration for it in its main drift and arguments. It is only on a single point that I have ventured to be critical.

I have just read Dr. W. A. Wigram's *Separation of the Monophysites* (Faith Press, 1923), in which he pleads very earnestly (chap. xiv) that the nominally Monophysite Churches of to-day, who reject Eutyches and affirm the permanent reality of two "substances," divine and human, in the incarnate person, should not be required formally to accept the definition of Chalcedon with its term "two natures," but that the Orthodox Churches and ourselves should be satisfied with their acceptance, which they are willing to give, of the Christological clauses of the *Quicunque Vult*, wherein the "two substances" are affirmed and which are identical in meaning with Chalcedon. I hope that this proposal will be met in the friendly spirit of Athanasius towards those who "mean what we mean, and dispute only about the word" (*de Synod.*, c. 41).

CHAPTER VIII

THE AUTHORITY OF HOLY SCRIPTURE

No doubt can be rightly raised that the Fathers of the Christian Church did see in the Holy Scriptures of the Old and New Testaments together "the word of God"—documents, therefore, of unique authority as the final testing-ground of doctrine, theological and moral, for every age of the Church; and also there is no doubt that they justified the assignment of this unique position to the Holy Scriptures by claiming for their writers a plenary inspiration of the Holy Spirit such as was claimed for no others.[1] Of course it was some time before the canon of the New Testament was settled. But before that had occurred, the words of Christ and the teaching of the Apostles had a final authority attri-

[1] See on this above, p. 173, where a few quotations are given and further references. But I may refer here to a luminous passage in St. Augustine's *de Bapt. c. Donat.*, i, 4 f., where he is arguing with the Donatists who appealed in justification of their schism to the authority of St. Cyprian. To this appeal Augustine makes a threefold reply. First, he exalts the supreme authority of Scripture. "Who is ignorant that the canonical Holy Scripture, both of the Old and New Testaments, is contained within its own definite boundaries, and is so superior to all later writings of bishops that no doubt or discussion can arise whether anything written there is true or right?" Secondly, he declares the writings of individual bishops to be subject to the criticism of others, whether individually made or in councils, and he subjects local councils to "plenary" or ecumenical, and earlier councils, even ecumenical, to later; "for the earlier are often corrected by the later, when by some evidence or experience [*experimento rerum*] what was hidden comes to light and what was unknown to knowledge." Lastly, he denies their right to appeal to Cyprian, who behaved so differently from them.

buted to them ; and during the process of defining the canon, the question whether any particular book was to be included appears to have been *generally* identified with the question whether it really was the work of an apostle or of the companion of an apostle, whose name it bore or to whom it was attributed.[1] Thus it is a matter of constant assumption that the standard of sound doctrine, to which the Church must always conform, is to be found in the Old Testament as supplying the foundation on which the Church is built, and in the New Testament as containing the teaching of the apostles, who were commissioned to deliver the faith in its fullness once for all.

But it is obviously a very different and a very exciting question whether such a claim for Scripture can be maintained to-day. And the question, if we come to look at it closely, appears to be not one but manifold: (1) Does the Bible, and especially does the New Testament, contain in fact one consistent doctrine ? (2) Can we reasonably maintain the finality of the apostolic interpretation of Christ ? (3) Can we deny that tradition, independently of "Scripture," may have handed down their teaching and be necessary to supplement it ? (4) Can we still ascribe to the writers of the Bible such a unique inspiration as the ancients did, and what is the meaning of this inspiration ? (5) Is the position reasonable which, affirming the finality and complete-

[1] Thus the work of no later teacher, Clement or Ignatius or Hermas, was admitted ; and the admission of the Epistle to the Hebrews meant its attribution to St. Paul or to St. Barnabas or one of the apostolic company. Eusebius seems to take it for granted that if the apostle John did not write the Apocalypse, it would fall out of the list of "acknowledged" books and be reckoned among the "spurious" (*Eccl. Hist.*, iii, 5) ; but see Sanday, *Inspiration*, p. 52, who quotes an (unusual) opinion of Jerome that "it does not matter who is the author of the Epistle to the Hebrews, as in any case it is the work of a church writer, and is daily read out in the churches" (*Ep. ad Dardanum*, cxxix, *P.L.*, xxiii, 1103).

ness of the New Testament doctrine, still demands that the tradition of the Church be appealed to to interpret it? These questions, obviously coming from very different quarters, are all important, and we must consider them all. If I do not include the question about the *limits* of the canon it is because in this book nothing is made to turn on whether Ecclesiastes should be inside and Ecclesiasticus outside, or whether 2 Peter is not wrongly included as the work of St. Peter.

I

Is then the claim that the Bible is so consistent in doctrine that it can be spoken of as conveying to us one "word of God" in the different stages of its delivery a really tenable claim to-day? The first volume of this series was largely occupied with the contention that, whatever changes historical science has recently rendered necessary in the conception of the Old Testament, it has in no way invalidated or even weakened its central claim to be the record of a real self-disclosure made by the living God to the people of Israel through the prophets. There is there presented to us a progressive and continuous doctrine about God and man, and a continuous anticipation, in which lies the predictive aspect of prophecy,[1] that the self-revelation of God was to find one day a climax and fulfilment. It is this prophetic doctrine alone which gives its special value and meaning to the Old Testament. And it is a matter of fact that Jesus of Nazareth presented Himself to men finally as the Christ—the consum-

[1] We are not, as will be contended below, bound to accept all the particular fulfilments of prophecy which the first Christians discovered; but some modern authors repudiate their interpretation of prophecy in general, as I think, unreasonably. See above, Appended Note A, p. 64.

mation of the Old Testament revelation—and it is upon the basis of the Old Testament that our Lord and His apostles and the whole Christian Church after Him have taken their stand. I will not labour this point any more.

But leaving now the Old Testament for the New, we find a number of modern critics denying the unity of doctrine in the New Testament which the Church has found there. Jesus Christ, it is suggested, never did in historical fact make any claim to Godhead, or to divine sonship, other than what belonged in idea to Israel in the Old Testament, or than belongs to every one of the sons of men, if he will have it so. The passages in the Synoptic Gospels which appear so plainly to imply a unique and essential divine sonship are explained away, or regarded as unauthentic, and the witness of the Fourth Gospel to the divine claim of Jesus is denied any historical value. The authority exercised by Christ is reduced to the prophetic type. The phraseology of the institution of the eucharist, which implies a Christ who is to impart His own sacrificed humanity to His people and to be their spiritual food, is declared unauthentic. The whole idea of the sacramental Church is ascribed to the influence of the Hellenistic mysteries. Then the belief of the first church at Jerusalem is explained as purely the Jewish apocalyptic belief transferred to Jesus. Even in St. Paul the conception of the incarnation of an eternal Son is not really to be found—only the supposed Jewish conception of the archetypal heavenly man or pre-existing Messiah, who is neither really divine nor solidly human. Out of this Jewish imagination, coupled with the conception of the Wisdom of God, operative in creation, St. Paul fashions his doctrine of Christ; who is to him always the glorified Christ and is identified with the Spirit. There is not to be found in St. Paul really the doctrine of a personal Spirit distinct from the Son. Only later in the Fourth Gospel is there any real conception of the incarnation of God in Jesus and of the personality of the Spirit. Thus the New Testament contains not one doctrine of Christ but three or four—the purely human or prophetic, the "adoptionist," the conception of the pre-existent man or Christ manifested on earth, and the doctrine of incarnation properly so called—and not one doctrine of the Spirit of God, but two. What has been central and fundamental in the theology of the Church, the doctrine of the Nicene Creed, is not in any way to be ascribed to Jesus Himself, nor to His first disciples, nor even really to St. Paul.

Now, in the second volume of this series and in the earlier chapters of this volume an attempt has been made to examine this set of ideas—which of course is presented by different critics in varying versions and with varying emphasis, but with a substantial identity of tendency—with real freedom of mind. And if any examination is to be free, we must not allow ourselves at starting to be so much impregnated with the atmosphere of current criticism as to lose the power of thinking for ourselves. Granted this freedom of mind, certain conclusions seemed to be fairly certain: (1) That no merely human measure will fit the Christ of the Synoptic Gospels, who certainly so presented Himself to His disciples as to come to have for them really the 'value' of God; and who certainly from time to time spoke of Himself as Son of God in some quite superhuman sense. (2) That St. Paul's testimony gives to the account of the institution of the eucharist historical value which cannot be ignored. (3) That though it is true the disciples were at first, after losing their risen Master from sight, so preoccupied with His glory, and then with the presence of the Spirit whom He had sent down upon them, as to feel no necessity to give account of His person, yet they treated Him, and called upon His name, as a properly divine being. (4) That when St. Paul interpreted His person, it was with a doctrine of the incarnation of the pre-existent Son of God—not of a pre-existent Messiah or heavenly man—a Son of God whom He co-ordinates with God and even calls God. (5) That this doctrine, afterwards confirmed and fortified by the writer of the Epistle to the Hebrews and the writer whom the Church has called John the apostle, prevailed without rival and without controversy—there is no "adoptionist" or other theory to be found in the New Testament. (6) That the Spirit is not by St. Paul, any more than in the Fourth Gospel, identified with Christ, though He is inseparably united with Him. And (7) that the institution of the Church and of certain sacraments must historically be attributed to Christ Himself. On all these points I do not ask for an unhesitating or uncritical verdict, but for a verdict in accordance with the evidence. And we have good reason for insisting on the necessity of freeing ourselves from contemporary prejudices. Dr. J. M. Wilson is a scholar whom we should not accuse of undue conservatism, but after speaking, in a recent book, of the effect on some writers of an *a priori* conviction that the supernatural cannot be true, he adds a warning which, I think, is needed. "It seems to me that some critics, to whom it would be absurd to attribute any such prepossessions, are so anxious not to allow themselves to be prejudiced in the opposite sense that they underestimate the obvious and clear arguments." [1]

If the conclusions just summarized, without being

[1] *The Acts of the Apostles*, p. 33 (S.P.C.K., 1923). The general warning quoted above is separable from its particular application to Blass's view of the 'Western' text of the Acts. See also Appended Note A on Dr. A. H. McNeile's *New Testament Teaching*, p. 278.

re-argued, are sound, then we have answered our first question. The Church was justified in appealing to the New Testament as to a book of many authors, presenting no doubt a variety of points of view and distinctions of emphasis, but presenting also really one doctrine, and not several—one doctrine gradually arrived at under the leadership of St. Paul, but the only one which really interprets certain authentic words of Christ and the whole impression He made on His disciples.

II

In seeking to answer the second question as to the reasonableness of ascribing finality to the apostolic interpretation of Christ's person, as we find it in St. Paul and the Epistle to the Hebrews and in St. John, we are still treading on ground already traversed.[1] If Christ is rightly interpreted in these documents—if no different interpretation can do justice to the fact of Christ—then the Christ so interpreted is essentially final. There can be no conception of God fuller or completer, given under the conditions of this world, than is given in Him in whom the Word is made flesh, and no union of manhood with Godhead fuller than is given in Him in whom "flesh," that is, human nature in all its faculties and progressive development, is the very organ of God. The resistance to this idea of finality comes from a desire to maintain a somewhat abstract belief in evolution, which implies that the past can never be the best. But we are learning that the abstract idea of evolution must submit itself to the facts.[2] It is a fact that the personality of Christ is

[1] *Belief in Christ*, chap. vi, pp. 315–19.

[2] Cf. Dr. H. R. Mackintosh, *The Person of Jesus Christ*, p. 309 (Edinburgh, 2nd ed., 1913): "If it be said the Gospel as involved in history must consent to be equally relative with other facts of

so unique that nothing can account for it but the belief that in the process of history, at a certain moment and in a certain historical person, the Absolute once for all manifested itself under conditions of time. Here is something in history which is supra-historical—towards which and from which all history, so far as it is religious history, must move and in which it must find its centre. The belief that this is so is what has been the strength of the Christian view of the world. As F. D. Maurice said[1]: "A clergyman" (let us say "a Christian"), "it seems to me, should be better able than other men to cast aside that which is merely accidental either in his own character or in the character of the age to which he belongs, and to apprehend that which is essential and eternal. His acceptance of fixed creeds (it would suffice to say 'the apostolic interpretation of Christ's person'), which belong as much to one generation as another, and which have survived amidst all changes and convulsions, should raise him especially above the temptation to exalt the fashion of his own time, or of any past one; above the affectation of the obsolete, above slavery to the present, and above that strange mixture of both which some display, who weep because the beautiful visions of the past are departed, and admire themselves for being able to weep over them—and dispense with them."

Of course we must never forget that the apostolic interpretation of Christ really quickens and inspires

the time series—that it has to choose, in short, between historicity and finality—the answer is that this is pure assumption, and assumption which must be changed if it conflicts with real phenomena. It may well be even bad metaphysics." See also p. 356: "It betrays a disabling bondage to *a priori* dogma, none the less hurtful that it is unorthodox, when men approach a stupendous problem with the tacit understanding that no results can be accepted which fail to conform to a fixed standard."

[1] Preface to Kingsley's drama *The Saint's Tragedy* (1849), see Kingsley's *Poems*, p. xvii (Macmillan, 1902).

religious development in mankind and does not dispense with it. It must take the whole of converted humanity with all its variety of gifts to show the full meaning of Him " in whom are hid all the treasures of wisdom and knowledge "; and only so can Christ be fulfilled in the Church. Nevertheless He is perfect and complete in His own person from the first, and the interpretation of His person which alone secures this must be final.[1] And it was so regarded from the first. Clement of Rome and Ignatius of Antioch, in sub-apostolic days, already look back upon the apostolic doctrine as formative and authoritative, almost before the collection of the canon of the New Testament was begun, just as Athanasius and Augustine do when it was practically settled. And in fact no one who is acquainted with the New Testament books and then sets himself to read those—such as Hermas or Justin Martyr—who in the second century with the best intentions sought to interpret Christ, can do so without feeling that he has come down to a much lower level of understanding and surefootedness.

III

But a curious question remains—whether the ancient Church was right in elevating the written books of the New Testament to a throne of solitary supremacy. Plainly our Lord resolved to entrust His gospel to men, not to written books, and He Himself wrote nothing. Then, when the books of the New Testament were written, many of them appear to be markedly occasional, and none of them

[1] I would refer to an illuminating article by the Rev. Richard Hanson entitled " History and the Historic Jesus," in the *Church Quarterly* of April 1923; see e.g. p. 100: " Christianity is the proclamation of a presence in history which is at once historic in that it appeared in time, and unhistoric in that it, by hypothesis, dominates and controls and gives an absolute value to history."

shows the intention of giving a connected account of Christian doctrine. Why then should not there be valuable parts of the apostolic teaching which were only handed down in 'unwritten tradition'? This, we know, is the theory of the Roman Church, which regards the Scriptures as only the chief source of the apostolic tradition. It requires supplementing by what was unwritten. And this idea of an unwritten tradition has in effect been used to render the whole appeal to Scripture and antiquity null and void. The living voice of the Church at any period, once established, *is* tradition, and must be assumed to have always been so. But this is to give to the idea of tradition a sense akin to the Gnostic idea of a secret tradition. The Fathers totally rejected this idea and countered it with the idea of an open tradition secured in the successions of the bishops. This tradition was in fact only for a little while 'unwritten.' It is written down in detail by Origen and less explicitly by Irenaeus. It was 'unwritten' (*agraphos*) only in the sense that it was not scripture (*graphé*). Thus we do know what the Church 'tradition' was from the second century, and we can boldly say that there was nothing of any doctrinal importance [1] in the tradition, and especially nothing which there was any tendency to make into a dogmatic requirement, except what is in Scripture. The Fathers are quite emphatic in giving to the tradition only an interpretative value.

Perhaps we might be disposed to argue that—granted that in Christ was uttered really the final word of God to man, which is to stand as His message or Gospel through all ages—it seems impossible to imagine that God would not have "devised means" to secure that the message should be delivered with sufficient fullness and plainness by its first com-

[1] See Appended Note B, p. 280, for an interpretation of this qualification.

missioned messengers and in such form that it should be accessible for constant reference. But we distrust such *a priori* arguments from the fitness of things. It is better to be content with the facts; and the fact is that there is nothing of importance, as *doctrine*, which can make a plausible claim to have been in the original tradition which is not also, plainly implicit at least, in the written books.

IV

Now there arises a very large question, which no book attempting to treat of the Holy Spirit in the Church can ignore—what do we to-day believe about the *inspiration* of those sacred books of the Old and of the New Testament to which, as we have seen, the Church assigned so sovereign an authority?

For the ascription by the Church of authority to the books was, we know, due to, or accompanied by, a belief that they were written under the inspiration of the Holy Spirit, and that they brought with them for this reason a divine guarantee of trustworthiness. This root conviction has expressed itself in the doctrine that every book and every sentence of the Bible is infallibly true—a doctrine which has prevailed alike among Catholics and Protestants. But the whole historical and critical world has risen up in arms against this conception and declared it impossible; and in describing at the beginning of these volumes the root causes of present-day unsettlement in matters of religious belief, I had of course to give a very large place to this cause.[1] Now, the whole purpose of these volumes has been to build up a constructive doctrine of God and Christ and the Holy Spirit in the Church without using the books of the Bible except as historical documents. Nothing has been said about them as if they were authorita-

[1] *Belief in God*, pp. 13 ff.

tive, because the subjects of a plenary inspiration. But we are now in a position from which the truth of Christianity, and its authority as the word of God, can be taken for granted. And its authoritativeness is so inseparable from the belief in the inspiration of Scripture that we must seek to determine what we mean by it and how it is to affect us.

The belief of the Christian Church in inspiration of course had its ground in the belief in the inspiration of the Old Testament which they inherited from the Jews. And this we are glad to find was primarily a belief in the inspiration of *prophets*, including Moses as the greatest and most creative of all. The evidence of this is to be found in the fact that no book was admitted into the Jewish canon which was believed to have been written after the time when the unbroken line of prophets ceased.[1] The value of this idea as evidence is quite independent of whether all the books of the Old Testament were in fact written before the line of prophets ceased and the Jews were left with only wise men. The idea is that the *prophet* is the inspired man. And we can notice at once that Philo's [2] identification of inspiration, in the highest sense, with the annihilation or expulsion of the human faculties of thought and reason—so that the inspired man is the purely passive instrument of the Divine Spirit, which dictates through him—does not at all correspond to the facts about the higher prophets of Israel and was never the view entertained by the Christian Church.[3] It was in fact derived from Greece and not from Israel. Those whom we name "the prophets" are occasionally represented as falling into trances, but this is rare,

[1] For the evidence of this see Sanday, *Inspiration*, pp. 110 ff. (Longmans, 1893)—surely an admirable book. The date suggested for the last of the prophets is that of Artaxerxes Longimanus, i.e. the date of the Book of Esther.

[2] For quotations see Sanday, *op. cit.*, p. 72.

[3] See *Belief in God*, p. 87, n. 3.

and even so they retain to the full their consciousness and individuality.

And the modern critical view of the Old Testament would lead us to see in the prophetic teaching the key to the whole. The traditional law of the *cultus* of Jehovah and the whole social law, in their final form, were permeated with the prophetic spirit. So were the histories. So was the Wisdom literature. So were the Psalms. It would appear that the Song of Songs was only suffered to be within the canon because it was interpreted mystically of God and His Church as husband and wife, which is a recurrent note of prophecy [1]; and Ecclesiastes only because, as the book stands, that doubting, pessimistic spirit is led back finally to the fundamental Jewish loyalty. "This is the end of the matter; all hath been heard: fear God, and keep his commandments; for this is the whole duty of man." The spirit of prophecy thus permeates the whole literature of the Old Testament. That the prophets were really commissioned messengers of the word of God and really "spoke as they were moved by the Holy Spirit" we accept with enthusiastic assent; and every book of the Old Testament, whether we accept the stricter Hebrew canon, or include the books which appear in the Greek Bible, which we call 'apocryphal,' partakes of the inspiration of the prophets in varying degrees. We may boldly say that the doctrine of the inspiration of the Old Testament stands as surely to-day as of old, in spite of changed views as to the character of the literature and the dates of its books. The Old Testament *is* not the word of God in the sense that everything there narrated as history is historically correct, or that we can isolate any particular text and say, "This is an infallible utterance of God"; but it *conveys to us*, in a variety of books of different kinds, one moral and spiritual message,

[1] Hastings's *Dict. of the Bible*, iv, p. 589.

really inspired by the Spirit of God, who both "spake by the prophets" and also penetrated through the whole assemblage of books.

No doubt the Jewish rabbis of our Lord's time held a strict doctrine of the infallibility of the sacred books in all their details. And their exegesis was already minute and, as we should feel, irrational and intensely literalist. But one of the most impressive facts about our Lord's teaching was that there was nothing of this spirit in His appeal to Scripture. We recognize there "the sovereign breadth of view and deep penetration of insight by which the Founder and Master of our faith was enabled to seize the spirit of the Old Testament legislation and to ensure that even the letter . . . shall be observed more effectively than it had been by striking down to the root of motive which the law could not reach."[1] He is indeed recorded[2] to have taught His disciples that "till heaven and earth pass away, one jot or one tittle shall in no wise pass away from the law, till all things be accomplished," and to have bidden them be strict Jews and not lax Jews, in preparation for the Kingdom. But already the hour of accomplishment had struck. "The law and the prophets were until John: from that time the gospel of the Kingdom of God is preached." And that gospel was profoundly disturbing to the tradition. It did not indeed destroy the law, but it fulfilled it by transmuting it into a new energy of the Spirit, which would proceed by a quite different method from that of minute enactments. Nothing, I think, is less justified on the whole than to represent our Lord as accepting the current Jewish interpretation of the meaning of inspiration, however true it is that it returned in great measure upon the Church in later days.

[1] Sanday, *op. cit.*, p. 411.

[2] Matt. v. 18, 19; cf. Luke xvi. 17 and note the differences.

It must be accepted as a fact that in dealing with the books of Scripture our Lord used the language and knowledge of the time, and showed, at least, no signs of transcending it ; just as He showed no signs of transcending the knowledge of nature which belonged to His age or country. That He should have done otherwise would have contradicted the whole manifest intention of Divine providence that men should only acquire for themselves by infinite pains the knowledge which is within their grasp. But I do not think it can be fairly urged that our Lord fixed upon us, whether about nature or about Jewish literature, the yoke of first-century knowledge. His teaching about God and man and the Kingdom of God is quite independent of any particular stage of mental development and human science. There must have been in our Lord's mind a world of ordinary "knowledge" which He shared with His contemporaries, by the use of which alone He could speak intelligibly to them, which was part of the furniture and limitation of His real humanity ; but this He did not teach. The only teaching which He gave, and gave with the note of infallible certitude, was drawn from a profounder and eternal source. On the only two occasions on which our Lord's argument appears to depend on either a question of authorship or the verbal authority of a text, the context makes it natural to suppose that He was only impressing on a certain group of objectors the duty of consistency in their arguments.[1] He was not giving any positive teaching at all.[2]

[1] I am referring to Mark xii. 35 and John x. 34–6. I have argued the matter in *Belief in Christ*, pp. 186–7, 191–3. See also on both passages Sanday, *op. cit.*, pp. 408–9, 417, 419, 483.

[2] Our Lord undoubtedly *taught* that the Old Testament Scriptures anticipated a suffering and dying Christ. If it were the case that no such prophesying can be found really in the Old Testament, it would be a very serious matter. But the case is not so : see above, p. 64.

When we turn from our Lord's teaching to that of the apostles and their companions, we are impressed with their prophetic insight into the real meaning of the Old Testament. Thus their moral teaching is the real flower of Old Testament morality. And St. Paul does really understand both the value of the law and its limitations. It was a preparation for the Spirit. It was to end in something not national but catholic. The doctrine of redemption and glory through humiliation, suffering, and death, which all the New Testament writers ascribe to the Old Testament, was a real note in the prophetic teaching which it was moral blindness to have overlooked. And the Epistle to the Hebrews is right about the sacrificial system. It was really essentially futile. "The blood of bulls and of goats could not take away sin." But it corresponded to something so deep in human need that it demanded an equivalent on a higher spiritual plane. Thus Christ really was the end of the law and the Church of the New Covenant the fulfilment of the Old. By comparison with the Rabbis the understanding of the meaning of the inspiration of the Old Testament shown by the New Testament writers is as light to darkness.

And the general account which they give of its inspiration is as acceptable to-day as it ever was. "The gospel of God, which he promised afore by his prophets in the holy scriptures." "God, having of old time spoken unto the fathers in the prophets by divers portions and in divers manners." "To him bear all the prophets witness." "Concerning which salvation the prophets sought and searched diligently, who prophesied of the grace which should come upon you: searching what time or what manner of time the Spirit of Christ which was in them did point unto, when it testified beforehand the sufferings of Christ, and the glories which should follow them."[1]

[1] Rom. i. 2; Heb. i. 1; Acts x. 43; 1 Pet. i. 10–11.

"No prophecy of scripture is of private interpretation. For no prophecy ever came by the will of man: but men spake from God, being moved by the Holy Ghost." "The Holy Ghost this signifying, that the way into the holy place hath not yet been made manifest, while as the first tabernacle is yet standing; which is a parable for the time now present." "Whatsoever things were written aforetime were written for our learning, that through patience and through comfort of the scriptures we might have hope." "Every scripture inspired of God is also profitable for teaching, for reproof, for correction, for instruction which is in righteousness: that the man of God may be complete, furnished completely unto every good work." [1]

But when we pass from the general interpretation of the Old Testament to the interpretation of particular texts by the first teachers of the Church, there is something different which has to be said in a considerable number of instances. Their minds were full of the interpretations of prophecies—"Thus it must have been, for so it was foretold"; thus it happened "that the scripture might be fulfilled which said"—and we feel again and again that we cannot recognize in the original text from the Old Testament which is cited, any prophecy demanding such a fulfilment.[2] We can cordially accept their

[1] 2 Pet. i. 20–1; Heb. ix. 8; Rom. xv. 4; 2 Tim. iii. 16–17.

[2] Such instances are fairly frequent in St. Matthew, e.g. ii. 15–18; and in him we find three or four cases where the supposed prediction is apparently allowed to modify the details of the record of fulfilment, e.g. Matt. xxi. 2 (the introduction of the ass beside the colt), xxvii. 3–10 (the introduction of the precise sum given, "thirty pieces of silver"), 34 (the gall). In Acts ii. 25 ff. the argument from the psalm is very precise as to the mind of David in writing it (cf. xiii. 35) and we cannot feel sure of the authorship, or feel that the original justifies the assumption that the psalmist is speaking *in persona Messiae*. Again, St. Paul's arguments from particular texts, as in Gal. iii. 13 and 16, Rom. iii. 10–18 and ix. 25, are, we feel, merely verbal and in no way borne out by the original context. See Dr. Strong's *Place of Scripture in the Church*, p. 38 (S.P.C.K., 1917).

general principle, viz. that the Old Testament as a whole anticipates and demands a climax or fulfilment in the future, and that this climax or fulfilment is really found in Christ, but their method of argument from particular texts belongs to their time and is quite superseded.

Here, however, we have passed from the inspiration of the Old Testament to the inspiration of the New Testament writers.

The most direct and definite claim to the plenary inspiration of the prophet, both in general and in detail, that is to be found in the New Testament, is that of John, the Seer of the Apocalypse (whether he be John the Evangelist or another); and I think that in that wonderful book we do see as vividly as anywhere the real effect of inspiration and its limits. John was really inspired to read the signs of the times and to see the meaning and issue of the conflict between the Empire and the Church, and to deliver to the terrified Christians the true message of encouragement. The visions are none the less real visions of God because the scenery is so plainly supplied by the mental furniture of the seer. It is a real foretaste of what must be, because God is God; but it is very far from being "history written beforehand," and those who have sought to interpret its mystical numbers in terms of historical years or temporal duration have gone utterly astray. We have not any reason to suppose that, if the seer, instead of giving us his successive visions, had endeavoured in cold prose to write down what he anticipated the course of historical events would be, he would have been found to be supernaturally enlightened, any more than the older prophets, except as to the meaning and issue of the struggle.

For the New Testament conception of the inspiration of an apostle we turn to St. Paul. He, no doubt, regarded the apostles, and the prophets who ranked with them or after them, as inspired.[1] Their inspiration is the greatest of the gifts of the Holy Spirit to the Church. Accordingly St. Paul regards his message as a direct and personal revelation of God,[2] though for the facts concerning Christ he appeals not to revelation but to the tradition received,[3] and sometimes he appeals to words of Christ as of final authority. But we notice that he regards the authoritative teaching as once for all received, so that he had no authority to alter it or add to it.[4] If he received subsequent "revelations," they were "unutterable."[5] And while he clearly claims divine authority for his message, and that of the apostles generally, he claims no special inspiration to write, and no infallibility for judgements expressed which are not covered by his gospel or for which he has no "word of the Lord" to rely upon. For instance, in regard to marriage he distinguishes sharply between the word of the Lord pronouncing the indissolubility of the marriage bond, and his own opinion on points of difficulty, which he gives not as the word of God, but as the judgement of one who has been found faithful, or "I think I also have the Spirit of God."[6] In respect of women's headdress he claims peremptorily that the discipline of the Church should be accepted obediently.[7] But he would not claim that a direct personal inspiration of God is to be found in his arguments. Again, with regard to the ministries to be allowed to women, St. Paul would certainly claim that women must accept the discipline of the Church, whatever it is[8]; and he would claim that the subordination of women to men was

[1] 1 Cor. xii. 29. The point is the variety of spiritual gifts in the one body; cf. Eph. iv. 8–12.

[2] Gal. i. 12. [3] 1 Cor. xv. 1–11, xi. 23 ff. [4] Gal. i. 8–9.

[5] 2 Cor. xii. 1–4—that is to say, they did not affect his message to the Church.

[6] 1 Cor. vii. 10–12, 25, 40.

[7] 1 Cor. xi. 2, 16. [8] 1 Cor. xiv. 34–36.

a divine law running through life as a whole. But I see no reason to believe that he would have us claim perpetuity for his particular enactments, whether against the ordination of men twice-married or teaching by women. Certainly he *would* claim perpetuity for the principle that all alike, women and men, must accept the discipline of the Church.

We are pleased to see that, like St. Paul, so the apostles from the beginning, and the historians of the New Testament, appeal for their facts not to inspiration, but purely and simply to evidence, the evidence of eye-witnesses.[1] And, if we may judge from the indications of St. Luke's preface, and St. John's manner of correcting tacitly mistakes in the Synoptic tradition, there was no strict infallibility assigned to the records, when they were written.[2]

When we pass from the New Testament into the records of the Church, we note two things. First, that as the canon of the New Testament forms itself by the selection of the Four Gospels, and the letters of Paul, and then of the rest of the documents, the same inspiration which was claimed for the Old Testament books was claimed, and rightly, for the New. Inspiration under the New Covenant was indeed something fuller and completer than inspiration under the Old; and the Church could not doubt, any more than we can doubt, that a real inspiration guided the Evangelists and the author of the Acts, though they claimed only the best information. But we note, secondly, that as for the Old Testament so for the New, the Christian Church *on the whole* took over from the Jewish schools an idea of inspiration which made it coincident with infallibility and completeness of knowledge.[3] Thus the tradition

[1] Luke i. 1–3; Acts i. 1–3 and 21, 22; 1 John i. 1–2.

[2] But it is in the Fourth Gospel regarded as a special function of the Holy Spirit in the hearts of the Twelve to quicken their memory of the teaching of Jesus (John xiv. 26).

[3] For quotations, see Sanday, *op. cit.*, pp. 31 ff.

18

equating inspiration with infallibility is primitive in the Christian Church and pre-Christian, in fact. This is to us moderns utterly unacceptable. We are sure that there is in the Old Testament, besides a great deal of very good history, also a good deal of legend and of "history as it ought to have been"; and that though the same Christ is presented in all the Gospels, yet there are many divergences of detail, both as regards the words and works of Christ, even among the Synoptists, and no infallibility in their use of Old Testament texts. By this we must stand.

And we would call attention to two points. First, that there are a good many signs of the "modern" spirit in individual Fathers and even in whole schools. Thus there is a widespread belief that the early chapters of Genesis were allegory or picture-writing and not history.[1] Again, the depreciation of the sacrificial system of the Jews has quite a tradition. It is asserted to be something which God tolerated, but did not ordain. It was in its origin pagan.[2] But this involves free handling of the record.[3] Again, the principle of gradual development in the divine education of man under the Old Covenant has a full tradition behind it. The "moral difficulties of the Old Testament" are to be explained in the light of the fact that God was doing the best for the education of a savage people, by leading them forward gradually into the true way.[4] Even in the Gospels St. Chrysostom would have us accept the consolation

[1] See *Lux Mundi*, p. 263, also p. xxv, n. 1.

[2] p. 241, n. 1; also Chrysostom on St. Matt. vi. 3.

[3] In St. Jerome's preface to the Epistle to *Philemon* he quotes the opinion of some who would refuse it a place in the canon on the ground that everything which occurs in St. Paul's Epistles was not written under inspiration, e.g. not "The cloak which I left at Troas," etc., or "But withal prepare me a lodging," or "Would that they that trouble you were cut off" (or "mutilated")—just as the prophets do not always write under inspiration, but sometimes as a *homo communis*. See Sanday, *Inspiration*, pp. 43–4.

[4] *Lux Mundi*, pp. 240–2.

that the discrepancies between them in detail only enhance the value of their common witness to the matters of chief importance.[1]

Also we need to notice that Origen makes it part of the authoritative tradition of the Church that the Scriptures, which were written by the agency of the Spirit of God, " have two senses, the plain and the hidden, whereof the latter can be known only to those to whom is given the grace of the Holy Spirit in the word of wisdom and knowledge."[2] And he revelled in this belief in a mystical and allegorical sense of Scripture, to the extent of delighting to point out statements in the Old Testament which could not be true in their literal sense and were only meant to stimulate us to discern their spiritual meaning. And though Origen's successors would not commonly have been ready to admit that the literal meaning could be untrue in fact, they used the key of the mystical meaning in a way that we should regard as totally arbitrary, to emancipate the Church from " the letter " of the Old Testament.

As we read the Christian Fathers, then, we find them to be men of very different intellectual statures and tendencies ; and we feel that in our modern controversies about the meaning and consequences of inspiration they would have taken different sides : that some of them, St. Chrysostom for instance, would have welcomed modern criticism, and some of them, for instance St. Leo, would have decisively rejected it ; and that St. Augustine would have accepted it as a matter of course before his conversion, and hesitated long afterwards about it, and finally, under the exigencies of controversy, rejected it. But this is, of course, conjecture.

[1] *In Matt.* Hom. i, 2, *P.G.* lvii, 16, 17, 18.

[2] *De Princ.*, i, prol. The school of Antioch, however, did not, or did but slightly, admit the legitimacy of recurrence to "the hidden" meaning.

The other point which we should wish to emphasize is that, in spite of manifold provocations, in early days the Church never formulated any binding dogma on the subject of inspiration, nor even contemplated such a course. Even up to the time of the *Encyclical* of Leo XIII, Newman can plead that "The Councils of Trent and of the Vatican tell us distinctly the object and the promise of Scriptural inspiration. They specify 'faith and moral conduct' as the drift of that teaching which has the guarantee of inspiration." It is with the doctrine of inspiration, as with the doctrine of the Atonement, that different theories have become dominant at different periods, and later have been more or less completely rejected by the common sense of the Church, and the old belief has been none the less maintained, but in a sense which has been—providentially—left quite undefined.

In many respects we are not at all the intellectual superiors of our remote forefathers. In some we are conspicuously inferior to the ancients of this or that period. But in some we have made real and immense advances. The science of history is one of these latter departments. In spite of all the extravagances and waywardnesses of some critics and historians, in spite of the real or supposed victories which tradition is said to have won over criticism, there is no question about it that an infinitely truer view of the length and scope and stages of history, and of the various kinds of literature in which the human spirit has expressed itself, is possible for us than was possible for the men of two centuries or less ago.[1] And just as it was fatal for the Church to claim the power to lay a restraining hand on the freedom of astronomical science, because its results were disturbing to those who had been taught to believe that all the statements of the Bible on all sorts of subjects were infallibly true, so is it

[1] See *Belief in God*, p. 13.

fatal for the Church to claim to restrict the sphere of historical criticism. It must be applied to the history and documents of the Bible, Old Testament and New,[1] as to all documents which claim to be human history and human literature. What we have a right to demand is that it shall be really *historical* criticism, and not inspired by a dogmatic belief, which has no claim to call itself historical science, that there can have been no such events as are called supernatural. But if we follow the course only of legitimate criticism, it leads to many conclusions as to sacred history and literature which are startling and revolutionary, just as it does in history that we call secular. We must welcome all the conclusions which are apparently assured, and when we have done so we find that a certain kind of belief about the effect of inspiration which was possible to our forefathers has become impossible for us. We must admit more of gradualness, more of fallibility and individuality in the human instruments, than used to be admitted. But when all this has been done, we dare to maintain that the grounds for believing in a real inspiration by the Holy Spirit of God not only of the prophets and apostles, but also of the writers generally of the Old and New Testaments, are not less strong than before. We have been led by the evidence to limit the scope of the inspiration to "the things of faith and morals"; and we have

[1] Some of us, who claim to be Biblical critics and also believers in the Christian Creed, are still annoyed by the imputation that we are ready to apply criticism freely to the Old Testament but not to the New (see G. C. Coulton, *Five Centuries of Religion*, p. 11). More than twenty years ago Dr. Driver and I repudiated this imputation, and I have done so since again and again. To make it implies that free criticism is always destructive of real historicity. But this is not so. As often it is constructive. It is so, I believe, when it is allowed to be really free about the documents of the New Testament. What is asked for the Gospels and Acts is only what criticism vindicates for the account in the books of Samuel and Kings of David's reign, viz. that it is good history. Criticism applied to different periods and documents reaches different results.

been led to recognize degrees of inspiration. We do not find nearly so much of the inspiration of God in Chronicles or Ecclesiastes or Esther as in the prophets. But we do find the movement of the same spirit in all the books. And the longer we put ourselves to school in the books of the Bible the more sure do we come to feel about the inspiration of their writers.

Something has still to be said about the two distinguishable uses of the Bible—as historical documents and as the books of inspired men; but before we come to this there is the last of the suggested questions which has still to be met.

V

Is the position reasonable which, affirming the finality and, in a sense, completeness of the New Testament teaching about the meaning and content of the Gospel message, still demands that the tradition of the Church be relied upon to interpret both it and the Old Testament?

It has been commonly remarked that the shock of modern criticism as applied to the Bible has been felt much less among Catholics than among Protestants. This cannot mean that the formal standards of orthodoxy about Holy Scripture have been less strict among the former. As we have seen, the doctrine of Biblical inspiration as stated by Leo XIII was of the severest and most rigid kind; and in the Church of England the Tractarian tradition was as strict as the Evangelical. But Roman Catholics in general have not had the Bible as an "open book." They have not been familiar with it as a whole; it has not constantly been read in their ears in public worship in their own tongues; it has not been normal piety to read it. "Who reads the Evangelists?" is even to-day a question by which the Italian Papini can rebut the objection that it could not be necessary for him simply to retell the story of Jesus, which is incomparably well told in the original documents. Certainly then, though among Roman Catholic students the strain has probably been great, it has not been much felt among the laity.

And generally it is true that a Catholic—in the sense of one who believes in the Church and the divine authority of its Creed—ought to have felt, and has in fact felt, the strain of the New Criticism less than the Protestant, whose traditional authority has been "the Bible and the Bible only." For the power of naked appeal to the infallible book—chapter by chapter and verse by verse—was exactly what the New Learning of our day has cut at the root. And popular Protestantism was in fact thrown into the deepest confusion. The mere appeal to the Book had tended to level all its parts [1]; and that upon the highest level of value and certainty. To say that man had developed out of the lower animals, or that Moses did not give the Law as it stands in the Pentateuch, or that there are inaccuracies in the Gospels, seemed to demolish the basis of faith. The Catholic was plainly better off. His faith rested primarily on the Creed of the Church. This gave him his point of view. It lifted into high relief certain events and ideas as the things to be believed. Granted the assurance that these things were so, he had still the solid ground under his feet, while the discussion about Biblical inspiration and the nature of the Old Testament books proceeded.

And the Catholic point of view is fundamentally the true one. In a sense Christ may be said to have left the Church with a book, but it was the Old Testament, and this was confessedly imperfect

[1] So it made the Puritans intensely Judaic. See Truslow Adams, *Founding of New England*, p. 80.

and superseded by the authority inherent in Himself. "It was said to them of old time . . . but I say unto you"; "The law and the prophets were until John." Thus the value of the Old Testament was chiefly prophetic. It had proclaimed a certain doctrine about God, and in various ways had prefigured and predicted what God was to do in the good time coming. Thus it "proved" that Jesus was the Christ; and it supplied the New Israel with a mass of moral warnings and instructions. But henceforth it could not be the final or central authority. "We do wrong to the New Testament," said Augustine, "if we put the Old on the same level with it." The final authority lay in the Lord Jesus. And He had written nothing, but He had reinstituted the divine society, the Church of God, and in the persons of the apostles had equipped it with a body of instructed men who were to be "his witnesses." Thus besides the Old Testament the Church had at first no book, but only "the teaching of the apostles," as orally delivered, in their memories and hearts. The Church was the bearer of the authoritative message, "the word of God." Gradually the books were written which came to form the canon of the New Testament. But for the most part they were books written to meet some special need in some particular church or individual member of the church. They were none of them written to uninstructed or unbaptized persons to give them their first understanding of the Christian faith. The "apostles' teaching," "the form of teaching whereunto ye were delivered," is always presupposed. This we note throughout the New Testament. The readers of the different books are to be those who already hold and understand the faith.

This is so with the narrative of the Gospels, as is witnessed by St. Luke's preface—"that thou mayest know the certainty about the things in which thou wast informed" (at the time of initiation into the Christian religion). The circumstances of St. Mark's composition of his Gospel indicate that the object of his writing was to record an oft-told tale. So St. John wrote the Fourth Gospel to confirm the Church in the faith, and apparently to supplement, and in detail correct, an existing tradition. In the Epistle which accompanied his Gospel, he reiterates that it is "the word which ye heard" (when ye became Christians) that he is writing. "Ye know all things," "I have not written unto you because ye know not the truth, but because ye know it," "That which ye heard from the beginning" is to abide in them. So it is with St. James: "Ye know this, my beloved brethren." So it is with St. Jude: he writes exhorting them "to contend earnestly for the faith which was once for all delivered." So St. Paul refers constantly back to an original "tradition," a word delivered, which not even he, not even an angel from God, can have authority to alter.

It is important to notice in studying the New Testament what it is that those who are to read or hear particular letters are supposed already to have been taught and to know; and in the case of St. Paul's converts we can discover this with some completeness, though so incidentally are the points mentioned that we must not argue from his silence on any particular point that it was not part of his preliminary teaching. But these 'elements,' or the 'tradition,' certainly comprised (1) a code of personal and social morality (1 Thess. iv. 1, 2, 9); (2) some teaching about the name of God—the Father, the Lord Jesus, or the Son, and the Holy Spirit, and the Incarnation of the Son and His present glory and future coming—knowledge of this 'doctrine' being plainly assumed; (3) certain facts concerning our Lord's human life—His birth of a woman, His death for our sins, resurrection and ascension, and

His appearances after His resurrection in detail; (4) the meaning of the sacraments of baptism (Rom. vi. 3) and the eucharist, the incidents of the institution being given at length; (5) the Church as the New Israel and the Body of Christ and the sphere of the Holy Spirit's action. This must not be taken as an exhaustive list of points on which St. Paul takes it for granted his converts have been already instructed. St. Luke's preface would seem to indicate that our Lord's birth of a virgin was already in the tradition—that is, among the things of which Theophilus had been informed. In the more strictly Jewish churches we cannot so easily judge the content of the first tradition. From the Epistle to the Hebrews—if we may assume that it was written to a Hebrew church—we learn that the first elementary instruction concerned "repentance and faith, baptisms and the laying on of hands, resurrection and judgement." But the words which follow about enlightenment and tasting of the heavenly gift, and being made partakers of the Holy Ghost, and tasting the good word of God and the powers of the age to come, imply a fuller instruction than the list suggests. Certainly the First Gospel must be taken as a document written for Hebrew Christians, and when that was written the threefold name of God—"The Father, the Son, and the Holy Ghost"—which implies a theology like St. Paul's and St. John's—was already associated with baptism by what was believed to be the word of Christ.

Assuredly, then, from the time when the first books of the New Testament were being written, it was the practice of the Church to give its converts fairly full instruction in faith and morals. The Creed of the Church is considerably older than the canon. And after the canon was formed, their Creed gave the Christians their *point of view*[1] in

[1] This is Athanasius' word, σκοπός.

listening to and reading the books. If in result it was agreed that "the Bible is to prove" the legitimacy of the Church teaching—i.e. is to be the final court of appeal—yet certainly it was the function of "the Church to teach" in the first instance. The convert after his baptism, and after the instruction which he received as a catechumen, found himself a member of a close fellowship saturated with a certain moral and theological and sacramental tradition. This tradition possessed him like an atmosphere, and it was as possessed by this atmosphere that he understood the Scriptures. This was the inevitable outcome of the method of Christ, who, writing no books, and giving no order for any to be written, founded a Church and instituted apostles to be the carriers of His gospel into the world.

And just as long experience has made it evident that the tradition needs the open Bible to keep it pure, so certainly it has made it evident that the Bible needs the guidance of the Church to introduce it to its readers. I do not mean that intelligent individuals—whether Greeks and Romans of old or Indians and Japanese and Chinese of to-day—have not been enlightened and converted to Christ by reading a New Testament all alone by themselves. It has been so and it still is so. But on the whole the isolated individual with the Bible is like the eunuch of Candace. He lacks guidance. And we have abundant experience to prove that the private interpretation of the Bible becomes the source of strange perverted doctrines based on misunderstood texts, isolated from the general context. As surely as history warrants us in saying that the books were not written to give the first knowledge of Christ, but presuppose "the tradition" accepted and known, so experience warns us the books should still be kept in their original context, as books interpreted by the Church for whose members they were written.

And if the history of sectarianism teaches us this lesson, so equally does the history of Biblical criticism at the hands of critics who either disbelieve the religion or treat it as—what it never can be—a matter purely for the speculative intellect: within their area we note the way in which the passion for new theories constantly prevails over the sober estimate of evidence; and we note also the extraordinary differences in the conclusions reached by different schools of criticism, and their rapid rise and fall. No one, I think, can study the history of rationalistic criticism without feeling that, though we owe it a great debt for the questions it has stirred and the real light it has constantly thrown on the problems, yet this is not the way to find the truth about religion, which, at its root, is still hid from the wise and understanding and revealed to the childlike. The Bible, if it is to be understood, must still be read in the same spirit in which it was written.

For the Christian religion is first of all a life based on a teaching accepted as the word of God, and constantly verified in an agelong and nearly world-wide experience. No doubt its message and claim must be constantly tested. For most men the testing must be mainly practical. Put to account by faith, the claim verifies itself as divine in moral and spiritual experience. But it must also be tested intellectually and in the field of critical history, and to do this is the special vocation of the scholar. He must do it with entire freedom, following the light where it leads him. But he will be the better equipped for enquiry, not the worse, because he understands his subject-matter with the sort of understanding that only faith, and the experience based on faith, could ever have given him.

VI

To conclude, then, there are two uses of Scripture which must be kept on the whole distinct. There is the evidential use ; and for this purpose we must treat the books of the Bible like any other books, without any regard to inspiration. It is indeed wholly illogical and out of order to introduce the claim of inspiration for the books of the New Testament before the faith in Christ is secured. And for this purpose again we must treat the books, not as collected into a canon of sacred scripture, but as independent books, the date and character of which it is the problem of criticism to fix. And all this must be done freely—nothing must be allowed to obscure the possibility of divergent opinions in the different authors, though (as has been said) it is true that the student who understands the religion from within is more likely to show a sane and balanced understanding of the books than one to whom they are merely as documents dug up by antiquarians out of the Syrian sand. Still, in the evidential use of the books the presuppositions of piety must not be allowed to hinder the adoption of any conclusion which criticism requires. The documents must be treated and estimated solely on their historical value and as witnesses to what the writers believed and had experienced.

But this is not their primary use. They grew up within the Church as documents in which inspiration —that is, the action of the Spirit of God on the soul of man—is seen at its highest. They are set before believing souls as documents of the highest spiritual authority. Each Christian is challenged to put himself to school with book after book, with the sure conviction that each one of the books has something to teach him, some special aspect of truth which his soul needs to mould it into the divine likeness. And this is the use of the Bible with which the preacher is mostly concerned.

No doubt "evidential" lectures should be delivered occasionally from the pulpit, and they should be boldly based on a frank and free criticism. No doubt also in the preacher's normal use of the Bible he should have the conclusions of criticism in his mind. He will not, in drawing rich lessons from the early chapters of Genesis, imply that they are historical accounts of particular incidents, because he knows better. He will not quote the passage about the Three Heavenly Witnesses, because he knows it does not belong to the original text. He will not quote St. Matt. xii. 40 or xxviii. 19—the formula of the threefold name—as words of our Lord if he seriously doubts whether they are so. But he will not obtrude his opinions. He will seek to preach positively, not negatively, and almost always in view of the object of preaching—to show men "the way," and the truths which are the ground of the way, and which assist us to follow it. And recognizing how wide and deep the function of "the Scriptures" as "instruments of the spiritual life" was intended to be, he will never be content to say merely "the Church teaches" so and so, still less to emphasize some fragments of Church teaching at the expense of the balance of the whole, but he will teach fully and richly out of Scripture as a man can do only if it is for himself the very treasure-house of truth.

And when we are thinking of the Bible as the book of the Church for the nourishment of the spiritual life we need to bear in mind the canon that "the Church may not so expound one place of Scripture, that it be repugnant to another." In the practical spiritual use of the Bible the Church has given this maxim a rather powerful extension. I feel sure that if we took the Epistle to the Hebrews as an isolated book, we should say that when the author wrote that "as touching those who were once enlightened . . . and then fell away, it is impossible to renew them again unto repentance," he meant to deny the possibility of repentance to deliberate apostates. But the Church insisted on its being interpreted in view of what is certainly the general sense for Scripture—that is, as not limiting the possibility of repentance in any case, or the right of the Church to restore any penitent. Again, St. Matthew twice appears to admit an exception to the indissolubility of marriage which St. Paul, St. Mark, and St. Luke do not contemplate; and here again we find the Church canonizing St. Matthew, but generally "explaining away" his exception. The fact that one of the Epistles and one of the Gospels should admit something which appears to be discrepant to the general sense of the New Testament is a fact which has to be taken account of in our estimate of inspiration, as not being equivalent to infallibility in detail. But concerning the Church as a teaching body, entrusted with a divine message, the maxim I have quoted, on which the Church has generally insisted, is full of right reason. It is the general sense of Scripture which must govern the teaching, rather than any isolated texts.

May I end this discussion of the authority of Holy Scripture by quoting some sane, serious words about the study of Scripture, words written by a Carthusian monk—Guigo of the abbey of Mont Dieu—about A.D. 1135 to his monastic brethren?

"Moreover," he writes, "you must get leisure for definite reading at a definite hour. Reading left to chance, and reading of passages at haphazard, does not edify, but renders the mind unstable. And what is lightly lodged there, lightly withdraws. But it must be dwelt upon with faculties concentrated; and the mind needs to become accustomed to the study. For the Scriptures require to be read in the same spirit in which they were written,[1] and can only so be understood. You will never enter into the sense of Paul until by the exercise of good intention in reading him and by assiduous meditation you have imbibed his spirit. You will never understand David till by actual experience the feelings of his psalms have become yours. And so with the rest. And in every scripture study is as different from mere reading, as friendship is from entertaining a guest, and social affection from an accidental salutation. . . . If in reading the reader seeks God, everything that he reads co-operates with him to this end, and it captivates his feeling and brings his whole sense of the passage into the obedience of Christ. If, on the other hand, the feeling of the reader declines upon some other end, it drags everything with it. And he finds nothing so holy or pious in Scripture as either by vainglory or a distorted feeling or a corrupt understanding may not minister to his harm or to vanity."[2]

APPENDED NOTE A (see p. 249)

ON DR. A. H. MCNEILE'S "NEW TESTAMENT TEACHING IN THE LIGHT OF ST. PAUL"[3]

I have read Dr. A. H. McNeile's book with much admiration and instruction on the whole; but though I have no doubt we believe alike, in total outcome, on doctrinal matters, I have felt surprised and unconvinced by many of his conclusions in detail. And I should like to ask those who have read my volume on *Belief in Christ* to read this book also and ask themselves such questions as these: Do they feel satisfied with Dr. McNeile's method of explaining, or as it seems to me explaining away, Matt. xi. 27 (Luke x. 22) and Mark xiii. 32 (Matt. xxiv. 36) on pp. 28 ff.? Is it at all an adequate statement that to

[1] This maxim, we see, is very much more ancient than the *De Imitatione.*

[2] See at the end of St. Bernard's works, Guigonis, *Ep. ad fratres de Monte Dei*, i, xi. I was led to this interesting little book by a reference of Dr. Strong's.

[3] Cambridge Press, 1923.

our Lord His Sonship to God " was Israel's moral sonship represented and consummated in His own human person " ? (p. 31). Again, admitting as Dr. McNeile does that St. Paul and St. John believed in Christ as the pre-existing Son of God (pp. 33 and 274), how does he find either room or need for the pre-existing Man (pp. 33, 265) of which I can find no trace in the New Testament (see *Belief in Christ*, pp. 76, n. 2, 87 f., 115, 313) ? Is not Dr. McNeile's explanation of St. Paul's use of ἐκένωσεν and ἐπτώχευσεν quite unsatisfying (pp. 63 ff.) ? Is it not a sign of arbitrariness, if out of the thirty-seven instances of the title Son of Man in the Synoptic Gospels he must discount eleven ; and amongst them all that fall before Peter's confession (pp. 46–8) ? How is the statement (p. 53) that κύριος is " nowhere in the New Testament a theological term for Christ connoting divinity " (p. 53) compatible with such a passage as Rom. x. 9–13 ? Or what do such passages as Rom. xiv. 10 and 2 Cor. v. 10 imply but some sort of resurrection of the wicked (p. 120) ? Again, is it true that " there is no other hint [in St. John's Gospel, i.e. except xxi. 22-3] of a future Advent " ? The statement seems to be implicitly contradicted on pp. 269, so far as concerns the Gospel as it stands. It is quite true that " Of the Ascension he [St. John] gives no record " ; but there are frequent allusions, iii. 13 (see *Belief in Christ*, p. 115, n. 2), vi. 62, xx. 17 ; and I see no justification for the statement that the traditional belief was " even more difficult than the Resurrection to place in line with St. John's Christian philosophy."

I have thought it right, though unwillingly, to call attention to a number of points, which can easily be added to, on which Dr. McNeile reaches conclusions the opposite of mine, because it seems to me these are just points on which his theory and mine of the developments and bases of the doctrine of Christ's person can be compared and tested in the judgement of my readers.

APPENDED NOTE B (see p. 253)

IS THERE ANYTHING OF DOCTRINAL IMPORTANCE IN THE CHURCH TRADITION WHICH WAS NOT ALREADY CONTAINED IN SCRIPTURE ?

I can think of nothing doctrinally important in the primitive tradition which is not already really implicit or explicit in the New Testament. But the following points may be regarded as partial exceptions.

1. The idea of Mary as " the second Eve." This was widely taught in the second century (see Justin Martyr, *Dial.*, 100; Irenaeus, *c. Haer.*, iii, xxii, 4, v, xix, 1, *Demonstr.*, 33; Tertull., *de Carne Chr.*, 17) in a sense which implied both a definite place for the Blessed Virgin in the divine plan of redemption and a position of " advocacy " for Eve. No doubt this doctrine may have an alarming superstructure built upon it. But in itself it seems to be based on scriptural facts; and also there was no movement to make it a dogmatic requirement.

2. The idea that the bread and wine of the eucharist were, as first presented on the altar, quite apart from what they were afterwards to become by consecration, already a sacrifice. This idea appears to be universal from Clement of Rome downwards. It may be, as Justin held, intended by our Lord's words *τοῦτο ποιεῖτε*. But in the event this idea or doctrine came to be quite overshadowed by the greater thought of what the elements became by consecration.

It is also of interest to enquire whether any customs of the Church, or anything in its practical legislation, implied or required a doctrine as having authority, to which Scripture does not allude. I do not think that the sanction given to sacred images at the second Council of Nicaea involves any such non-scriptural doctrine, nor prayers for the dead, nor requests on the part of the Church to be helped by the prayers of the saints, though it led no doubt to perilous developments.[1] But there is one piece of ecclesiastical legislation which does seem to

[1] See below, pp. 291, 311, on these points.

involve a certain doctrine—I mean the admission of the validity of baptisms and ordinations and (by implication) eucharists in heretical and schismatical bodies. On this the New Testament books are certainly quite silent. " Separated churches " are not in any way contemplated. But the matter was one which had to be decided one way or the other. Under St. Augustine's leadership the more liberal view prevailed in the West. It became, after considerable resistance, obligatory on the bishops to act in a certain way. But there was no emphasis laid on any implied doctrine, except on the doctrine that in every sacrament it is the Holy Spirit who is the real agent, and not the possibly sinful or heretical earthly minister—a doctrine which is certainly scriptural. In the East the practice has never been fully received.

Certainly it remains true that nothing in the ancient or undivided Church has ever been made an article of faith (as distinct from a pious opinion or a religious practice) which is not to be found plainly in Scripture.

CHAPTER IX

WHAT IS OF FAITH ?

My readers and I have been seeking in these volumes to pursue a long process of continuous reasoning ; and those who, on the whole, have followed with assent, or at least provisional assent, to the conclusions reached find themselves in this position—they believe that the conception of God which dominates the Old Testament and which we owe to the Hebrew prophets, and which reaches its fullest expression through Jesus Christ and the mission of the Holy Spirit, reposes upon a real self-disclosure of God, which is to be received in faith as His word ; which is more satisfying than anything which men could have arrived at for themselves by the exercise of their speculative reason, and fuller than anything which can in any sense be called divine revelation to be found elsewhere in the world. It is thus rightly, from man's present point of view, described as a supernatural revelation. But the supernatural does not mean the unnatural. It is indeed but the restoration and recovery of the deeper and truer nature of man and of the universe. For what we call the "word of God" proceeds from the same fountain of truth and light as has given to man his natural reason. It is the nature of man to seek to know God and have fellowship with Him. There is a movement of God from within man, which sin has never obliterated, as well as a movement of God upon him from above. And the supernatural revelation comes therefore not to overwhelm and bewilder or eclipse the natural reason, but to augment it and to satisfy and to emancipate. Thus in accepting the supernatural revelation we at the same time glorify God our creator by refusing to ignore the claims of reason in the largest sense, whether as shown in philosophy or science or historical criticism, or in the spiritual experience of mankind.

Further, we had been led to believe that "the grace and truth" which "came by Jesus Christ" was not cast abroad in the world without any preservative organ or channel. It was committed to a society which was to be the organ of the Spirit and the Body of Christ. This society is the Old Israel, the old people of God, reorganized by Christ; but whereas in the old Israel the self-disclosure of God was confined to that one people, the New Israel is free and open to all the world, a Catholic Church. Such a Church is by its very nature destitute of those links which bind nations and most human fellowships together, such as a common country or language or racial tradition or common occupation; but we have found it to be provided from the beginning with special links to preserve its continuity and cohesion —especially three: (1) The authority of an apostolic ministry which perpetuated itself in various grades and which everywhere was to be regarded with the reverence due to divinely appointed "stewards of the divine mysteries." (2) Certain sacraments of fellowship in which all were bound to participate, because they are the divinely given occasions and instruments for the bestowal of specific divine gifts, which all alike need, such as regeneration, and the possession of the Spirit, and the indwelling of Christ. (3) The common teaching or rule of faith or tradition, which was to be accepted by all the members of the Church as the word of God.

Finally, we have been occupied in examining the nature of the authority claimed by the Church for its tradition, and for its officers as the responsible exponents of its tradition; and inasmuch as there have risen into prominence in Church history varying estimates of its range and character, we have been seeking to discriminate the true from the false or exaggerated estimate of the authority of the Church; and in particular to vindicate a certain regulative supremacy and finality which the ancient tradition assigned to Scripture, as adequately embodying the teaching of the apostles.

But now we may reasonably be asked another question. What, according to you, is the content of this authoritative tradition of which the Church is set in charge—what is "of faith" for those who believe, as you would have them believe, in the authority of the Catholic Church? Some answer to this question we require for our own peace of mind, and because from all sides some further definition of our position is demanded of us in a world as full as our world is of intellectual questionings and contending creeds. What then, more or less in detail, do you understand by Catholicism considered as a dogmatic or doctrinal system? We intend to try to meet this challenge by considerations as purely objective and historical as possible, leaving aside—only for the moment [1]—any consideration of the difficulties which arise when we seek to apply our conclusions to the present circumstances of the world. But before we set out on this rather formidable enterprise there are one or two reminders which we should do well to give ourselves at starting.

1. First, we must quite dispossess our minds of the expectation that authority will best show its divine origin by the assurance with which it can answer all sorts of questions. The Christian religion came into the world as a life to be lived, and not primarily as a doctrine to be received. It came into

[1] See chap. xi.

the world to exhibit the true life of sonship and brotherhood—to show men the real meaning of humanity. It was, and still is, enabled to do this in virtue of truths which it has been taught about God and His purpose, and by a real and continuous experience which only these truths can explain. "The life" is based upon "the truth"; and it is the content of the "word of truth" which alone can make faith sure, or hope vigorous, or love active. And concerning all that is really needful for that moral and practical purpose, there is no very serious question as to what the Church is commissioned to teach. But religious curiosity has not been at all satisfied with that. It has wanted to know a great deal about the unseen world and the state of the dead, and the glory of the saints and of the Virgin Mother, and about the manner of the sacramental presence, and many other "secret things"; and these questions —for which the ancient tradition had no answers— have received answers 'on authority' by a process of (somewhat miscalled) development. And there can be no question, I think, that the drift of all this additional teaching has been to satisfy curiosity about the other world, at the expense of attention to this. The Church has strangely forgotten its function to establish a visible example of the Kingdom of God here and now in this world. And you do not help to a right direction of the Church's interest in this world by increasing the amount of information supposed to be authoritative about the other. And the growth of required dogma, involved in answering questions to which the apostles had no answer, has been to many noble and generous souls, who are surely friends of Christ, a sore addition to their intellectual burden. The tendency of such a consideration is to make us wish to minimize rather than to maximize the dogmatic requirements. We must seek without evasion to interpret the faith as authoritative tradition has handed it down. But we shall pay great attention to the marked reserve of the scriptural revelation. Assuredly, according to that, "we know in part, and we prophesy in part." As with those who lived under the Old Covenant, so still with us under the New, "The secret things belong unto the Lord our God" and "the more part of his works are hid."

2. We should never forget that the faith is the faith of the great Church before it is the personal conviction of an individual. No doubt the Church has demanded of its candidates for baptism (or in their name in the case of infants) a strong profession of personal faith in the clauses of the Apostles' Creed, "All this I steadfastly believe,"[1] and a renewal of this profession in the visitation of the sick. In the case of the neophyte in baptism I suppose this means that he has been taught the creed of the Church and accepts it on its authority. In visitations of the sick we know that the prescribed examination of the sick man's faith causes, in not rare cases, such difficulty that the priest must content himself with something much less stringent—"Lord, I believe: help thou mine unbelief."[2] What is wanted is the profession of the desire and intention of the individual to unite himself to the faith of the Church. St. Thomas Aquinas says:

"The confession of faith is made [*traditur*] in the creed as in the person of the whole Church which is united by faith. But the faith of the Church is an instructed faith [*fides formata*] . . . and therefore the

[1] This is the Anglican form; but it is, in substance, the ancient requirement. In the proposed revision of the Prayer Book an alternative form is offered, according to which the minister asks: "Dost thou in [this child's] name profess the Christian faith? *Answer:* I do. *Then shall be said by the Minister and Godparents the Apostles' Creed.*"

[2] Some provision is made in this sense in the revised form for the Visitation of the Sick.

confession of faith is made in the creed in terms suitable to an instructed faith, so that, even if there are individuals among the faithful who have not an instructed faith, they should [at least] desire to reach it." [1]

Further, the Church from time to time in its early history made specific requirements, especially upon its bishops, of adhesion to the doctrinal decisions of the Councils, and in later times has required a specific profession of personal faith from all those who are to be appointed its officers. Such requirements may be criticized in detail,[2] but it can hardly be regarded as unreasonable that those who are required to teach a particular creed should be required also to express their personal adhesion to it. With those exceptions the Church has made no inquisition into men's private minds and no specific demand on the laity. On the whole, I cannot help thinking that we should make the purpose for which the Creed is recited in public worship more evident if we were to say it in the form in which the Council proclaimed the Nicene Creed—beginning not "I believe" but "we believe," [3] which would mean, "This we acknowledge to be the Catholic faith, to which through all failures of faith we intend to unite ourselves."

[1] *Summa Theol.*, 2ª 2ªᵉ, 9, 1, art. 9.

[2] In the case of the Anglican Church these requirements were largely revised in 1865, and an excellent revision is now proposed of the Declaration about Faith in the Scriptures, which it is proposed should run: "*Bishop:* Do you unfeignedly believe all the canonical Scriptures of the Old and the New Testaments, *as given of God to convey to us in many parts and in divers manners the revelation of Himself which is fulfilled in our Lord Jesus Christ? Answer:* I do." The change proposed consists in the addition of the words italicized.

[3] It has often been said that, while in the Western Church the Creed occurring in the services begins "I believe," in the Eastern Church it begins "We believe." But this is a mistake. In the Eastern Orthodox Church also it begins "I believe" in the Liturgy of St. James (Brightman's *Liturgies*, p. 42) and St. Mark (p. 124) and St. Chrysostom (p. 383, cf. p. 320). In the Liturgy of the Abyssinian Jacobites, however (p. 226), it is the plural "We believe"; so also in that of the Nestorians (p. 270), and in that of

I

What, then, is the content of this Catholic faith? Its root lies in the doctrine concerning God and man and the divine purpose for the world which we owe to the Hebrew prophets. I shall seek in the next chapter to emphasize the dominant importance of this fundamental doctrine, on which our Lord undoubtedly built and which controls the whole Christian Creed. And the Church of the early centuries gallantly contended for its distinctive features, both as regards the divine nature and the freedom of man, in its long struggle both to use and to correct the principles and phrases of Greek philosophy. But I think it cannot be denied that some of these principles or assumptions—such as the immutability and impassibility of God—were allowed rather seriously to obscure the Old Testament conception of a God who has limited Himself by the creation of free beings, and accommodates Himself to a situation which sin has introduced, quite contrary to His will, and consents to struggle for man's good against man's rebellion, and to be afflicted in the afflictions of His people—a conception of God which, of course, reaches its climax in the thought of the incarnation and passion of Him who is "very God." We certainly need a careful examination of the treatment by the theologians of the divine attributes.[1] However, it is

the Armenians (p. 426), and in the Liturgy of the Syrian Jacobites (p. 82) the priest is to say "We believe," and each of the faithful "I believe." I suppose that in the service of baptism the confession of faith made by the candidate was universally in the singular, "I believe." See Brightman in *Early History of the Church and Ministry*, pp. 343 ff.

[1] I think also that, in the doctrine of human nature, the proposition that the soul of man is in its essence incorruptible and so necessarily immortal (St. Thomas, *Summa Theol.*, p. 1, qu. 75, art. 6: "Respondeo dicendum, quod necesse est dicere, animam humanam, quam dicimus intellectivum principium, esse incorruptibilem") is derived from Greek philosophy and not from Scripture.

from the Bible chiefly that we are to learn about God, and the metaphysical scruples of the theologians have not been allowed in any way to affect the Creeds and the dogmas of the Church. It is none other than the God of Israel and the God and Father of our Lord Jesus Christ who is still our God.

For the revelation given to Israel received its culmination in the Incarnation. And the faith of the Church in God is the outcome of the whole process of divine self-disclosure, by which the name of the one God became the name of the Father, and of the Son—Jesus Christ—and of the Holy Ghost. It was through their experience of the man Christ Jesus that the first disciples came to believe Him to be Lord and God. But this belief in Jesus as the eternal Son incarnate, and in the Spirit, whose presence within men is God's presence and Christ's presence, involved the belief in the Trinity in unity. The doctrine of the Incarnation is explicit, but the doctrine of the Trinity is certainly implicit [1] in the New Testament; and both alike received explicit statement in the Nicene Creed [2] and were protected by four definitions of Ecumenical Councils, repudiating four different attempts to explain the person of

[1] I have lately read the deeply interesting and entertaining record of *The Travels of Fa-hsien* in the excellent translation of Professor H. A. Giles. But he writes a preface in which he speaks of the Christian doctrine of the Trinity (p. vii), and he chooses to say that "nothing was heard of it in the early centuries of the Church, and it was first enunciated in detail as a mystery in the so-called Athanasian Creed, of (?) fourth century A.D.," etc. It would be hard to compress more mistakes into a single sentence. Any history of doctrine would have enlightened Professor Giles as to the facts. If a theologian were to make an equally ignorant statement about (say) Buddhism, he would be justly chastised and his reputation would suffer. But it appears that men of learning in other departments are allowed to say what they please about theology.

[2] Surely it is pedantic to insist on speaking continually of the expanded and modified Creed of Chalcedon as "Nicaeno-Constantinopolitan" (which is very likely inaccurate) or by any other periphrasis.

Christ which were found to be fundamentally subversive of the Christian faith.

Certainly the Catholic Church is committed in the deepest sense to this Creed with its affirmations both of facts and principles, and to these definitions. In their appeal to the New Testament on behalf of their definitions we must acknowledge that the Fathers are abundantly justified. Certainly there is to be found there the faith in the real deity of Christ, and in the continuity and unity of His person, before and after His incarnation, and in the full and permanent reality of the humanity which He assumed and in which He was glorified. No doubt the dogmas have been misused; but only in so far as it was forgotten that they were primarily negative, and that for our positive picture of the Christ we must constantly go back to the Gospels. But as to this I believe enough has been said elsewhere.[1]

No doubt a good deal of human nature at its worst is to be found in the history of these Ecumenical Councils; if there had been less of human sin at work the definitions need not have involved such serious and permanent schisms as did in fact result. Nevertheless, nothing of substantial value for the Church has emerged from Arianism or Nestorianism or Monophysitism since they became organized in separate churches, and nothing, we may thankfully recognize, which was right in the theological intentions of those who supported these heresies, or hesitated to condemn them, has been in result excluded from the Catholic faith. On the other hand, I think it is impossible to consider how strong a tendency there was inside the Church to reduce the meaning of the "flesh" of Christ into a mere veil of a divine theophany, or a mere medium for the sacramental

[1] See *Belief in Christ*, chaps. vii and viii. Also above, Appended Note, p. 228, where the objections of Dr. Mackintosh are considered at length.

communication of God to man, without feeling that the Holy Spirit of truth was overruling the Church through all the period of the Councils, producing that strong determination which the Church showed to insist on the full reality and complete activity of the manhood in Christ, in reason and will and spirit as well as in body, and guiding the mind of the Church to the production of a protective formula of balanced antithesis. We recognize that the Fathers might truly say, "It seemed good to the Holy Spirit and to us."

II

I have spoken in the main about four Councils—Nicaea, Constantinople, Ephesus, and Chalcedon—because the fifth (second of Constantinople, A.D. 553), which condemned certain writings of theologians long dead who had fostered Nestorianism or condemned the theology of St. Cyril, did not add anything to the theological definition of Ephesus, and need not receive the attention of the 'layman' in technical theology[1]; and the sixth Council (third of Constantinople, A.D. 680), which balanced the fifth, as Chalcedon had balanced Ephesus, though its affirmation of the reality of the human will and complete human activity in our Lord (as well as the divine will and divine activity) was really important, yet substantially added nothing to the work of the second and fourth Councils. So that for our present purpose we can ignore them.

But something must be said about the seventh council (second of Nicaea, A.D. 787). Its claim to be called ecumenical has been seriously disputed, and by such men among our theologians as William Palmer and John Mason Neale—but not convincingly, if it be

[1] See, however, Appended Note, p. 315, on the fifth and seventh Councils.

judged by objective tests, for it was finally received universally as ecumenical like the second Council. The Eastern Orthodox Churches in particular hold to it with even a fanatical devotion; and I do not think its conclusions need be rejected on the ground that they are unscriptural. Its object was to vindicate afresh the making and venerating of sacred images (icons) against the imperial and military iconoclasts. The theologians upon whom the Council relied, of whom the greatest was St. John of Damascus, were surely right in saying that the Incarnation had introduced an important modification into the sense of the second Commandment. It could not be wrong to make artistic representations of the human form and acts and sufferings of Jesus Christ. Such pictures are "the books of the unlearned," and for all men are intended to serve as memorials of events with which our redemption is bound up. And similar memorials of the saints must be allowed, and of angels (who have appeared as men). So the Council affirmed. When the customary respect and veneration is paid to the image, it is not paid to the material object, but to its unseen prototype. And adoration (*latria*) is to be given, not to any saints nor to any image, even of Christ, but only to God as He is in Himself. The Council was occupied in vindicating a Church practice, passionately clung to, rather than in establishing a theological principle. But there is a theology involved and declared by the Council, and I do not think it should offend us as unreasonable or unscriptural. It would indeed have been well if the Church had always sought to keep the devotion of its people within the limits prescribed by the Council.[1]

Nevertheless—in respect of devotional practice—the whole-hearted acceptance of the principle of images and of paying them ceremonial homage, does

[1] See Appended Note, p. 315.

represent a change of attitude as compared to that of earlier teachers of the Church. St. Augustine could not have written as he did against the veneration of images among the pagans, repudiating as a subterfuge the distinction proffered between grades of worship,[1] if the Church of his day had accepted the principles of the second Nicene Council. There was in fact a strenuous effort on the part of some of the Fathers—who were very familiar with pagan idolatry—against a tendency of human nature to make and venerate images and pictures of holy persons, which is not necessarily idolatry, but runs easily into it ; but the tendency proved too strong to be resisted, and what the second Nicene Council sought to do was to approve the practice of making and venerating images, with the enthusiasm of men who had just been relieved from persecution for their inherited religious customs, and at the same time to safeguard it against running into idolatry. That the barriers it raised did not prove wholly effective does not condemn the Council. And there are very few to-day who would condemn the making of images of Christ or of the saints.

III

We have mentioned all the definitions which the whole Church in ecumenical council has formulated and made obligatory upon its teachers or in a less direct sense upon all its members. But there is of course a large body of coherent "articles of faith" which have either never received definition at all, or at any rate have never received definition of the like ecumenical authority. Thus St. Paul taught the Church very explicitly to believe that not only are

[1] See *Enarr. in Psalm* cxiii, Serm. ii, 4–6: "Quis enim adorat vel orat intuens simulacrum, qui non sic afficitur, ut ab eo se exaudiri putet, ab eo sibi proestari quod desiderat speret?"

individual men sinners, but that mankind as a whole, all the children of Adam, are involved in sin, before any actual sins of their own, inheriting a nature biassed towards evil and enslaved to evil, so that they need, every one of them, not merely enlightenment and encouragement, but a fundamental renewal of their nature and redemption from bondage, which it is the purpose of the free grace of God to give them in Christ, transforming them from the old manhood to the new. St. Paul is explicit about all this; and the doctrine of "original sin" is implicit in the Bible generally, and it is an underlying assumption of theology, Eastern as well as Western,[1] though the Easterns are more constantly occupied in asserting man's remaining freedom. When the denials of Pelagius forced the question to the front, Augustine became the vindicator-in-chief of the idea of man's inherently sinful state, but he also startled the West by his exaggerations of our depravity and helplessness. What has a right to be called Catholic teaching on the subject received moderate expression at a small Council of Orange in 529, which, as confirmed by the Pope, became authoritative in the West and also represents the doctrine of the East. In the decrees of this Council original sin was emphatically dissociated from St. Augustine's terrible affirmation of "the predestination of souls to evil by the power of God," which is condemned with horror; and the free will in man is declared to be "warped and weakened," but not destroyed; and it is not suggested that the fault or defect of our nature is itself *guilt*, which seems to be an especially personal word. I have tried at an earlier stage of our discussion[2] to show how the doctrine can be freed

[1] Thus Origen takes for granted that all men are fallen, even when he relegates the fall to a previous state of existence. This idea of a prenatal fall was his earlier, though apparently not his final, teaching.

[2] *Belief in Christ*, chap. ix.

from the exaggerations and associations of gross injustice which have been allowed to encrust it, and can be expressed in terms which do not leave it in collision with biological science. So freed and so re-expressed I dare to say that the experience and conscience of men respond to it and confirm it. Here I am only concerned to maintain that it has behind it the authority of Scripture and of the Catholic tradition.

There are two other doctrines to be named which have behind them the whole weight of Catholic authority—the Atonement made once for all for the sins of men by the sacrifice of the cross, and the inspiration of the writers of Scripture by the Spirit of God. Both are barely alluded to in the Nicene Creed in the words "crucified *for us*," and "I believe in the Holy Ghost . . . *who spake by the prophets*"; but in spite of marked differences of theory about the former which have prevailed in different ages, and of considerable differences about the second in the early centuries, nothing has been done, either by ecumenical council or even by general consent, to define either the one or the other. The former has in the most emphatic sense the authority of Scripture, and the enthusiastic assent of the Christian world as a whole; the latter has, for the Old Testament the emphatic authority of the New, and for the New Testament the belief of the Christian Church from the beginning. The former has been, like the doctrine of the Fall, even monstrously encumbered with associations of injustice which have revolted the consciences of good men; and in ages before the rise of historical criticism, the latter has been given an extension of meaning and identified with infallibility in a way which criticism has made impossible for us. But, as has been said, the Church has not defined their meaning, and they can be disencumbered of features which are contrary to our moral conscience or our reason without any real loss of spiritual value.[1] So disencumbered they do not, as I have argued already, present any real obstacle to our intellects, while both of them in Christian experience have received the widest and deepest confirmation.

IV

It is certainly remarkable what doctrines were *not* inserted in the Creeds. But it has to be remembered that both the Nicene and Apostles' Creeds were originally baptismal creeds, and the clauses were expansions of the threefold name of God—the name of the Father, and the Son, and the Holy Ghost—in which baptism was conferred. This—the faith in the name—was in a pre-eminent sense the Catholic faith, and still in the *Quicunque Vult* (as in the *Te Deum* and the *Gloria in excelsis*) this only is so proclaimed. The corollaries of this faith, about which there was no dispute, could be taken for granted. So it was that there is in the Creeds only the barest allusion to the doctrines of the Atonement and the inspiration of Scripture. So also, while *I believe in the Holy Ghost* received expansion in *I believe in one holy catholic and apostolic church* (which is the organ of the Holy Spirit), or as in the early African creed, *I believe the remission of sins and eternal life through the holy Church,* nothing was said in the Creeds about the sacraments except (in the Nicene Creed) *I acknowledge one baptism for the remission of sins.* That is all. And yet this meagre mention of one sacrament, and the absence of any attempt at authoritative definition of any sacrament for more than a thousand years, stands

[1] This has been argued earlier: see *Belief in Christ,* chap. x, for the doctrine of the Atonement; for the doctrine of the inspiration of Scripture see in this volume, pp. 254 ff.

in even startling contrast to the intensity of the belief in their spiritual efficacy which possessed the Church from the beginning. That the Church is the home of the Spirit, and that membership in Christ and all His rich gifts are imparted to men in the sacraments of the Church, was their belief and their experience, grounded, as we have seen, on the apostolic teaching.[1] Thus they believed that baptism was their new birth—that by the action of the Holy Spirit in that sacrament they passed into a new spiritual status "in Christ," and their old sins were washed away. Baptism was both "their grave and their mother." They believed also that in the rite of the laying on of the bishop's hand, in which baptism was completed, there was imparted to each individual the anointing of the Holy Spirit, which gave him his full standing in the royal and priestly body. There is no subject on which the early teaching is richer and more spiritual than on the subject of baptism; and no part of the expressive ritual of the Church was more full of meaning than the rite of baptism. Nor during all the early period, when to become a Christian was a dangerous adventure, was there much peril of a mechanical or magical idea of baptism. The moral requirement was unmistakable, and it was expressed in the current dread of post-baptismal sin, which made men doubt whether more than one absolution for gross sin after baptism was even possible.

No doubt, when Christianity became the established religion, baptism became largely a convention and the belief in its efficacy largely non-moral. But this was purely an abuse against which the language of the rite of baptism, as of the New Testament, was a continual protest. In fact it ought to be no more possible to draw a *contrast* between the requirement of baptism and the requirement of faith and con-

[1] See above, chap. iv.

version than to draw a contrast between food and digestion. As the healings of Christ in the Gospels required both the power which passed out from Him and also the faith of the recipient to appropriate it, so in baptism, and in the sacraments generally, the external rite embodies the power of the Spirit and supplies the spiritual food; but its efficacy to effect the spiritual enrichment of the soul of the recipient depends upon the faith of his converted will. There is need of equal emphasis on both factors.

About the doctrine of baptism there was not any appreciable variety of opinion. But that was not so about the doctrine of the eucharist. I am not attempting here to write a history of theology, but only to enumerate the "articles of the faith" as the constant tradition of the Church presented them. Elsewhere I have endeavoured to give a conspectus of those different types of explanation of the eucharist which we find in the ancient Church.[1] But behind those different attempts at explanation there was the constant realistic faith concerning it, which first finds clear expression in St. Paul. Thus Justin Martyr, in the middle of the second century, in the "apology" for the Christians which he addressed to the Emperor Antoninus Pius, writing of the eucharistic feast of the Church, says:

"This food is called among us Eucharist, and no one is allowed to partake of it unless he believes that what we teach is true, and has been washed in the laver for the remission of sins and for regeneration, and is living as Christ enjoined. For we do not receive these things as common bread or common drink, but just as Jesus Christ our Saviour, by the word of God made flesh, had both flesh and blood for our salvation, so we have been

[1] *The Body of Christ*, pp. 59 f. (Murray). To this book I must refer for a fuller discussion of all the questions concerning the eucharist.

taught that the food over which thanks have been given by the word of prayer which comes from Him, that food from which our blood and flesh are by assimilation nourished, is both the flesh and the blood of that Jesus who was made flesh."

So Irenaeus writes: "The bread and the mixed cup, receiving upon themselves the word of God, become Eucharist, that is, the body and blood of Christ."[1] That from the first was the faith of the Church about its sacrifice and sacrament.

So also they believed in the sacramental efficacy of the judgements of the Church upon the "mortal" sins of its members, and of its absolutions, as carrying with them the judgement and absolution of Christ. This belief, founded on our Lord's words as St. Paul interpreted them, was the basis of the Church system of penance—later called a sacrament—through all the variations in the use of it. Also they believed in ordination as a sacrament; that is, they believed that through the laying on of the bishop's hands a spiritual gift was really imparted, qualifying a person for ministry in the various grades of office. Also they believed in the indissolubility of marriage in a sense that may be called sacramental, though after the establishment of the Church the principle began to be seriously compromised in the East. And finally, the ceremony of anointing the sick with a view to their recovery, enjoined by St. James, came to be regarded as in some sort sacramental. Thus, though they did not for more than ten centuries talk about seven sacraments,[2] yet all these rites of the Church, environing the life of man with spiritual blessings from the cradle to the grave, were regarded as having in somewhat different senses a sacramental power. But the rites first called "sacraments" (or "mysteries" in Greek) were baptism with confirma-

[1] For references see *Body of Christ*, pp. 4 ff., 81 f.

[2] See above, Appended Note B, p. 149.

tion, and the eucharist, and sometimes ordination; and though there were no precise dogmatic definitions,[1] as indeed there were no such denials as evoke definition, the faith in sacraments, as ceremonies of the Church which were instruments of divine gifts, was universal and undisputed. It was inseparable from the Catholic faith and life and it was rooted in the New Testament.

V

When we say "I believe in one holy catholic and apostolic church" we mean that we believe a visible society, however full of human infirmity, is yet the special organ of the Holy Spirit and of the living Christ in the world. This belief I have sought to vindicate as representing the real intention of our Lord. But here I am only concerned to point out one of its corollaries. A visible society which, because it is to be diffused throughout the world, lacks all the links of fellowship which belong to a nation, must have links of its own; and one of the chief of these was, in fact, a ministry, proceeding down the generations by succession from the apostolic fount, and taking shape in a hierarchy of bishops, presbyters, and deacons in each local church. In the intercommunion of the bishops was to be found the link

[1] When I say there were no precise definitions I am speaking of the early centuries or the undivided Church. The dogma of transubstantiation was indeed a precise definition, but I have already (briefly above, p. 193, more at length in *Dissertations*, iii, "Transubstantiation and Nihilianism"), given the reasons which seem to me convincing why we should not accept it as a dogma or indeed as a true opinion. It was in the seventeenth century accepted by the Orthodox Church, though in the case of the Russian Church without the accompanying theory of substance and accidents; but it would appear to have been accepted half-heartedly and certainly without following it out to its consequences. I am led to believe that our not accepting it would be no bar to union with the Orthodox Church. And the reasons for not accepting it are fundamental.

of Catholic fellowship, and in their due succession the guarantee of continuity. That the ministry of the Church, so constituted, was, with extraordinary unanimity over the whole Christian world, believed to have divine authority, so that membership in the Church could only be maintained by adhering to it, is an undoubted fact of history from the middle of the second century to the period of the Reformation. Its authority ranks with the authority of Scripture and the authority of the Creeds. This fundamental law of order was equated in importance with the fundamental rule of faith. If there is anything on which the "binding" and "loosing" power granted to the Church can be said to have been exercised it is on the necessity of the episcopate. Those teachers who, like Jerome, minimized the difference between bishops and presbyters, as a matter of ecclesiastical arrangement, yet did not doubt that authority had in fact restricted to the bishops the power of granting the ministerial commission. If we take account of the disruptive tendencies of human nature in ancient as in modern times, we must confess that it was the episcopate, and the principle of the apostolic succession, which saved the unity of the Church, so far as it was saved.

As we have seen, Ignatius of Antioch at the beginning of the second century can proclaim the threefold ministry to be (1) necessary to the constitution of a church; (2) an ordinance of the apostles; and (3) as world-wide as the Church itself. It would appear that in this last point he was not quite well informed. There were churches still without a monarchical bishop. And it is an obscure matter exactly how the Church constitution, as Ignatius describes it, developed out of the constitution of the Church as it appears in the Acts and the Pastoral Epistles. But there is really nothing in the New Testament to support the idea that any church had the right to elect and appoint its own officers without the intervention of the apostles, or those who held quasi-apostolic authority, like Timothy and Titus, to ordain to the ministry with the laying on of hands. Both the evidence and the probability are against it. Thus we have very sure grounds for maintaining that our Lord constituted a ministry in His Church in the persons of apostles; that it acted as a ministry intended to be self-perpetuating; that in fact it took shape in the threefold ministry known to Church history without any signs of confusion or controversy; and that the authority of the Church universal has been as deeply as possible committed to the principle of the apostolic succession.

Elsewhere I have endeavoured at length to develop the evidence. Here I would only say that there is no subject on which it is more necessary to take a wide view of the evidence as a whole, if one is to avoid being misled.

VI

Now we have to consider a quite different part of the Christian faith—that which concerns the life beyond. "I look for the resurrection of the dead, and the life of the world to come." "I believe in the resurrection of the body [flesh] and the life eternal." There is no question raised that the Catholic Church has held it to be essential to believe that there is an immortal life beyond death, and that this is not merely an immortality of the soul, but a persistence of the whole human personality, body as well as soul, of which the resurrection of Jesus Christ supplied the prototype. There was, however, considerable ambiguity in the way in which this belief was expressed. Had Christ been raised "in the flesh"? St. Paul apparently would say No: He was raised in the body, but not in the flesh; "flesh and blood cannot inherit the Kingdom of God." That is to say, he identifies "flesh" with the present corruptible condition of the body. On the other hand, St. John [1] appears to assume a Christ existing still in flesh and blood,[2] though "the flesh" and "blood" have now become "spirit and life." Ignatius, some fifteen years after the appearance of the Fourth Gospel, passionately affirms this. It is thus a question of the definition of words whether we are to speak of the glorified body or of the glorified flesh. But no doubt can be entertained that, in days when, though in some respects there was a high level of enlightenment, there was crass ignorance of what we have come to call "science," it was easy for men to assume that what would happen at the resurrection would be a recollection of the materials of our present body; and the expression "I believe in the resurrection of the flesh" was, in fact, interpreted and insisted upon in this sense. Even then, however, wiser men, such as Origen and Gregory of Nyssa, refused so gross an idea; and it is probably in deference to such, more rational, opinion that the Nicene Creed when it was enlarged did not contain the words "I expect the resurrection of the flesh" (or even "I expect the resurrection of the body"), but "I expect the resurrection of the dead."

A group of our Modernists to-day have been pressing us with the prevalence in ecclesiastical writers of the grosser view, and endeavouring to claim that it has full Catholic authority, in order to discredit authority altogether. But that is not just: we must always scrutinize current theology in the light

[1] And St. Peter in Acts ii. 32.

[2] See 2 John 7. Christ is still *to come* in the flesh: see Westcott's note. The permanence of the "flesh" and "blood" of Christ is also assumed in some sense in John vi., and the flesh and blood there spoken of are declared to be the flesh and blood of the ascended and glorified Christ, and are therefore to be thought of as "spirit and life" (ver. 62–3). St. Paul and St. John do not differ substantially at all.

of the formally expressed doctrine (where such exists) and of the New Testament. There were, we know, two currents of explanation of the doctrine—the grosser and commoner, and the more refined. And the Church inserted in its most authoritative Creed—the Nicene—an expression which markedly does not commit us to the common view, and justifies us in taking the Western expression "I believe in the resurrection of the flesh" in the sense in which, I suppose, St. John would have adhered to it.

But it is even more important to appeal to the New Testament, and especially to St. Paul, who alone has expounded at length what he would have us understand by the resurrection of the body, and has expounded it in a sense which certainly does not suggest the recollection of the material atoms. St. Paul, then, does not attempt to analyse what happens to the body after death or at the resurrection scientifically; and he is not concerned (as we shall see) with the "intermediate state" of the disembodied soul at all; but he contemplates in all cases a transition from our present "natural" and corruptible bodies to the condition of what he calls the "spiritual body." This, no doubt, on the pattern of our Lord's, he conceives of as material; but the materiality must be such as would be no impediment to spirit: that is, we must suppose, it is a refined sort of materiality, in which matter is wholly the vehicle and subservient instrument of spirit, as appears in the Gospels to have been the case with our Lord's risen body.[1] St. Paul speaks quite indefinitely, however. But he insists that in all cases the transition from the natural to the spiritual body will take place. "We shall not all sleep [die], but we shall all be changed,"[2] and he contemplates three different cases of this transition: the case of

[1] See *Belief in God*, pp. 268–9, and the whole section pp. 262 ff.
[2] 1 Cor. xv. 51.

our Lord, whose body saw no corruption, but was transmuted within the period when He lay in the grave ; the case of those who are to be alive at the Coming, which he still hoped would be his own case, for whom he contemplates—using vague words, as about a "mystery"—a sudden transformation "in a moment, in the twinkling of an eye"; and the case of those who have died and been buried, and whose bodies have therefore presumably rotted in the grave. And in their case the language he uses does not at all suggest the recollection of material particles, but, as in the case of the seed corn, the continuity of a vital principle clothed by God in a new embodiment. So we will boldly, with St. Paul, hold to the faith in "the resurrection of dead men" as the Creed expresses it, or "the resurrection of the body" as St. Paul suggests it, interpreting in this sense the more Johannine phrase "the resurrection of the flesh," without for the moment allowing ourselves to be encumbered with notions derived from a pre-scientific age, and without any claim to understand by what exact method what we believe in will be accomplished.

And we shall rejoice to recognize that in believing, not in the immortality of a bare soul, but in the resurrection of the whole person, we are in harmony with the spirit of science. For science, in the true sense, shows us such an intimate dependence of spirit on body in man as to make the idea of purely disembodied spirits very difficult. We have lost, or ought to have lost, all the old Greek and Oriental horror of the body as such. What we look for is the perfecting of the whole creation for the fulfilment of spiritual purpose, through whatever final catastrophe. "Nature itself also shall be delivered from the bondage of corruption into the liberty of the glory of the sons of God"; and for these sons of God what we look forward to is indeed a glory unimaginable, when He who is our Redeemer, at His final coming or manifestation, shall have "fashioned anew our bodies of humiliation that they may be conformed to the body of his glory, according to the working whereby he is able even to subject all things unto himself." The figures in which His coming is described to us are doubtless symbolic, but its essential and moral meaning is unmistakable.

Almost all the Christian outlook upon the life to come in the New Testament is directed to the great end. We are assured of personal immortality in its completest sense, but its completion is associated with the Last Day, the Day of Resurrection and the world to come. Generally the resurrection is spoken of in the joyful sense in which it is to happen to those who are "in Christ." But in our Lord's parable of the Day of Judgement, and in the Fourth Gospel, and in the Apocalypse we hear of a resurrection of those who have rejected Christ and God, of the unjust as well as the just, and St. Paul appears to anticipate the same.[1] And if we are to give serious meaning to the words of our Lord—none the less awful because figurative—and of St. Paul and St. John, we must recognize a final assessment of all human lives, a final judgement of God, and an awful possibility of final and irretrievable condemnation.[2] Life is essentially probation. Acts form habits and habits form character and character tends to become fixed. And there seems to be bound up with the reality of responsibility the possibility that the personal will may so identify itself with evil as to have lost at the last the faculty for good, and to have become finally incompatible with God. In such a case, to

[1] St. Matt. xxv. 31 ff.; John v. 28–9; Apoc. xx. 11 ff.; Rom. ii. 5–16, xiv. 10; 2 Cor. v. 10.

[2] I have endeavoured to summarize conclusions and give references on this tremendous subject in *Expos. of Romans*, vol. ii, App. C, p. 210.

recall the tremendous words of Isaiah, the near coming of the divine holiness has become intolerable and elicits nothing but the cry, "Who among us shall dwell with the devouring fire? Who among us shall dwell with everlasting burnings?"[1] The consideration of this horrible possibility of final ruin and misery chills us to our very bones and is meant to chill us. For my own part, I cannot understand how anyone, who considers human nature broadly, can doubt that in moments of almost irresistible temptation, when yet we have time and will to think, the thought of the infinite and timeless issues of wilful sin—the undying worm and the unquenchable fire—has, and is meant to have, an overpowering effect upon us. "Fear him," said our Lord, "who after he has killed hath power to cast into hell; yea, I say unto you, Fear him." And the repudiation of this sort of fear seems to me to be one of the silliest features in modern religion.

The imagination of men from very early days occupied itself in drawing gruesome pictures of hell, which revolt us or make us laugh; and doctrines which condemned men to hell—unbaptized infants, or all the non-Christian world, or all the non-elect, or all who, however sincerely, had reached heretical conclusions—in such indiscriminate fashion as to be wholly contrary to justice, have discredited the teaching about hell, so that the popular Christianity of to-day appears almost to have "left it out." But it is there in the authentic teaching of Christ and in the innermost testimony of the enlightened conscience. There is language in St. Paul about "eternal destruction," and language which seems to identify the ultimate issue of things with the absolute and universal triumph of good—when God shall be "all in all"—which has made some thoughtful men conceive that the state of the lost may carry with it

[1] Isa. xxxiii. 14.

the ultimate dissolution of personality and personal consciousness. For my own part, I thankfully accept this as a possibility. "Eternal" does not always mean "everlasting," and "eternal fire" is only strictly interpreted in terms of everlasting time in the images of the Apocalypse,[1] where temporal images are almost always to be translated into non-temporal ideas, if we are to understand them truly. So I cherish this hope, finding the idea of actually everlasting torment unthinkable.

But this is an uncertain interpretation. What is of the greatest importance is that we should recall the attention of men to the awful warnings of our Lord as to the ultimate possibility of self-chosen ruin, calling to mind at the same time that we know the character of Him who is to judge the quick and dead, and that we cannot associate with Him injustice or inconsiderateness, or any refusal to do the best possible for every soul that He has created; and, for the rest, to acknowledge our ignorance and the absence of any attempt on the part of the undivided Church, in spite of a great deal of provocation, to define authoritatively what is to be understood by "eternal punishment."[2]

Certainly the belief in the ultimate judgements to be passed on all human souls at the Last Day has a tremendous effect on human life. That, however, has come to seem far off, and meanwhile human curiosity has largely exercised itself not on those ultimate issues, but on the immediate future after death. How is it with those I love, who have de-

[1] Apoc. xx. 10.

[2] It is certain that universalism—which I hold to be really incompatible with the New Testament—was very prevalent in the East, and yet received no formal condemnation by any Council, except in connexion with Origen's idea of pre-existence, which was condemned at the Council which formulated the XV anathemas; but there was hardly any consideration given to conditional immortality in any form.

parted this life, here and now? Do they know what is happening to us on earth? Can I speak to them or in any way reach them? And imperfect as they were, are they not still under education and cleansing?

And to all such questions there is in the New Testament and in the early tradition very little answer. The blessed dead are in "Paradise," or in "Abraham's bosom." These phrases, taken over by our Lord from the later Jewish tradition, were retained and loved by the early Church. Again, St. Paul assures us they "have fallen asleep in Jesus," and are "the Lord's" as much as those who are alive, and are "with Christ" in some "far better" sense than we are in this world.[1] And their sleep is plainly not unconsciousness. The "spirits of just men" have been "made perfect,"[2] though they still await their consummation at the resurrection of the just. It was in view of this consummation that St. Paul prayed for his apparently dead friend Onesiphorus, "The Lord grant unto him to find mercy of the Lord in that day."[3] And the early Church prayed unhesitatingly and abundantly for the dead, but in a sense which suggests always that rest and light and peace and refreshment are the thoughts which were associated with Paradise. As to the occupations and interests of the departed we are told nothing. If there is a providential purpose in the silence of Scripture, it is plain that it is not intended for us to have our minds preoccupied with the state of the dead. Our main business is to be with the building of the Kingdom in this world.

From very early times, however, as was natural, men's minds were directed to the question whether, imperfect as even good Christians are when they die, the state of the dead must not be a state of being purified, and whether purification must not be rela-

[1] 1 Thess. iv. 14; Rom. xiv. 8–9; Phil. i. 23.
[2] Heb. xii. 23. [3] 2 Tim. i. 16–18.

tively painful.[1] On this matter there was a good deal of speculation, beginning with Clement of Alexandria. A number of the Fathers from Clement and Origen to Jerome and Gregory of Nyssa were "universalists"—that is, they hoped that all would ultimately be saved—and for them the idea of hell was that of a shorter or longer cleansing by fire. But this was certainly neither in Scripture nor in tradition. The tradition, as Origen states it, was simply that in the world to come the souls of men, clothed in their spiritual bodies, will inherit eternal life or suffer eternal punishment according to their works. And there was a further speculation, based (surely) on a misunderstanding of the phrase "saved yet so as by fire," as to a cleansing of all alike in the fire of the Great Day.[2] These were speculations. And we cannot but speculate. It seems an inevitable conclusion of reason that the intermediate state must be somehow a state of cleansing, and cleansing must be somehow painful. But the fact remains that Scripture is silent on the subject and the authoritative tradition of the Church. There were those, on the other hand, who held that souls at death are *suddenly* changed into the wholly good or wholly evil. Augustine, as has been shown, in whom the idea of a purgatory for the imperfect *in the intermediate state* first clearly appears, plainly knew that there was no tradition behind him. He believes in purgatory, but he says "it is not incredible," it is a matter of "perhaps."[3]

I have said something about the way in which

[1] Origen, *de Princip.* i, praef. 5. [2] See above, p. 198.

[3] It must not be left out of sight that, though all the emphasis in the New Testament is laid on the day of salvation being "now" and "the time" being "short," yet in 1 Pet. iii. 18—iv. 6, we have an intimation, so far distinct, that waiting souls in the unseen world, rebellious as they had been, could hear the gospel and live. If it was possible in their case, may it not be so in that of others?

Gregory the Great, in the light of his blood-curdling visions, laid the basis of the mediaeval Western belief in purgatory, as a place where the temporal punishment due to our forgiven sins has to be expiated in torments; and there was superimposed upon this the doctrine that the power of the Church in dispensing "the treasury of merits" could extend "indulgences," that is, remissions of temporal punishment, even into the unseen world. These twin doctrines had a portentous effect; they altered the whole character of the Church's outlook upon the world of the faithful departed, and added enormously to the idea of the Church's power—with results which we all know. But certainly neither in Scripture nor in tradition is to be found the ground for either the doctrine of purgatory or the doctrine of indulgences applicable to the dead.[1] Accordingly they cannot be part of the authoritative faith.

There are many things we should like to know, which apparently the divine wisdom has not thought it good that we should know. We cannot doubt that the departed pray for us. If they are conscious and in Christ, we feel it cannot be otherwise. The great saints who have fought the Church's battle and cared for her with all their souls cannot forget her in their prayers in Paradise. Thus surely the Church has most rightly prayed to God that we might be helped by the intercession of the saints and of the Virgin Mother; and that such prayers were left out of our service-books at the Reformation is indeed lamentable. Defect is certainly no less culpable than excess. And if the mediaeval cultus of the saints was excessive, our neglect of their communion

[1] There is an interesting article in *Theology*, No. 41, November 1923, by Mr. A. Lewis James, on "The Intermediate State." But our best book, as I have said, is Dr. Arthur Mason's *Purgatory*, etc. (Longmans). Even if we do not agree with all his opinions, we find there all the most relevant passages from the Fathers carefully translated and commented upon.

has been equally hard to pardon. There is, however, no sign in the New Testament of the direct invocation of saints and martyrs. A word to indicate that the first Christians asked the prayers of Stephen and James, the first martyrs, would have seemed natural. But it is not there. There are early inscriptions on tombs, such as "Gentianus, pray for us; for we know that thou art in Christ," which are instinctive and touching, and invocation began to become a common practice in the fourth century. It is surely not to be condemned, provided we recognize that the knowledge which could have authoritatively sanctioned it is withheld from us. And though we should delight to acknowledge the glory of the Virgin Mother and the Saints, it must be owned that their cultus in the Middle Ages was built up largely on a basis of mythology and quite unhistorical imagination,[1] and admitted features of the pagan tradition with a dangerous freedom. So much is admitted by all careful scholars. We do not need to attempt to lay natural piety in fetters; but we do need to preserve the type of New Testament devotion.

I should add that among the elements which Origen enumerates, in his summary of the tradition of doctrine received from the apostles, is the belief in good and evil spirits and their influence upon men —"that every rational soul is a free agent, plotted against by evil spirits and comforted by good angels, but in no wise constrained."[2] This element in the tradition certainly represents the teaching of the apostles and of our Lord Himself, and there is no rational ground for treating it with contempt.

[1] Cf. *Belief in God*, p. 261. I cannot see any ground for believing that the later habit of the Church—to canonize certain persons as saints, thus anticipating the judgement of the Great Day—is within its legitimate functions. It is quite another thing to let natural gratitude and devotion mark out certain people as saints, and to desire to have their prayers.

[2] Origen, as above, summarized.

And now I have perhaps sufficiently fulfilled my task of enumerating, as Origen did long ago, the items of the doctrinal tradition of the Catholic Church, which it claimed to have received from the apostles, and which are certainly confirmed in the New Testament. Speculation in ancient days sometimes ranged widely beyond the limits of tradition; but we hold fast to the contention of the ancient Church that nothing which was not in the original tradition can be laid upon the faithful as a dogmatic requirement. The function of the Church with regard to the tradition is to defend it and to explicate it, but not to add to it.

With regard to Church discipline in matters of practice, with which we have not been directly concerned, the case is different. Here the Church was always believed to have a freer hand. It could legislate with a much greater freedom in view of the requirements of the times; and it could freely alter or ignore the decisions of even ecumenical councils where circumstances had changed or the earlier decisions been found impracticable. So it was that the prohibition of the translation of bishops from see to see, and the prohibition of kneeling at Easter, passed into desuetude. And we should cling to the assertion of our Article that "Every particular or national Church hath authority to ordain, change, and abolish, ceremonies or rites of the Church ordained only by man's authority, so that all things be done to edifying." Thus in fact the Anglican Church not only allows a married clergy, contrary to the previously attempted discipline of the Western Church, but also, contrary to the ancient canons, allows the clergy to marry after ordination, which, I believe on the whole, was "done to edifying." Even disciplinary rules enacted by the apostles need not be regarded as permanently obligatory, such, for instance, as St. Paul's regulation of women's dress and his exclusion of the twice-married from the clergy. And canonical legislation can pass into desuetude as well as be formally abrogated. Nevertheless great reverence is surely due to Catholic customs and canons, in proportion to their universality. We may respectfully ask whether it was not presumptuous on the part of both East and West to abandon the apostolic rite of the laying on of the bishop's hands in confirmation, and equally presumptuous on the part of the Western Church to abandon, contrary to what was plainly our Lord's own intention, the administration of the chalice to the communicants at the altar. And the general and needless disregard of Catholic customs amongst ourselves has surely been most culpable. But I will not pursue the subject, which is not really that with which we set out to occupy ourselves.

I conclude with two remarks: (1) In the conspectus which I have been seeking to give of the doctrinal tradition as it was recognized of old, the conclusion at which we arrived in a previous chapter has been constantly taken for granted—that it is a mistaken idea of doctrinal development to suppose that it consists, or ought to consist, in the gradual accumulation of dogmas by a logical or quasi-logical process of deduction. In substance the revelation was once given and has never been augmented. The thinkers and saints of the Church may ponder and speculate, and pious opinions may be uttered and pass into vogue. But as far as concerns the authoritative revelation, what the ancients did not in substance know cannot become part of it, nor what is not really affirmed or implied in the New Testament. This, we saw, is the safeguard of intellectual liberty for the individual, and leaves the Church free to enter each new age and country unencumbered by anything except the original message. And the justification of the appeal to antiquity lies also in this: the Church started on its career, and maintained it for three centuries or longer, in marked distinction from the world or the State. After Church and State became one, a fusion took place the effect of which is unmistakable. It is right we should call the early centuries "the pure centuries," in the sense that in them the current of Church life and teaching was running substantially distinct.

(2) The Church has allowed a place of unique authority to the General Councils. It has been often said that "the authority of the Church diffusive is no less binding than that of the Church collective."[1] But this is not quite the case. The authority of the ecumenical councils has a pre-eminence, because there a particular doctrine, which had already agitated the Church and been very fully discussed, was brought into distinct light, and the collective mind of the Church was brought to bear upon it, in a sense which gives their decisions an importance and precision which uncontested tradition cannot quite reach.

APPENDED NOTE (see p. 291)

ON THE FIFTH AND SEVENTH GENERAL COUNCILS

The most handy volume to begin with for the study of the General Councils is *The Seven Ecumenical Councils* in the "Nicene and Ante-Nicene Fathers," by Dr. H. R. Percival (Oxford: James Parker, 1920). No one reading the documents and history concerning the fifth Council will find them very edifying. But, as I have said, in substance it added nothing to the definition of Ephesus, while accepting Chalcedon. It only aimed at rehabilitating the theological reputation of St. Cyril.

The only doubtful question which arises out of it is the question whether the great Origen was condemned by the Council in a string of heretics. This is probable but not certain. There are strong arguments against

[1] I assented to this proposition in *Roman Catholic Claims*, p. 55.

it (see *op. cit.*, p. 314). Anyway, we must agree with Hefele that "the XV anathematisms against Origen" cannot be attributed to this Council. And, when we read them, we shall feel that it is only a phantom of the real Origen which was under the consideration of whatever council issued them. The specific opinions then condemned there are few to-day who could be found to maintain. And it is remarkable that Origen's opinions concerning Holy Scripture are not noticed, nor is his belief in the final restoration of all souls repudiated except in connexion with his belief in their pre-existence, before they became human beings.

The seventh Council is very explicit that God "wholly and alone is to be worshipped and revered with adoration" (p. 541); that icons are to be made only of Christ as He appeared in the flesh, and of the angels who appeared as men to men, and of the saints. All the misleading pictures of the Holy Trinity as three men, or two men and a dove, which are so sadly common in the West, or of the Father as an old man, are apparently contrary to the decrees of the Council. And as to the proper attitude of Christians to the icons we read—

> "To these should be given due salutation and honourable reverence (ἀσπασμὸν καὶ τιμητικὴν προσκύνησιν), not indeed the true worship of faith (λατρείαν), which belongs only to the divine nature; but to these, as to the figure of the precious and life-giving cross, and to the book of the Gospels, and to the other holy objects, incense and lights may be presented according to ancient pious custom.[1] For the honour which is paid to the image passes on to that which the image represents, and he who reveres the image reveres in it the subject represented" (p. 550).

[1] This, as Bishop Basil of Ancyra said at the Council, was customary also with images of the emperors, when they were sent to cities or rural districts, in order to honour not the image but the emperor himself (p. 535).

CHAPTER X

THE TEST OF RATIONAL COHERENCE

IN the last chapter I have sought, like Origen, simply to enumerate the "articles of the faith" which constitute Catholicism, considered as an intellectual system, and I have endeavoured to proceed by purely objective tests. These enumerated doctrines have behind them in history the whole weight of Catholic authority and of Scripture, as well as the wider assent of Christian experience. But there are many such articles of belief; and the sensitive modern spirit is apt at once to catch fire and protest with vehemence that it is impossible to expect agreement on so many theological propositions. It is in anticipation of such a protest that I now want to bring into prominence a consideration which is reassuring to our nervous critical reason—viz. that the propositions enumerated turn out not to be really many, but in principle one, so that in accepting one we are accepting all, or at least in accepting the root doctrine about God and man we are led on to feel that the rest cohere indiscerptibly with it. This idea of solidarity is of course conveyed by the term "articles of the faith." For "article" means first a little limb or joint, a component element in a living whole, and in its transferred sense, as meaning an element in an intellectual system, it retains the notion of solidarity as between one element and another. So Chrysostom says of the Christian faith that, granted the Incarnation, all the rest "follows in rational sequence."[1]

[1] *In Matt. Hom.* ii, *P.G.* lvii. 27, τούτου δὲ γενομένου, τὰ μετὰ τατα απαντα κατὰ λόγον καὶ ἀκολουθίαν ἕπεται.

This test of rational coherence, considered as an evidence of truth, is of course subordinate to other tests—the test of experience, the test of historical evidence for historical statements, the test of agreement with the whole of our knowledge, and the test of authority; but it is in itself an important and illuminating consideration which it is worth while to pursue.

I

We must begin then with the idea of God which the first volume of this series strove to vindicate.[1] When Christianity came out into the world it found, as we saw, a monotheism of a kind in occupation of the minds of the intelligent. It was the Stoic pantheism, the doctrine of the immanence of the divine reason. Some doctrine of divine immanence Christianity, in the persons of St. Paul and St. John, showed its readiness to assimilate, as indeed Judaism had already claimed it for its own; but only as subsidiary to the doctrine of God which it inherited from the Hebrew prophets. This is the conception of God as not only in the world but over the world and prior to it, in independent perfection, the absolute creator of all that is, personal in the profoundest sense and possessing definite character, being in Himself essentially righteous and good. For this distinctive doctrine of God, and not merely for some kind of monotheism—which might sound more Christian than it really was—the early apologists found themselves constrained to struggle. They were surely quite right. It is on this doctrine that Christianity as a whole depends. Granted this, the whole follows in "rational sequence"; and if this is not adhered to, the whole fabric crumbles.

[1] But see Appended Note, p. 334, "The Rationality of the Belief in the Christian Doctrine of God."

And there is bound up with this Biblical idea of God a certain idea of man—that rational man is not part of God, nor essential to the being of God, but a creature of God, absolutely dependent upon His will ; so that, however great the distinction in dignity may be between man and the irrational creation of which he is the crown, the distinction is not comparable to that which lies between the only one self-subsistent being, God the Creator, and everything else that exists—the creatures of His will and love.

On the other hand, man has been highly exalted. He was created in God's " image and likeness," that is, a rational being with a limited but real freedom, which God has allowed even to condition and restrict the action of His own almightiness. He has placed man in a sense as His vicegerent in the world, and has enabled him to co-operate in His divine purpose—the Kingdom of God. That is his great vocation. But man's freedom is ambiguous—it involves not only the opportunity of correspondence but also the opportunity of lawlessness or rebellion. And in fact mankind has on the widest scale and with the utmost universality so asserted his self-will against God's will as violently to disorder the moral world, and, superficially at least, the physical world which he in a measure controls.

This idea of human nature is inseparable from the Biblical conception of God. Both ideas are set before us with majestic simplicity under symbolical forms in the early chapters of Genesis, are continually emphasized and developed in the tradition of prophetic teaching, and form the foundation of our Lord's teaching and of the New Testament. It seems to me that the whole intellectual problem of belief is summed up in the acceptance of this doctrine of God and of man without which the Bible goes for nothing. Granted this, all is in sequence.

I always experience a slight shiver when I read in modern books about Christianity being essentially Christocentric. It is true, no doubt, that God has revealed Himself finally in Christ, but Christ always points us beyond Himself to the Father—to God; and faith in God did not begin with the historical Christ; and the object of Christ's manifestation, when He came, was that in the fullest sense our "faith and hope might be in God."

I say, then, grant the fundamental Biblical conception of God and man, and the whole Christian creed follows, and makes its rational appeal to us as one coherent unity. The appalling disorder of God's creation which sin has introduced—and dimly in the background we discern forces of rebellion other than human—demands the redemptive action of God. This again is an idea which pervades the Bible. And the conception of redemption is that of a re-creative activity of God—the activity of a Creator, free to take action to prevent the ruin of His work. As I have argued earlier, if God be simply the soul of the world, the immanent spirit of its order, it may be contended *a priori* (whatever that argument would be worth) that the divine action cannot be anything else than an inevitable development of this natural order. But certainly no such argument can hold if God is not only in the world but over it, independent and personal, and free from every restriction except what lies in His own perfection. In a unique emergency He can, on the analogy of every rational being, act uniquely. So it is that the summary act of divine redemption in Christ is presented as miraculous—as a re-creative act of God vindicating His original purpose. "I will up, saith the Lord." It is this conception of redemptive love which makes the evidence for the miracles of the Gospel intelligible and credible.

In this connexion I would call attention to a

criticism of my earlier argument which seems to me both interesting and strange[1]:

"If Dr. Gore's work has one inherent defect . . . it is that he is over-ready to treat the claim of the historical critics as merely what it professes to be, the claim of impartial students of fact, and to suppose that when he has met that claim, he has disposed of the whole Modernist case. As a matter of fact, historical criticism is always more or less a philosophy in disguise, and, though Dr. Gore very truly points this out, he hardly does justice to the philosophy in question. . . . Insisting on the uniformity of the natural sequences which govern events, it may reconcile the uniformity with belief in God, by urging that God's method of action is the penetration of what is natural and human from within, not interference with it from without. A Christian interpretation of the doctrine of immanence will go on to point out that the method of penetration without intervention is peculiarly consonant with the conception of God as love, and of His supreme self-revelation as taking place in and through a natural human life. But it must hesitate to accept anything in the nature of a miracle strictly so-called, because this seems to imply a direct intervention from without upon the natural order, the idea of which is alien to its religious philosophy."

And the writer goes on to intimate that the Modernists' philosophy may be interpreted as more congruous than any other with the conception of God as essentially *love*.

"It can see the Godhead incarnate and supremely revealed in the human goodness of Jesus Christ and in the love which suffered, unsaved by any miraculous intervention, upon Calvary, but not in an apparent breach of the natural order of human birth, or in the resuscitation of a dead body. . . . Such things, it maintains, are alien both to the apparent constitution of the world and to the method and character of love pure and supreme."

[1] Canon Oliver C. Quick in the *Quarterly Review*, October 1923, p. 380.

Now, there are phrases in this interesting passage—which, I do not forget, expresses not the point of view of the writer, but a point of view, different from his own, which he is representing—which would demand detailed criticism. I deprecate the phrase "interference from without" because the miracles of the Gospel are rather represented as the action of the Holy Spirit working from within; and the word "resuscitation" is not at all the word to describe the transformation in the case of Jesus of the natural into the spiritual body. But I have reproduced the passage not to criticize details. What I wish to criticize is simply the main idea that the purely immanental conception of the action of God is more congruous than any other with the idea of His love. And I write with feeling, because all my life has been a struggle to believe that God—the only God—is love. That is to me, as to many other men, not only the governing dogma of the Christian religion, but the only really difficult dogma. It has its source in the Bible, and nowhere else is it affirmed with the same courage of assurance. And in the Bible, I contend, it is wholly bound up with the conception of God as transcendent and sovereign, over and beyond nature. There are marks of goodness in nature to which our Lord and St. Paul call our attention, as signs of the goodwill of "your Father which is in heaven," or of the sovereign Creator. But it is not chiefly to them that appeal is made. "Herein is love . . . that God sent His Son to be the propitiation for our sins," or "to be the saviour of the world." If we think of our Lord's teaching in the parables about God's love, we find it represented as something free and personal, bound by no restrictive law—the shepherd's preference for the one sheep at the risk of the ninety and nine, the father's preference for the prodigal son, which provoked the rational remonstrance of the elder brother. If we consider it, all His teaching about God is found to be naïvely on the lines of the sovereign Being, without the suggestion of immanence. It is "your Father which is in heaven." If at the great crisis He is not to be saved from death, it is not that the Father could not or would not do it, but that He Himself will not ask for it.

Then outside the Gospels, the New Testament identifies the original assurance of the revelation of God in Christ with the evidences of His resurrection. Without this, it appears, no gospel of divine love would have gone out into the world. This it was "that marked Him out in power as the Son of God." This gave the disciples their "assurance" of His lordship. "If Christ has not been raised, your faith is vain; ye are yet in your sins." "God raised him from the dead and gave him glory; so that your faith and hope might be in God." Can it be seriously contended that if the supposed event was an illusion, the value of that assurance would remain? Also can it be doubted that, through the whole New Testament, the conception of God's love in Christ is wholly bound up with the conception of God as coming forth in a great re-creative act, from beyond the process of nature, in which the miracles were a natural feature?

Then leaving the ancient sources of witness, and coming to our own day, surely it is just in respect of God being love that the conception of the immanent God—God in the process of nature—proves to be so defective. I scrutinize great nature anxiously and find it full of ambiguity. I cross-question the philosophers of immanence and the poets of nature and get no satisfaction. I do not say I could not retain a hope that the great inscrutable power which works in nature might turn out to be good. But I do say that any confidence of faith depends on a belief in the transcendence and liberty of God. It is such a God we need as can come forth to re-create and renew what sin has so deeply defaced and spoilt. It is such a God as can do a new thing, because a desperate situation demands it, and the "process of nature" is inadequate to remedy it. And if the Christ is this unique thing, the Divine Saviour come into the world in our nature, it seems to me most natural to believe that when sin murdered Him, God should vindicate Him; and that the birth of Him who was not only man but the New Man, should have been signalized by discontinuity as well as continuity with the humanity out of which He emerged.[1]

II

Well, then, I contend that the fundamental Biblical conceptions of God and of man and of the result of sin in disordering the world lead naturally on to the belief in a divine act of redemption which has miraculous accompaniments. Viewed in its total effect, this redemptive activity of God is not contrary to nature, but is the reconstitution of nature in its proper relation to God, actually in the region of the redeemed humanity and potentially in the whole world. And it is not contrary to the idea of a gradual development of divine purpose in the world. Quite otherwise: what it has done is only to effect the removal of what made the actual development something even grotesquely unlike the divine purpose. "Grace is not contrary to nature, but is rather the restoration of nature." Nevertheless grace, the personal action of divine love, postulates a God who

[1] In answer to a note of Canon Quick's on p. 381, I would say I thankfully believe that *God is love* as *God is spirit* and *God is light*; and that we should hardly say *God is justice* or *God is power*, because justice and power appear to be modes of action or attributes of Him whose essence is "love" and "spirit" and "light." But I decline altogether to identify love with purely "natural" processes. Love has always and specially the capacity for doing something over and above the ordinary.

is not enslaved to His own ordered method, but can act freely.

And the same Biblical conception of God leads us on to approve the Catholic conception of the incarnate person, Jesus Christ, as it gains expression in the New Testament and as it finds definition in the Creeds and Councils. Christ is the Word, or Son, of God incarnate. Thus He is the mediator between God and man—but because He is both God and man. There can be no middle term between the Creator and the creature. There can be no demi-god. If the Son, Jesus Christ, is to be worshipped as God, and if by union with Him we are united to God, then He must have come personally from beyond the fathomless depth which in idea separates the one creative nature from the creatures. He must belong essentially to the one divine being. He must be of one substance with the Father. That is the verdict against Arius. And again, if He is—as the Gospels show Him to be—truly and completely man, that must be "not by confusion of substance, but by unity of person," by the taking of manhood into God. No conception of Christ as becoming God, or as gaining for us the values of God because He is perfect man, is consistent with our root conception. The nature of man, the creature, is godlike and can therefore become the organ of God. But it can never become the nature of God the Creator. The two natures must remain in their fundamental distinction. What we welcome then is the conception of God, who had made man in His own image, remaining God, but for our redemption taking unto Himself our nature and living and acting and suffering, by a divine self-suppression, as man, so as to redeem him from within. And no formula can be found to guard the reality of Deity and the reality of manhood in the unity of one person but the Catholic formula.

So with the doctrine of the Holy Trinity in Unity. I have very often repeated the suggestion that in the process of divine self-disclosure the doctrine of the Trinity was "overheard rather than heard." There was no moment of proclamation. In the process of experiencing redemption men found themselves believing in God as Father, Son, and Holy Ghost. So we find the idea of the Trinity implicit in the New Testament, and, after delays and hesitations and many bungling attempts at formulation, made explicit to the mind of the Church. The Church, one must acknowledge, though it believed that the name of the One God had become the name of the Father and of the Son and of the Holy Ghost, as a matter of experienced fact, yet found it very difficult to express the truth, even inadequately. Nevertheless, however imperfectly it admits of being expressed in human language, the conception of God as subsisting in three "persons" has proved to be the only conception of God which can make us able even remotely to conceive of God, as our fundamental Biblical faith demands that we should conceive of Him, as alive and personal, independently of nature and prior to nature, and the creator of all that is. For will and thought and love, which are the essential qualities of personality, have no meaning for us except in the relation of the individual subject to another. Will and thought and love alike demand an object. And the only way in which men have found themselves able to think of God in Himself, as eternally alive in the fullness of personal life, is by welcoming the glimpse into His eternal Being which the process of redemption has given them, and finding there the reality of an eternal fellowship in which the Father expresses Himself eternally in the Son and in the Spirit, and finds the reciprocity which will and thought and love demand. Only so can we avoid the fatal weaknesses, intellectual and moral, of the conception of a God dependent upon nature for self-expression and consciousness.[1]

Once again, the Biblical conception of God seems to lead inevitably to the anticipation of a "Last Day" or "End of the World." No doubt the vision of the End in the New Testament—the great catastrophe of nature, the rending sky, the angel-messengers, the form of the Son of Man descending in majesty to judge the world, the last trump, the multitudes of humanity of all the ages gathering for judgement, the opened books, the final verdict, and the localized heaven and hell—all this is symbolical. Apparently we can only be taught in symbolical forms about the things which lie outside our present possible experience. But the symbols enshrine a necessary truth—the truth that God is to come into His own at last in the whole creation, and the truth that it is in the historical Jesus that He does come into His own. God has a purpose in all history. That is one of the great contributions to the thought of humanity, which we owe to the Hebrew prophets. This purpose has been flouted and thwarted by sin. Nevertheless as God is God, so at last He must vindicate Himself, and in Jesus is to be found not only the central point in history, but its end.

III

In intimate coherence with the Biblical doctrine of God is, as I have said, its doctrine about man. It gives no place for foolish pride. Man is purely a creature and, as such, absolutely dependent. But the position of man is as far as possible from being abject. He is made in the image of God. He is destined for co-operation with God and for sonship. God deals with man not as an arbitrary autocrat

[1] See *Belief in God*, pp. 69 ff., 148 ff.

with a slave, but as a father with his children. "O my people, what have I done unto thee ? and wherein have I wearied thee ? testify against me." "Wherefore, when I looked that it should bring forth grapes, brought it forth wild grapes ?" Job's indignant questioning of God, based on the deep-lying assumption that, if he can only get to God, He will listen to his reasonable and just plea, is treated as meritorious, not as insolent. In our Lord's teaching the tone is never autocratic—it seems to be taken for granted that, if only men are sincere and open-hearted to the light, they will welcome what He says as right and true. The true type of Christian authority must, as we said, always make its appeal so as to commend itself to the conscience and reason of men. Personal responsibility and freedom, wherein lies man's true dignity, is not to be destroyed. If souls are to be finally lost, that is only because they have used their divinely given prerogative of freedom to harden themselves into an obstinate refusal of the light. There is to be no absolute compulsion even to save man from ruin. There is no imperious grace or divine call which *cannot* be resisted. The paradox always remains in the theology that is really Christian : "Work out your own salvation ; for it is God who worketh in you, both to will and to do of his good pleasure" ; or again, Accept the Church's message as what it is in truth, the word of God who cannot lie ; but accept it because your own heart and conscience and reason tell you it is true.

The whole of Catholic theology at its best is full of this two-sided conception of man as both an absolutely dependent creature, and also a son and not a slave.

There is another feature in the Biblical doctrine about man in his relation to God which seems to me fundamentally to determine our attitude in favour of Catholic theology—that is, its treatment of man as individual, with the responsibility of an individual, but also as social; so that God deals with him not as a man only but as man. As we know, it is only gradually that the sense of individuality emerges in the Old Testament; but it does emerge decisively, and the New Testament is full of the sense of the individuality of men and of the responsibility and equal spiritual worth of all individual men. But the sense that mankind is also a social and corporate unity is never weakened. Thus it is impossible to read the New Testament and not feel the bearing of this both on man's sin and on his redemption. Sin lies in the will; its seat and source is moral; it is man's fault, not his nature, and the secret of guilt is not to be found in the material body. All this tends to emphasize individual responsibility. We are bound to say that only where individual knowledge and responsibility begin does personal guilt begin. Nevertheless, alike in the Old Testament and in the New, behind the individual is the nation and the race. It is mankind that is sinful, and every individual is born into a sinful world. This double aspect of man, individual and social, appears in the moderate Catholic doctrine of original and racial sin, which, I have contended, really corresponds with the facts of experience[1]; it also appears in the doctrine of redemption. The redemption is corporate. Christ is the new Man, the second Adam, the head of a new race, which in purpose and intention is to extend to all the world. So it is potentially on behalf of the whole race, and effectively for all who will believe in Him, that Christ acts as the Redeemer. Thus our corporate redemption has its root in the great representative act of sacrifice and reparation to God by which the new covenant of God with man is inaugurated. "He taketh away" (by expiation) "the sin of the world," and not merely

[1] See *Belief in Christ*, chap. ix.

the sins of the individuals. He is "the propitiation for the whole world."[1] So it is ideally that mankind is redeemed by Christ as a race; and actually the covenant is with the Church of the believers, and in the doctrine of the Church and the sacraments is found the sanction and the security of corporate redemption. Corporately man is fallen and corporately he is to be redeemed.

So it is, I think, that doctrines which look at first sight as if they were detached propositions—like the teaching of heaven and hell, and the teaching about original sin, and the doctrine of the virgin birth and the vicarious atonement, and the doctrine of the Church and the sacraments—are seen all to cohere with one another by having their common root in the fundamental Biblical conception of man in himself and in his relation to God. The doctrine of hell is a necessary corollary of his indestructible freedom; original sin is the expression of human solidarity; the fact of the virgin birth coheres with the fact of Christ as the second Adam, the new man, both continuous and discontinuous with the old humanity; the vicarious reparation corresponds to the idea of Christ as acting on behalf of all of us who are to be reborn in Him; the Church and the sacraments express again the solidarity of man. Men are not to be saved as individuals by themselves.

Once more the fundamental Biblical idea of creation involves a high estimate of the physical creation and the human body. Whatever God made was "very good." The Oriental and Hellenistic idea of matter as somehow evil, and of association with the material body as the source of pollution to the soul, is quite alien to the Bible. Sin is rebellion, and its seat is in the will. Once the will is brought back to its right relation to God, the whole body is on the way of redemption. So when the thought of

[1] John i. 29; 1 John ii. 2.

God's justice, and the sense of the fellowship with God into which the individual soul is admitted, forced the Jew forward to believe in life beyond the grave, his faith took shape in a belief not in the immortality of the bare soul, but in the resurrection of the body. And the actual resurrection of Christ, in which this faith in a corporal resurrection found its confirmation, is regarded in the New Testament not only as the pledge of the like destiny for men who are Christ's brethren, but also as the pledge of a glorious future for the material world as a whole. Again, in Christ's person the Word, who is God, is made flesh. Thus the dignity of the material nature is vindicated by its becoming for ever the organ of Godhead ; and the same great principle interprets the sacraments. In them also material nature and the human body receive their consecration, and the material is seen as the organ of the spiritual.

There is a coherence and solidarity, then, in "the articles of the faith," and one fundamental doctrine of God and of man is the key to the whole Catholic building. A Christian philosophy will start by the vindication of these Biblical conceptions, and proceeding from this standing-ground, will be able to exhibit the whole doctrinal and moral structure of the faith as the harmonious expression of one or two luminous principles.

IV

It is obvious, I think, that there is a similar cohesiveness among the characteristic doctrines which we group under the name of "Modernism." The root conception is again found in the doctrine of God—but now it is the idea of God as immanent in the order of the world which is allowed to dominate, either absolutely to the point of denying His transcendence, or only so far as to produce a marked reluctance to appeal to it. The disclosure of God then is to be found in the order of the universe ; anything which seems to break in upon that order is found repellent. Sin is either in principle denied by a doctrine of determinism, which makes the idea of responsibility and sin fundamentally a delusion, or it is minimized. There is an inevitable upward tendency, as in the world as a whole, so in the individual soul. Sins are the mistakes or the delusions which experience and enlightenment will overcome. What is wanted is nothing else than more light and guidance. Jesus Christ comes as the Light of the World, but He comes purely in the natural order. The goal of the world is the incarnation of God in humanity. It is a gradual process of which Jesus is the foremost specimen. He is in truth a purely human personality and non-miraculous. He is the noblest and most perfect specimen of our race, the sinless son of man, and therefore Son of God. He is divine just because He is simply and perfectly human. What we need from Him is a perfect example and a fresh inspiration. We do not need vicarious sacrifice to make reconciliation for sin—only the fuller evidence of divine love. We ask to be shown the true way of human life and to be stimulated to follow it. Christ is pre-eminently Son of God and the Word made flesh, but so are all men in a measure in their fundamental nature, and are to become so more and more under the influence of Christ. The Spirit of God which worked preeminently in Him dwells also in a measure in all of us. It is the universal spirit of humanity which He stirs into consciousness. The corporal resurrection as the first disciples believed in it was, no doubt, an illusion ; but it was a symbol of the real resurrection, which is the assurance of human immortality. The story of the descent of the Holy Spirit at Pentecost is the symbol of a universal presence which we only need to realize. Similarly the sacraments of the Church are symbols of fellowship, human and divine, by which our faith and consciousness are quickened. Again, the expectation of the Second Coming was an illusion, bred of Jewish tradition, in the minds of Christ Himself and His disciples, but it was also symbol of the truth that the issue of human development is to be the permeation of all institutions and civilizations by the Spirit of Christ which is the universal Spirit of God; and the one God who is manifested in the whole world as Father, and in the correspondence of the human will as Son, and in consciousness as Spirit, will be "all things in all."

We are all familiar with these ideas, expressed separately, at this point and at that, by the theologians who are solicitous that we should revise our creeds. But in fact they constitute a sequence of ideas dependent upon the substitution of the idea of divine immanence—God in nature, as the dominant or exclusive conception of God—for the idea of the transcendent Creator, not as the only, but as the controlling idea. All the 'Modernist' conceptions which I have sought to set in consequential order follow very closely the Biblical and Catholic conceptions and have a like sound. But really they represent much more closely the ideas which historical Christianity combated and dispossessed, revised in the light of the modern category of development.

It must be confessed that they depart very widely from the historical Creed. The root of the divergence lies in the conception of God which is made dominant; and the effect of the divergence is to derogate from the sense of the liberty and majesty of God and the heinousness of sin, on which, in the Catholic religion, the appreciation of His love has been based. We must hold to the ancient Creed, which has history and experience on its side. But we must never allow ourselves to forget that what has given the modern reaction against the Creed of the Church its strength has been in great measure the Church's own defects. And like the Greek Fathers in their time and the Schoolmen in theirs, we must see to it that nothing which makes a legitimate appeal either to the reason or the conscience or the aesthetic faculty of man is allowed to seem alien to the world-wide scope of the religion which calls itself Catholic.

APPENDED NOTE (see p. 318)

THE RATIONALITY OF THE BELIEF IN THE CHRISTIAN DOCTRINE OF GOD

In *Belief in God*, after reviewing briefly the grounds of Theism (pp. 46–61), I endeavoured (1) to show the inadequacy, both intellectual and moral, of any belief in God which represents Him as simply the immanent Spirit of the universe and ultimately as much dependent upon nature as nature is upon Him (see pp. 61–6 and 69–73); (2) to vindicate the idea of positive self-revelation on the part of God as an idea which cannot be rationally excluded (pp. 66–9 and 74–5)—I think it is extraordinary how little consideration the philosophers are willing to give to it; (3) to give the reasons—to my mind the overwhelming reasons—for believing that such a revelation has actually been given, especially through the Hebrew prophets and in Jesus Christ (pp. 75–109); (4) to vindicate the intellectual results of this revelation (pp. 111–32) as consistent with the whole of our knowledge (pp. 133–70, 230–51); (5) to call attention to the moral power consequent upon the acceptance of the Biblical faith.

Since the above volume was written I have been criticized for taking too little into account the arguments of the psychologists. But I think the argument of the psychologists against the objective reality of God turns out to be equally destructive of the objective reality of all things and persons. And I do not think any argument is ultimately formidable which would undermine our confidence that real things and persons exist independently of us, and are by us knowable. This is the kind of realism—involving no doubt in some sort a fundamental act of faith—which "common sense" requires, and which philosophy must accept. This is Lord Balfour's point in *Theism and Thought*.[1] On the subject of the psychological argument I would refer to a popularly written, but deep-thinking little volume, by Mr. Balmforth, *Is Christian Experience an Illusion?* (Student Christian Movement, 1923).

Since *Belief in God* was written I have found myself much assisted by Professor E. W. Hobson's Gifford Lectures, *The Domain of Natural Science* (Cambridge, 1923), which with rigid impartiality seeks to show us what exactly the claim of natural science amounts to in the interpretation of the universe. It seems to me to be a valuable contribution to thought. Also I have been greatly impressed by a book which has not received sufficient notice, *The Natural Theology of Evolution*, by J. N. Shearman (Allen & Unwin, 1915). Anyone who is disposed to think that the doctrine of biological evolution has disposed of the "argument from design" should read this book.

I fear I cannot agree with Dr. Arthur Robinson's optimistic estimate of *The Trend of Thought in Contemporary Philosophy* (Longmans, 1922). It is hard to say whether it has any decided trend. The idealism of Bradley and the physical realism of Alexander appear to be irreconcilable with one another and with the Christian idea of God. And the "new psychology" is, I suppose, inconsistent with all three. But certainly the absence of agreement among the schools of philosophy, and the marked tendency among the men of science to regard it as outside their province to interpret the meaning of nature and life as a whole, ought to give us Christians courage to study and proclaim our message, and show its power to interpret experience, and its coherence with all that can claim to be called knowledge.

[1] Gifford Lectures (Hodder & Stoughton).

CHAPTER XI

PRESENT-DAY APPLICATION

I

We have come to the end of a very long train of thought. We began by considering the intellectual and moral situation of to-day, especially as it appears in the English-speaking countries. We found that there has occurred, within the course of the last two generations, a collapse, on a very large scale, of the old religious tradition in all classes of our society. The intellectual causes of this collapse we found to be fairly easy to indicate. Equally obvious are the social causes which have produced a widespread alienation, both of " the workers," and of all those who are convinced that our industrial and international life have been built up on rotten principles, from " the Churches " which they identify with the established order against which they are rebellious. These intellectual and social movements have been accompanied with a wave of moral rebelliousness, fostered by the war, which has been " up against " the Commandments as well as the Creed and the Bible. And the result of these disintegrating influences is apparent in a general condition of religious and moral unsettlement, and an almost chaotic individualism of belief or scepticism or blatant disbelief. Strongholds of tradition remain, reiterating conservative formulas and warnings. But the area of confusion is very wide, and it is reflected and fostered in popular literature.

The intellectual remedy for this confusion, if remedy there be, must be sought nowhere so much as in the deliberate reconstruction of belief from its foundations, inspired by a fearless trust in real freedom of thought. The signs of the times are adverse to anything like the prospect of a mass-recovery of faith. It must be a matter of individual recoveries or re-assurances of faith, resulting in groups of men and women, larger, more numerous, and more confident than exist at present, who know what they believe and why they believe, and can find a new power and meaning in the old Creeds and institutions of the Church. It is therefore at the reconstruction of belief in individuals that these volumes were aimed.

The natural starting-point for religious belief is authority. Of those who to-day are deliberate believers in the Christian religion the vast majority have received it on authority, and, so far as they have verified it, have verified it in practice. But among those who are more or less educated and interested in intellectual questions, the feature of the day is that the insurgence of new knowledge along the channels of natural science and historical criticism has discredited religious authority, and generated a profound suspicion that the grounds of belief have been shaken or destroyed. Against such suspicion an appeal to authority is in most cases of no use. The violent changes from atheism and immorality to a credulous and uncritical acceptance of Catholicism, which appear to be common in France, are, if not unknown, yet not familiar to us here. What is familiar is a gradual change of mind in honest and good men. To promote such a gradual movement what is needed is that religious belief should vindicate its reasonableness afresh, and its consistency with the whole of knowledge and experience. Indeed, if religious authority is to be true to its own best traditions, its validity must be vindicated, not only by showing its power to inspire and redeem human life, but also by demonstrating its adequacy in the court of reason and free enquiry; as was done of old, when it succeeded in making of Platonism the instrument of its own theology, and later in converting the revived Aristotelianism of the Middle Ages. In the same spirit its task is now not only to convert and sanctify souls, as it has always been doing, but to show itself at home in the modern world of science and criticism and sociology.

Thus we set ourselves to this task—to seek to build up a fabric of belief in God and in Jesus Christ without any conscious appeal to authority, solely by reference to rational and historical standards. In *Belief in God* we investigated the grounds of theism and found its philosophical foundations in the general sense still unshaken. But the God whom philosophy offers to our faith we discovered to be profoundly unsatisfying to the demands of the soul of men. We also saw that the belief in God on which our Western civilization as well as our religious life has been based was, in fact, directly derived from the prophets of Israel and from Jesus Christ, and claimed to be, not a conclusion drawn from the reasoning of philosophers, but a gradual revelation or self-disclosure of God to man. We must not allow ourselves to put revelation and reason in sharp contrast; for reason is confessedly the light of God within us. But we found no justification for dismissing as irrational the idea that the God after whom reason gropes and whom it dimly discovers should be such a being as can meet the aspirations of reason by positive self-disclosure from His own side. And when we studied the record of the prophets and of Jesus, we found the conviction become irresistible that here we really have, as nowhere else in the world, the word of God.

This is the first challenge we addressed to those who would think freely: Can you, trusting your own best conscience and judgement, stand face to face with the long line of prophets and with Jesus Christ, and reject their claim to be the vehicles of a real self-disclosure of God, as being at bottom only an illusion? Can you do this, having in view not only the weight of their own testimony, but also the profound difference which its acceptance has made in the experience of innumerable men and the no less profound difference which the withdrawal of this faith would make? For the moral effectiveness added to life, over long periods and wide reaches, by a particular belief cannot be left out of sight in the estimate of its truth.

The question whether the very distinctive and unique doctrine about God and man which we owe to the prophets of Israel and to Jesus Christ must be taken for truth is, in reality, the most fundamental of all questions for religion, and the one on our answer to which our answers to subsequent questions will in the main depend. The Hebrew faith in God, as intensely personal, as possessing moral character, as being at the last resort eternal Love, as the absolute Creator of all that is, prior to the universe which He sustains by His presence in it, and the judge of all free and rational spirits, we found to be in no conflict with our knowledge as a whole, and to be alone capable of interpreting and sustaining the higher moral and spiritual experience of man. Thus those who, on the whole, followed along with the argument of our first volume accepted this faith, provisionally at least, as a faith to be applied to experience and put to account in life.

On the basis of this faith we set to work to answer the question: What think ye of Christ? Here we found ourselves in the presence of so wide a conspiracy of our intellectuals, refusing dogmatically to take into consideration anything but a non-miraculous and purely humanitarian conception of Christ, that we were compelled to recall to mind the fallibility of philosophers, and to stimulate afresh our resolution to think freely. We saw reason to refuse the conceptions of a *merely* immanent God and a closed system of nature, and vindicated for the Creator the freedom to take fresh action to redeem a world which sin had ruined. We took note that famous "critics," who have biassed their criticism by *a priori* refusals of the supernatural, are in consequence driven to treat the Gospel evidence with great violence, and produce in effect strangely divergent pictures of the historical Jesus. We sought with openness of mind to trace the development of the first faith in Jesus Christ, and we saw reason to believe that the faith in the Incarnation, as St. Paul and St. John proclaim it, is the faith which corresponds to and interprets the facts as a whole, as no other estimate of His person can do; and the faith of the Catholic Church, as it found expression in the Creed and Councils, we recognized as in substance neither more nor less than the faith of St. Paul and St. John, only now formulated in opposition to certain radically hostile tendencies of thought. It is true that the traditional faith has been at times associated with uncritical history, and with an impossible theory of the effect of inspiration, and with estimates of Christ's Godhead which tended to efface His real manhood, and with doctrines of redemption against which our moral nature rebels. But we sought to purge the idea of the Incarnate Person and His work of all such associations, and to maintain a doctrine of His person and work which is fully in accord with the historical evidence, which is in no respect an offence to our reason or conscience, and which in its whole substance is just the faith of the New Testament and the Church which has been verified in an almost world-wide experience. This was the aim of *Belief in Christ.*

It remained for us in this volume to confront another claim of the critics—that is, to separate the doctrine of the Holy Spirit in the Church, and the doctrine of sacramental Catholicism, which is now commonly acknowledged as the teaching of St. Paul and St. John, from the teaching of Jesus Himself. He, it is contended, had no idea of founding a church or instituting sacraments. This position solidly contradicts the assumption of the Acts and the Epistles (chap. i). There is no more unconvincing treatment of evidence, I think, than is to be found in the denial that St. Paul's "tradition" about the Last Supper was, like his tradition about the resurrection of Christ, something which he had "received" at his conversion—"from the Lord" as its source, but through the Church which delivered it to him. It is true, we saw, that our Lord did not found a new Church; but all the evidence converges to show that He refounded the old Church on a new basis, and re-equipped it with officers in the persons of the twelve apostles and with certain sacramental rites of fellowship (chap. ii). And the suggestion that "sacramentalism," as it appears in St. Paul's Epistles, with the doctrine of salvation through the immanent Spirit and glorified Christ, was something alien to the historical Jesus and His Jewish disciples, and was assimilated in the first Gentile churches from the mystery religions of Paganism, we saw cause to reject as violating both the evidence and the principles of probability. We recognized in the mystery religions an influence which contributed materially to the spread of the gospel and the Church—as part of what older scholars called "the divine preparation" for the catholic gospel—but the source of the original doctrines and practices of the New Testament we found to lie unmistakably in the Jewish tradition, and in the experiences through which the first Christians had passed in the school of Jesus Christ (chap. iii).

Having thus reached the conclusion of our reconstructive argument, it remained for us to consider what the acceptance of the faith not only in God the Father, and in the Incarnate Son Jesus Christ, but also in the Holy Spirit, and in the Church as the temple of the Holy Spirit and the body of Christ—what this faith involves and means. Thus we analysed the idea of the Church and of the sacraments, as it is found in the Epistles and the Acts, and we found there, unmistakably, the conception of the one visible society as the only covenanted sphere of Christ's redemption. Membership in Christ and membership in the Church are represented as the same thing in different aspects, inasmuch as union with God is not otherwise offered to us than in the fellowship of the believers. The principle of the sacraments we saw to be that they are social ceremonies, in which the grace of the Spirit is attached at point after point to the community life. And the unity of the community, the Catholic Church—threatened from the first by disruptive forces—we found to be secured by three main links: the apostolic ministry to which all must adhere, the sacraments of the society in which all must participate, and the faith or "word of God" which all must hold in common (chap. iv).

We then passed on to discuss the nature of the authority of the Church (chap. v). The primary purpose of the Church is to represent the Kingdom of God in the world—that is, to exhibit such a type of human life, individual and social, as shall both glorify God and be a moral attraction to mankind. But this life draws its motives from a certain doctrine, and the doctrine on which it is based proclaims itself as a divine revelation—a word of God. This word of God as taught by the apostles constitutes the tradition of the Church and is the basis of its authority. We took note of the very conservative and moderate character of this authority, as the ancient and especially the Greek-speaking Church conceived it. It was content to hand on and defend the original tradition, and to make its appeal to the original Scriptures now being gathered into a canon. It was so confident of the scripturalness and reasonableness of its tradition that it regularly sought to stimulate enquiry by constant appeals to reason and Scripture; and it was very sparing in dogmatic requirements.

Then we contrasted with this the imperialist conception of centralized authority, and the love of uniformity and regimentation, which have more and more characterized the Roman Church (chap. vi). Doctrinally considered, we found that this spirit has expressed itself in dogmas which are neither consistent with history nor justified by the ancient canons of tradition. The religion of the Roman Catholic Church presents all the appearance of a one-sided development of catholicity in the direction of autocracy, and the Eastern Orthodox Church in rejecting its claim has simply been abiding by the tradition. Then (chap. vii) we examined the plea of development, in the larger sense, by which alone the dogmatic claim of Rome can justify itself, and we found in it really a false idea of development. The true development of the Church does not lie in the heightening and extension of the dogmatic claim by a logical process, which more and more tends to make the burden upon the intellect intolerable and swamps the freedom of the spirit; it lies rather in the constant self-adaptation of the Church to new demands of new races, new knowledge, new conditions of society. For this sort of development the *minimum* rather than the *maximum* of required dogma is for the advantage of the Church. There is no doubt a constant system of doctrine which constitutes Catholicism. But it is intolerable to suppose that the Church should become more burdensome to the intelligence and narrower in its appeal as it goes down the generations and widens out into the world. Thus we would find our ideal in the minimum rather than the maximum of dogmatic requirement.

Then (in chap. viii) we applied ourselves to the authority of Scripture. We found that the appeal to Scripture as supplying a final testing-ground of legitimate doctrine is the main safeguard against the tendency to multiply the dogmas which authority would seek to impose upon the conscience. The function of the Church is to teach the faith with authority; and the function of the "open Bible" coupled with free enquiry is to preserve the faith from illegitimate accretion. We found also that a recognition of the unique inspiration of Scripture and a profound reverence for it is compatible with the critical treatment of the documents.

Then a summary was offered of the doctrines which constitute Catholicism, estimated by the ancient standards (chap. ix). And as a list of such numerous articles of faith is alarming to our intellects, it was shown (chap. x) that these articles, or little limbs of the body of doctrine, are not really separable affirmations, but depend with rational consistency upon the affirmation of the central principles concerning God and man which consitute the message of the prophets and of Jesus our Lord, and which found their fulfilment in the Incarnation of the Son and the mission of His Spirit. One fundamental act of assent to this word of God carries with it the general position of orthodoxy.

II

Our argument has been largely historical. We have been occupied in considering what the religion of Christ has in fact been, as it is represented in the New Testament and in the tradition of the Church from the beginning. This appeal to our origins, which is distasteful to the modern mind, saturated in a popular philosophy of development which is a misunderstanding of its scientific meaning, is nevertheless essential to Christianity. It is involved in the fundamental principle of the finality of the Christ.[1] In Him we have the final expression of God, or the Word of God, in terms of humanity, and the final expression of humanity in union with God. And this was found to imply, and does imply, a fixed creed about God and man and redemption, to which adequate expression was given in the New Testament. The developments of Christianity will be rich and manifold, as rich and manifold as are the capacities of humanity in all its tribes and phases to bring out into prominence its aspects and meanings; but the fundamental faith, with its positive implications of idea and fact, must remain the same. In a changing world it is yet in the main to the unchanging needs of the human soul, in its aspirations after moral freedom and eternal life, and in its struggles with sin and suffering and death, and to the unchanging requirements of human fellowship, that the catholic gospel appeals. There is a "general heart of man," and therefore there can be a catholic and substantially unchanging gospel. And there has been such demonstrably in history. There is something in Christendom, below all its divisions, which responds to the test of "*ubique, semper, ab omnibus*" in the sense of its author, though the break-up of Western

[1] See *Belief in Christ*, pp. 315 ff.

Christendom at the Reformation has introduced, as we shall recognize directly, a complication into the appeal. Thus, in a religion which proclaims the finality of Christ, the appeal to antiquity is inevitable.

Moreover, since the Church became the established religion of whole nations, there has been an inextricable confusion between the standard and polity of the Church and the traditional standards and political tendencies of nations and races and classes. If we want to understand the essence of Christianity we must look at it, long and steadily, as it emerged from Palestine and ran in a broadening stream, but substantially unconfused, into the great world of the Roman Empire.

Thus we are unashamed in our appeal to antiquity and Scripture. And those who, on the whole—though, it may be, only provisionally—have accepted the argument of these volumes, have in their minds a clear understanding of what the Catholic Church of Christ has meant ; and it is with this in our minds that we turn back to the confusing spectacle of the present day.

. . . . .

"Men's hearts are failing them for fear, and for looking after those things that are coming on the earth," and "there are many antichrists." Such is no doubt the condition of things to-day. But in the midst of all our social and international anxieties there is, and that in many countries, a widespread conviction that there is no redemption for human nature—whether socially or individually—but in the name of Jesus of Nazareth ; and there is a feeling associated with this conviction that the cause of Christ is infinitely weakened by our religious divisions, in acquiescing in which for so long we have "done despite unto the Spirit of grace." We do well to pay heed to these two thoughts or emotions which are widespread among the best men and women belonging to very various religious traditions.

Now, I see no prospect of reunion among Christian denominations on any wide scale within the measurable future. It may be that times of Antichrist lie ahead of us, in which disaster and suffering and loneliness may drive Christians into unity. But whatever the future holds, there is, it seems to me, one thing which can be seriously undertaken at once, the importance of which it is hard to exaggerate, that is, the union of Christians in their various sections for moral and social witness and service.

It is in this that our traditional Christianity has been so lamentably and increasingly partial and one-sided. Christianity is, first of all, "The Way." It is a life—a social life to be lived. It is as a life, rather than a doctrine, that in the New Testament it makes its tremendous and difficult claim upon men. The doctrine is only the necessary background of the life. There can be no question that our Lord intended His Church to make its appeal to the world mainly by the life which men saw it living. In this way His disciples were to be the salt of the earth, the light of the world, the city set on a hill. And when the Church recovered herself from her first moral peril, due to the vast invasion from the Gentile world, she maintained her moral standard, her standard alike of self-control and brotherhood, through the long days when Christianity remained a dangerous venture. It was in the main as "The Way" that she conquered.

"Established Christianity," whether in the civilized Roman Empire or in half-barbarous tribes or in modern nations—the sort of Christianity which claims to embrace the whole society, which it costs men nothing to profess, and into which children are practically baptized as a matter of course—appears to be as audacious a departure from the method of

Christ as can well be conceived. Whether it was a venture made under the guidance of providence, or the greatest of all the mistakes or corporate sins of the Church, it is not for us to decide.[1] In imagination we ponder inevitably over the question of what the history of the Church and the world would have been if in the days of Constantine the Church, while gratefully accepting from the Emperors full toleration, had obstinately refused to accept the imperial power as an instrument for propagating and maintaining religion, had jealously maintained its independence and its former standards of moral discipline, preferring reality of profession to numbers; and if later it had altogether refused to baptize the Franks in platoons in the suite of their chief, as if they were only just changing their old hero gods for a better and stronger one. We can dream of the difference it would have made in the history of the world and the Church, but we can only dream. The facts were otherwise. What price was paid for the assistance of the strong arm of emperors and kings we know. Christianity began to cost men nothing to profess; or, rather, it very soon cost them their life to profess anything else. The difference in the average moral level of church membership was immediately apparent. We see it already in the sermons of Chrysostom in the East and Augustine in the West. The average moral level had become what it is to-day.

We must not refuse to recognize the glory of the mediaeval conception of Christianity, or the work which it did in the taming of the nations, or the witness which it bore to the solidarity and brotherhood of men and nations in the catholic society, or the grandeur of the moral and social principles of

[1] But I find it very hard to doubt that the Church in fact unconsciously succumbed just to that temptation which its Master resisted when He refused to accept "the kingdoms of the world and the glory of them" at Satan's price

the Schoolmen and moralists of the Church, or the constant influence of the saints. Nevertheless, it remains true that in fact the Church accepted, what our Lord so systematically refused, a double standard, the standard for saints and the standard for average sinners or conventional Christians; and the practical attention of the Church was to an extent difficult to exaggerate, and more and more, directed to saving individual souls, by getting them into purgatory at their death and then redeeming them from purgatory by powers it was supposed to possess, though they had never made any serious attempt to live the life which Christ prescribed to His disciples.

Of the moral witness of the Church in our own country we know the record: it is in many respects an honourable record; but in many respects it has been startlingly deficient. It has been content, flatly contrary to the spirit of our Lord, to draw a marked distinction between respectable and disreputable sins—stigmatizing drunkenness and violence and fornication, while it has practically condoned avarice and the love of money, and contempt of social inferiors, and selfish luxury, and injustice—as to which 'respectable' sins we know the mind of our Master. Politically it has been strangely content to be merely nationalist and patriotic. It is pitiful, indeed, to think of the extent to which nationalism has been allowed to eat the heart out of the catholic religion, not in England only, or Germany, but in the Orthodox Churches; and to mark how the greatest of international societies, the Roman Catholic Church, has borne no witness in these last days—no audible witness, at least—against nationalist and militarist excesses in France and Italy. It is pitiful to contrast the enthusiasm of the Church in many lands for the great war with the feeble support it has given to the cause of international peace.

I do not want to weary my readers by saying constantly the same things. But I write under a profound sense that the first duty of the Church to-day, in all lands, and particularly in our own, is to re-erect the ethical standard of Christianity not only with regard to sexual relations and the control of our passions, but also with regard to commercial morality and the obligation of truth both in commerce and politics, to the right and (much more) the duty of property and the sin of avarice, and to the meaning of brotherhood and the equal spiritual value of all human souls. On most of these subjects we have had committees which have produced reports. There is, however, still much to be done by scholars and thinkers. And there is much more to be done in reducing their conclusions to something like a popular moral creed, and converting the conscience of the Church to its acceptance. What we have to remind ourselves of is that the Christ who is to judge the world—both the living and the dead—is the same Jesus of Nazareth who spoke the Sermon on the Mount and the parables of judgement and mercy, and that He does not change His character with the changes in the Church's disposition.

I know that such a fundamental ethical reform in the Church's teaching would be very unpopular in many directions. It would encounter many prejudices. It would alarm many vested interests. What sort of restoration of moral discipline it might lead the way to, I do not know. But I feel certain of one thing—that it, and it alone, would attract and win a great body of men and women such as would have been among the disciples of Jesus of Nazareth; that it would cut right across all our denominational divisions; that it might unite all the most real friends of Christ in co-operative effort even at once, while the long process is gone through of thinking out afresh our theological principles; and that it, and it alone, will make the world understand what the Catholic Church is for.

III

I trust that the interpretation of Catholicism which this volume has sought to give will be acceptable to a considerable number of the theologians of the Orthodox Churches, and will at least prove no obstacle to the reunion with them for which we Anglicans pray. If we can agree on the necessary doctrine, and on the necessary conditions of valid ordination and administration of sacraments, I hope it may prove possible to be mutually tolerant of great diversities of custom and ceremonial. We feel a profound sympathy with the Orthodox Churches in their present calamities, all the more that we know we have not done what we ought to have done to avert them; and we venerate the spirit of martyrdom which they have never ceased to display. But we recognize that there is a long tradition of mutual alienation and misunderstanding between us which only time and friendly intercourse and much prayer can overcome. We must not be impatient. What I trust is that those who share the point of view which this book has sought to express may look hopefully forward to ultimate reunion between Orthodox and Anglican.

As we look toward the great Church of Rome, we know that in the main we Englishmen owe to her our Christianity, and we should delight to acknowledge the primacy of the Bishop of Rome among the churches of Christendom. As we read the record of the separation of the sixteenth century we wonder wistfully whether, if religion had not been so much mixed up with politics and with the passions of imperious monarchs, the separation need have occurred or need have become inveterate. But these are idle dreams; and as things stand at present no way towards reunion seems to be open. Since the early sixteenth century the breach has become wider and the obstacles larger and more definitely fixed. We can but wait and pray, in faithfulness to the truth as we see it.

I know that a great deal in this book will provoke and distress English Free Churchmen and Scottish Presbyterians and those of other lands who symbolize with them. I desire to acknowledge with all my heart the wonderful and continuous evidences of the work of the Spirit of God among them; and to express the gratitude which thousands among us feel for theological and spiritual help received from them. But I am sure that at the Reformation they broke certain fundamental principles and laws of the Catholic Church. There is very much in their spirit, their traditions, and their institutions which the Catholic Church needs, and which in a reunited Church must be retained; but there cannot, I am convinced, be a reunited Church except on the basis of the Catholic Creeds, and the acknowledgement of the sacramental principle as well as the due administration of the sacraments, and the recognition of the episcopal succession as the link of connexion and continuity in the Catholic body. Here again, then, unity seems a long way off. I do not know if anything can heal the breaches, unless very evil times force us together. But meanwhile the best preparation for future unity lies, I believe, in the detached and disinterested study of our Christian origins and in close fellowship for social service.

IV

And now I come finally to our own Anglican communion. I confess that I cannot rank myself among those who can speak of the Church of England as "on the whole the most glorious church in

Christendom" or of her Book of Common Prayer as "incomparable." I find that her history in many of its aspects and characteristics makes me feel ashamed and depressed. But if there is in history the stamp of a divine providence on any society, it is set on the Anglican Church. It was marked out in the sixteenth century to hold together the ancient Catholic tradition both in creed and order with the appeal of the Reformation to the open Bible as the final court of reference for Christians; and so to present a type of Catholicism which the world had forgotten, which should have priests but not be priest-ridden, and should accept the Catholic tradition but keep it purged by the free use of reason and an all-pervading scripturalness.

Those who hold this ideal for Anglicanism will probably agree in certain determinations and desires.

1. That while we accept provisionally the situation fixed for us in the 'settlement' of the fifteenth and sixteenth centuries, and embodied in the Book of Common Prayer, as being one under which it is tolerable to live and work, we should insist on making our constant appeal, not to the particular arrangements and compromises of our Reformation, but to the ancient Catholic tradition as verified in the New Testament. The particular settlements arrived at in the reigns of the Tudor sovereigns were manifestly compromises conditioned by the determination to keep together in a National Church under the headship of the Crown the contending theological parties and the silent, moderate, and conservative mass of the nation. In detail the compromises had in them sometimes much more of temporary policy than of abiding principle. But the underlying principle was never abandoned, and was brought to the front again by Hooker and the seventeenth-century divines—to maintain the Catholic tradition conditioned by the appeal to Scripture, and to exclude the Romanist

accretions which had imperilled the legitimate liberty of national Churches, and rendered nugatory the appeal to antiquity and Scripture.

2. To be true to this principle we need reforms in our service-book, or if that is impossible without doing violence to the Evangelical conscience, then, as is now proposed, the recognition of alternative forms within the existing rite, which shall give sufficient expression to undoubted features in the Catholic tradition. Such would be the restoration of a 'canon' in the eucharist less meagre and more conformable with tradition; and the recovery of public prayers for the dead, and a fuller commemoration of the saints, and prayers to God on the ancient model that we may have the assistance of their intercessions; and the alteration of the preface to the Confirmation Service which obscures the sacramental character of the rite. We shall also ask for the removal of passages from the service-book which are not really scriptural and which are a stumbling-block to many men's consciences, like the phrase which describes infants as "children of wrath" and the text of the Three Heavenly Witnesses in one of the Epistles. The full list of needed changes or additions would be a fairly long one. Some of these reforms it seems likely we shall have speedily granted. For some of them we may have to wait. But we must not cease to make our reasonable wishes known.

3. I am stating an opinion which I know to be shared by many among us of different schools of thought when I say that the Thirty-nine Articles of Religion, while remaining in respect as an interesting historical document, ought to cease to be regarded in any sense as a theological standard. They belong markedly to an epoch of controversy which has passed away. They contain a number of expressions or statements which are needlessly repellent to the modern spirit, and others equally so to the Catholic

spirit; and at many points they sought to serve their pacific purpose by a vagueness of statement which makes them both valueless and perplexing. It is true that they are 'patient' of a tolerable meaning by the help of a great deal of explanation; it is true also that since 1865 the assent which the clergy are required to give to them is vague and general—the common talk of the clergy "signing the articles" being simply a survival from the former period; but nothing, I think, is gained by their retention which can be compared to the disadvantages of a theological standard which has ceased to carry either serious obligation or theological enlightenment. I would have those who are being ordained required to express their assent (not to the Thirty-nine Articles, but) to the Nicene Creed, and the Book of Common Prayer, and the Ordering of Bishops, Priests, and Deacons; and also, with a solemn sense of responsibility, to give the required answers to the questions in the Ordination Service which affirm the truth of the Scriptures [1] and their position as the final testing-ground of necessary doctrine.

4. Conditions are not favourable to trials for heresy; and even if our Church Courts were reconstituted on tolerable lines, we should do well to shrink from them. But we sorely need a revival of the spirit of what I would call a rational loyalty to accepted obligations. I dare say that in twenty years' time it will have become evident that as regards the person of our Lord the alternative is between a frank Unitarianism on the one side and a frank adherence to the Creeds both as regards facts and doctrine on the other. Meanwhile, the claim of a few of our Modernists to retain their positions as ministers of the Church while they profess opinions which appear to be quite inconsistent with the Creeds they recite

[1] The question being modified by an explanatory addition as now suggested: see above, p. 287, n. 2.

and the service-book which they use has undoubtedly a very demoralizing effect. We have a few others on the opposite flank of the Church who affirm apparently the whole of the Roman teaching, excepting, with a strange inconsistency, the central point of the jurisdiction and authority of the Pope, which affects so fundamentally our right to teach and administer the sacraments. No doubt these relatively small groups bulk too large in the public eye. But they have generated among the laity a sense of the hollowness of the formal professions of the clergy, which makes them distrust our honesty. On the Catholic side this suspiciousness is even more justified by the apparent ignoring on the part of many of the clergy of the solemn declaration, in virtue of which alone they can be admitted to any clerical office—"In public prayers and administration of the sacraments I will use the form in the said book [the Prayer Book] prescribed and none other, except so far as shall be ordered by lawful authority." Let us give the freest interpretation to the last exceptive clause, and recognize that no clergyman can be blamed who uses whatever dispensations from the obligation contracted his bishop thinks himself entitled to give him ; but let it be a definite and public dispensation, so that all can be cognizant of it ; and, granted this modification, the rites of the Prayer Book, whether we like them or not, must be followed, with whatever varieties of accompanying ceremony, as binding upon us. 'Devotions' of various kinds, and deviations from the prescribed standard, more or less lawless, do undoubtedly attract a number of people. We should wish to go as far as possible in meeting spiritual needs of different kinds. Nevertheless I question whether what has been thus gained can be set in comparison with what has been lost by the scandal which seeming lawlessness is causing. There is no doubt that there is among the laity a widespread questioning of clerical honesty which is doing the most serious moral harm and which is due to what they see or hear of in the most opposite sections of the Church. What we need is a revived sense of rational loyalty to that particular portion of the Church we belong to, as well as to the great Church Catholic which lies beyond. (And in matters of rite and ceremony it is the particular Church to which we specially owe obedience.) And we need even more a deepened sense of the moral seriousness of formal obligations contracted before God and man. There appears to be a noxious form of party spirit current among us, which emboldens us to stand by one another in doing what, alone before God, we could not justify.

5. I should be untrue to convictions which I share with, I believe, only a few if I did not say, finally, that, whatever is to be said in other ages and other situations for established Churches, I believe the existence of an Anglican Establishment to-day in our country is inconsistent with the actual state of beliefs in the nation, and a real disadvantage to religion on the whole. And I cherish the belief, well-grounded, I feel sure, that if we were disestablished, our internal cohesiveness would prove to be surprisingly great, The solid block of the Anglican communion means to abide by its principles and will hold together.

. . . . .

It will have been evident that the writer of this book is very much alive to the faulty character of all parts of the Catholic Church. Certainly where he says *I believe in the Holy Catholic Church*, he means with St. Thomas *I believe in the Holy Spirit vivifying the Church.* For underlying all laxities, defects, exaggerations, and unworthy accommodations to the world, of which Church history is so lamentably full, there is a divine movement, of which the Church

Catholic is the organ, which had its beginning in the call of Abraham and the redemption of Israel, and its consummation in our Lord and the mission of His Spirit, and has had its development in all the history of the Church. To the faith on which this movement rests the saints of every generation and country are the witnesses, and with it the moral and spiritual hopes of humanity are bound up. There are many of us who are at times tempted to disloyalty or assailed by doubt. "Yea," we cry with the psalmist, "I had almost said even as they"—the adversaries and the sceptics: "but lo, then I should have condemned the generation of thy children." That is the true reply in all such temptations. I cannot repudiate the fellowship of the children of God, or forget the great cloud of witnesses who watch how I play my part in the great conflict.

> "It should seem
> Impossible for me to fail—so watched."

Nor, while we labour and pray for the restoration of visible unity—"the bond of peace"—among the divided sections of Christ's Church on earth, shall we ever suffer ourselves to forget that the actual principle of unity in the Church is the Holy Spirit; and though our divisions lamentably mar the exhibition of that unity to the world, they are not deep enough to extinguish it. For in spite of them, and beneath them, He is at work binding all the members of the one body who are still on earth into union with their Lord in heaven and with the whole company of the faithful in the heavenly places.

TABLE OF SUBJECTS

INDEX OF NAMES

www.ingramcontent.com/pod-product-compliance
Lightning Source LLC
LaVergne TN
LVHW020525100826
845148LV00010B/1348

* 9 7 8 1 6 0 6 0 8 1 1 9 8 *